# Closing the Gap isn't working

# Closing the Gap isn't working

Billions of dollars of aid hasn't
helped First Nations People

Chris Gilford

Copyright © 2023 by Chris Gilford.

Library of Congress Control Number:        2022922683
ISBN:              Hardcover              978-1-6698-3353-6
                   Softcover              978-1-6698-3352-9
                   eBook                  978-1-6698-3351-2



This book is a work of non-fiction. Unless otherwise noted, the author and the publisher make no explicit guarantees as to the accuracy of the information contained in this book and in some cases, names of people and places have been altered to protect their privacy.

Any people depicted in stock imagery provided by Getty Images are models, and such images are being used for illustrative purposes only.
Certain stock imagery © Getty Images.

Print information available on the last page.

Rev. date: 13/12/2022

**To order additional copies of this book, contact:**
Xlibris
AU TFN: 1 800 844 927 (Toll Free inside Australia)
AU Local: (02) 8310 8187 (+61 2 8310 8187 from outside Australia)
www.Xlibris.com.au
Orders@Xlibris.com.au
847749

This book contains details of many medical conditions and is designed to show how many of them can be prevented or mitigated. The advice given is general in nature and may not apply to individual circumstances. The book contains data from reports from many sources including Australian government bodies, but this does not imply that it has been endorsed by any of them.

# CONTENTS

# LIST OF FIGURES



All the figures, apart from the author's photographs, have been obtained from websites and reports with a Creative Commons licence or are in the public domain, except for Figure 13, for which permission was obtained from the Department of Health and Aged Care, which owns the copyright.

# LIST OF TABLES

# LIST OF ABBREVIATIONS

| | |
|---|---|
| ABS | Australian Bureau of Statistics |
| ACTH | Adrenocorticotropic hormone |
| AIC | Australian Institute of Criminology |
| AIDS | Acquired immunodeficiency syndrome |
| AHW | Aboriginal health worker |
| AIHW | Australian Institute of Health and Welfare |
| ATODS | Alcohol, Tobacco, and Other Drugs Service |
| BCE | Before the Common Era (formerly BC [before Christ]) |
| BMI | Body mass index |
| BMR | Basal metabolic rate |
| CDC | Centres for Disease Control and Prevention (USA) |
| CE | Common Era (formerly AD [anno Domini]) |
| CMV | Cytomegalovirus |
| CTG | Closing the Gap |
| DTs | Delirium tremens |
| ED | Emergency Department |
| ESKD | End-stage kidney disease |
| GBH | Grievous bodily harm |
| GBS | Group B streptococcus |
| GFR | Glomerular filtration rate |
| HIV | Human immunodeficiency virus |
| ICOP | Indigenous Cardiac Outreach Programme |
| IHD | Ischaemic heart disease |
| IQ | Intelligence quotient |
| IROC | Indigenous Respiratory Outreach Care |
| NACCHO | National Aboriginal Community Controlled Health Organisation |
| NHMRC | National Health and Medical Research Council |

| NWRH | North and West Remote Health |
| --- | --- |
| PCYC | Police Citizens Youth Clubs |
| PBS | Pharmaceutical Benefits Scheme |
| PSGN | Post-streptococcal glomerulonephritis |
| PTSD | Post-traumatic stress disorder |
| RFDS | Royal Flying Doctor Service |
| RHD | Rheumatic heart disease |
| SIDS | Sudden infant death syndrome |
| STIs | Sexually transmitted infections |
| SUDI | Sudden unexpected death of an infant |
| THC | Tetrahydrocannabinol |
| UNESCO | United Nations Educational, Scientific, and Cultural Organisation |
| UNICEF | United Nations Children's Fund |
| WHO | World Health Organisation |
| WHR | Waist-hip ratio |
| WQPCC | Western Queensland Primary Care Collaborative Limited |

THE TERM 'INDIGENOUS' has been used for most of the last forty years when referring to descendants of the original inhabitants of Australia. However, in the last few years, they have elected to call themselves 'First Nations' peoples, and so that is the way they will be referred to here, apart from where I am using quotations from other sources or when it is used in an international context.

I have used metric units throughout this book, but there are instances in everyday life when imperial units are used. The exception is for calories and joules, when I have given both. The other conversions are given here:

Heights

| Centimetres | 160.0 | 167.5 | 175.0 | 183.0 | 190.5 |
|---|---|---|---|---|---|
| Feet and inches | 5'3" | 5'6" | 5'9" | 6' | 6'3" |

Weights of babies (chapter 6)

| Kilograms | 2.5 | 3.5 | 4.5 |
|---|---|---|---|
| Pounds and ounces | 5 lb 8 oz | 7 lb 11 oz | 9 lb 14 oz |

# CHAPTER 1

# Introduction – The Closing the Gap Campaign

I N THE LAST sixty years, there has been a huge change in society's attitudes towards First Nations peoples. This has been a cultural shift, and it is impossible now not to be aware of their presence and the fact that they have been here for so long. Many meetings start with a 'Welcome to Country' or 'Acknowledgement of Country', an example being 'I begin by acknowledging the traditional custodians of the land on which we meet today and pay my respects to their elders past, present, and emerging.' Television programmes often provide a similar acknowledgement and identify the owners of the land where the programme was developed. The 'Sorry' speech was given in Parliament in 2008, there has been the Uluru Statement in 2017, and there is likely to be a referendum on a Voice to Parliament in 2023. First Nations peoples' rights and interests in land are now formally recognised over more than 40 per cent of Australia's land mass.

Many more people are identifying themselves as being First Nations, and we are seeing more and more First Nations people in prominent positions. The combined federal and state parliaments now have an estimated twenty-six members of Parliament who identify as First Nations (3.1 per cent of all federal, state, and territory parliamentarians). This percentage is almost the same as the proportion of people who identified as First Nations in the 2021 census (3.2 per cent).

However, well before now, before the end of the twentieth century, there was a realisation by governments that First Nations peoples were behind the rest of Australians in standards of health, education, and employment. The state governments had been putting extra resources into these areas, but the federal government started targeting First Nations people for increased funding early in the 2000s. After a few years, the term 'Closing the Gap' was coined as an umbrella term for this funding.

Closing the Gap now refers to a campaign that was formally established in 2008 and aims to reduce First Nations disadvantage in the areas of health, education, and employment and was under the direct supervision of the Department of the Prime Minister. Targets have been set to monitor the outcomes. The targets agreed to in November 2008 were to

- close the gap in life expectancy within a generation;
- halve the gap in mortality rates for Indigenous children under 5 within a decade;
- ensure all Indigenous 4-years-olds in remote communities have access to early childhood education within five years;
- halve the gap for Indigenous students in reading, writing, and numeracy within a decade;
- halve the gap for Indigenous students in year 12 attainment or equivalent attainment rates by 2020;
- halve the gap in employment outcomes between Indigenous and non-Indigenous Australians within a decade.

The targets have been modified since then, and an extra one (school attendance) was added in 2014, so they were then as follows:

1. Halve the gap in mortality rates for Indigenous children under 5 within a decade (by 2018)
2. Ensure 95 per cent of all Indigenous 4-year-olds are enrolled in early childhood education (by 2025)
3. Close the gap between Indigenous and non-Indigenous school attendance within five years (by 2018)
4. Halve the gap for Indigenous children in reading, writing, and numeracy within a decade (by 2018)

5.  Halve the gap for Indigenous Australians aged 20–24 in year 12 attainment or equivalent (by 2020)
6.  Halve the gap in employment outcomes between Indigenous and non-Indigenous Australians within a decade (by 2018)
7.  Close the life expectancy gap within a generation (by 2031)

Notice that life expectancy, which was originally top of the list in 2008, was relegated to the bottom in 2014.

Each year a report on progress with Closing the Gap was prepared for the prime minister and Parliament, and the reports are made available on the website www.closingthegap.gov.au; the latest one on that website is dated 2020 and was tabled in Parliament on 12 February 2020. After that report, extensive changes were made to the campaign, and there are now seventeen outcomes with associated targets. The report writing was transferred to the Productivity Commission, which produced their reports in July 2021 and 2022.

Additional reports have been prepared by the Lowitja Institute, Australia's National Institute for Aboriginal and Torres Strait Islander Health Research, funded by Oxfam. Their 2022 report, Transforming Power – Voices for Generational Change, is a 'small collection of the hundreds of stories that catalogue the success of Aboriginal and Torres Strait Islander-led initiatives'.

The new reports by the Productivity Commission are somewhat deficient in hard data. There are now seventeen targets, and in many cases, there is little comparison with the previous indicators. I shall therefore discuss the 2020 report in detail and come back to the 2021 and 2022 reports at the end of this chapter.

The original inhabitants of Australia arrived about 65,000 years ago, and their descendants now number about 800,000 according to the 2021 census. Torres Strait Islanders (TSI) are ethnically distinct being of Melanesian origin and arrived in Cape York, the northern tip of Queensland, from the island of New Guinea. There is debate about when they first arrived in Australia, with no clear consensus. There are currently about 28,000 TSI people in Australia, most being in Cape York.

There is a third group of people that might satisfy the description of being Indigenous but probably not First Nations. These are now known as South Sea Islanders and are the Australian descendants of Pacific Islanders, mainly Melanesians but some Polynesians. They were kidnapped or recruited between the mid to late nineteenth century as labourers in the sugar cane fields of Queensland. At its height, the recruiting accounted for over half the adult male population of some islands. Their numbers are thought to be in the range of 10,000 to 20,000. Queensland Health published a report on their health in 2011, and this showed significantly poorer health than non-Indigenous people, but they are not covered by the Closing the Gap campaign.

## 1. Mortality Rates for Children

According to the 2020 report, the key points on childhood mortality were as follows:

- In 2018, the Indigenous child mortality rate was 141 per 100,000 – twice the rate for non-Indigenous children (67 per 100,000).
- Since the 2008 target baseline, the Indigenous child mortality rate has improved slightly, by around 7 per cent. However, the mortality rate for non-Indigenous children has improved at a faster rate; and as a result, the gap has widened.
- Some of the major health risk factors for Indigenous child mortality are improving. There is a need for further research to understand why these improvements have not translated into stronger improvements in Indigenous child mortality rates.

The report shows a graph showing the change in child mortality rates:

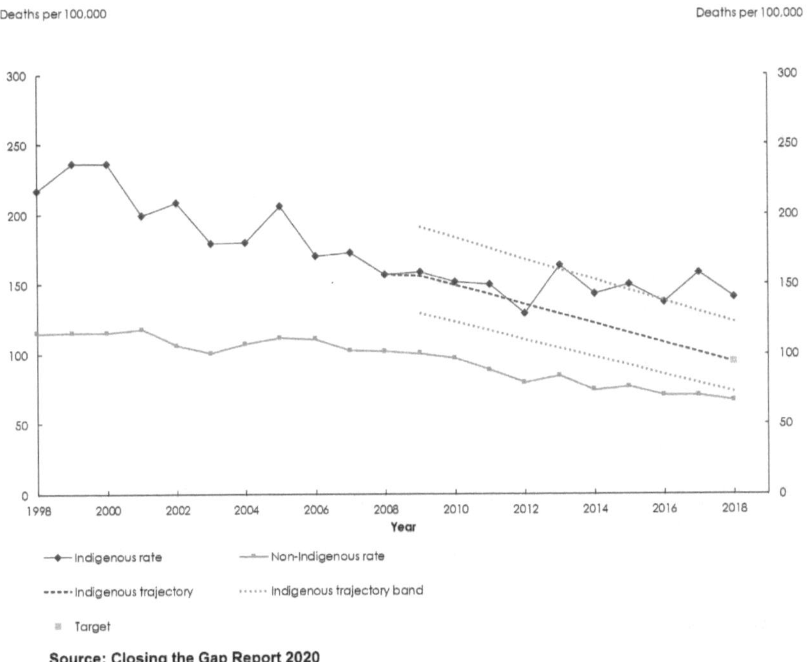

**Source: Closing the Gap Report 2020**

Figure 1: Child mortality rates

The comment in the report is that 'Indigenous child mortality rates have improved (by 7 per cent) between 2008 and 2018. However, this improvement was not as strong as prior to the 2008 baseline'. The report does attempt to explain the volatility of the data between 2012 and 2015, but no reason is given for its stagnation in subsequent years. It seems to me that there has been no improvement at all since 2009. Paradoxically, the improvement in non-Indigenous mortality was actually greater in 2008–2018 than in the previous ten years. This can be seen in my reinterpretation of the graph:

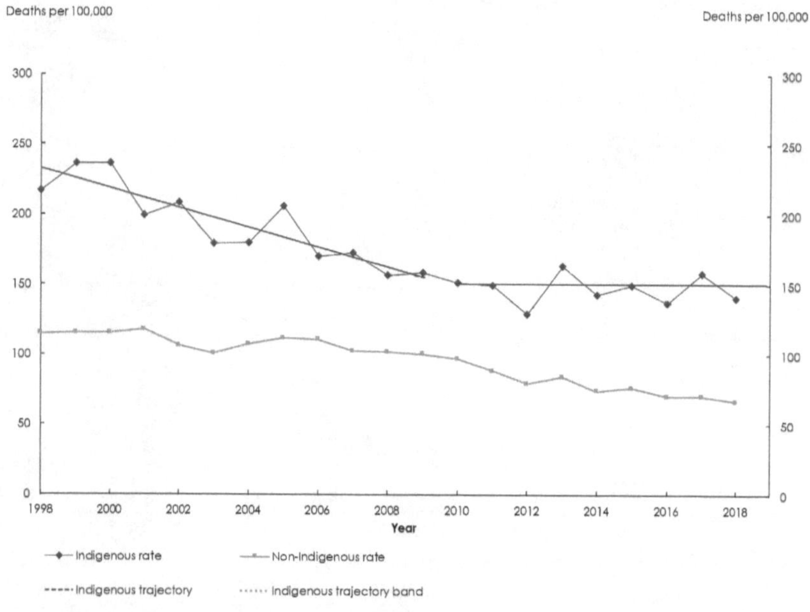


Figure 1a: Child mortality rates – modified

The Closing the Gap programme regarding child mortality can only be described as an abject failure as its achievement was to completely halt the improvement that had been made over the previous ten years.

## 2. Early Childhood Education

The target is for 95 per cent of all Indigenous 4-year-olds enrolled in early childhood education (by 2025). The key points in the 2020 report were the following:

- In 2018, 86.4 per cent of Indigenous 4-year-olds were enrolled in early childhood education compared with 91.3 per cent of non-Indigenous children.
- Between 2016 and 2018, the proportion of Indigenous children enrolled in early childhood education increased by almost 10

percentage points. There was a slight decline of less than 1 percentage point for non-Indigenous children.

- The attendance rate for Indigenous children was highest in inner regional areas (96.6 per cent), almost 17 percentage points higher than the lowest attendance rate in very remote areas (79.7 per cent).

The report only provides data for 2016, 2017, and 2018 and shows that there has been encouraging progress. It also shows that the gap between First Nations and non-Indigenous might have already closed. However, it is unlikely that the target of 95 per cent enrolment will be achieved by 2025, given that the figure for non-Indigenous is 91.3 per cent in 2018.

The change in target between 2008 and 2014 from 'having access to early childhood education' in 2008 to 'enrolled in early childhood education' in 2014 is interesting. Even the newer target should be fairly easy to attain. All it needs is for someone to get a list of all the 4-year-olds in a community and visit all their parents and sign them up on the spot. Surely, the target, and therefore the challenge, should be the percentage of who actually attend early childhood education.

## 3. School Attendance

The target is to close the gap between Indigenous and non-Indigenous school attendance within five years (by 2018). The key points from the 2020 report are as follows:

- The majority of Indigenous students attended school for an average of just over four days a week in 2019. These students largely lived in major cities and regional areas.
- School attendance rates for Indigenous students have not improved over the past five years. Attendance rates for Indigenous students remain lower than for non-Indigenous students (around 82 per cent compared with 92 per cent in 2019).

- Gaps in attendance are evident for Indigenous children as a group from the first year of schooling. The attendance gap widens during secondary school. In 2019, the attendance rate for Indigenous primary school students was 85 per cent – a gap of around 9 percentage points. By year 10, Indigenous students attend school 72 per cent of the time on average – a gap of around 17 percentage points.

Although the second key point above stated that the rate 'had not improved', the reality is far worse, particularly in the Northern Territory, where the rate actually declined by 7 percentage points. In every other jurisdiction, the rate also declined but 'only' by about 2 to 3 per cent, with most of the decline between 2017 and 2019. This is seen in the graph that the report supplied:

**Figure 2**     Indigenous student attendance rates, by jurisdiction, Semester 1 2014–2019

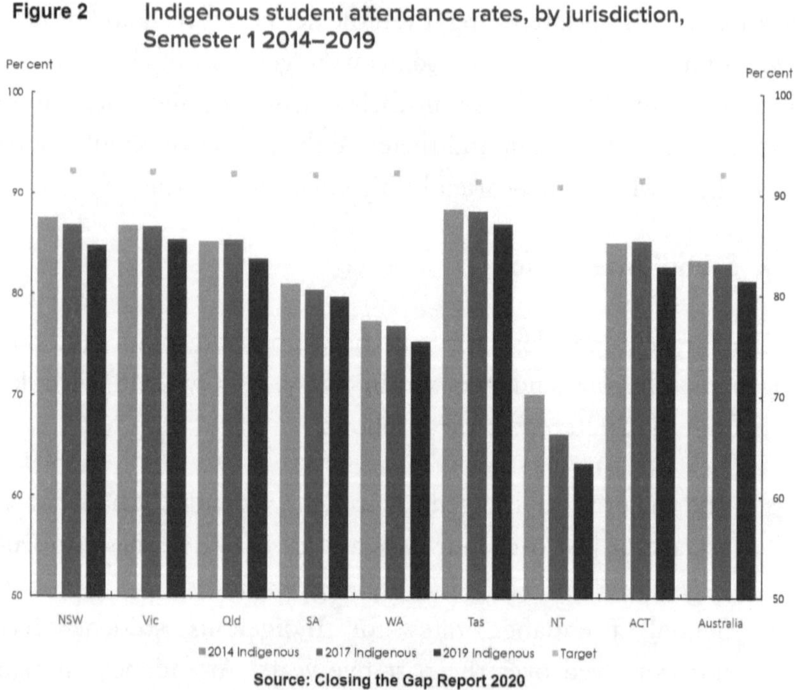


**Source: Closing the Gap Report 2020**

Figure 2: School attendance by jurisdiction

Remoteness is a major factor for the variation in attendance.



CHRIS GILFORD

Attendance was generally about 83–85 per cent for those in major cities and inner and outer regional centres. However, it was about 75 per cent in remote areas and 65 per cent in very remote areas. There was little comment on this in the report as it did not consider the difficulties for a child to attend a school. It may, in fact, be easier for a child to attend a school in a very remote First Nations community than in the leafy suburbs of a major city. In Mornington Island, the school is right in the middle of the township, so over 95 per cent of the population live less than one kilometre from the school, an easy ten- to fifteen-minute walk. I think that it is likely that the same is found in most remote communities. The exception, of course, is for those families who live on remote cattle stations, and they could well have an hour's drive to get to school. However, many of these would be non-Indigenous, and the alternative is to enrol in the School of the Air, no doubt now using Zoom.

**Figure 3**     The gap in attendance widens throughout secondary school, Years 1–10, Semester 1 2019

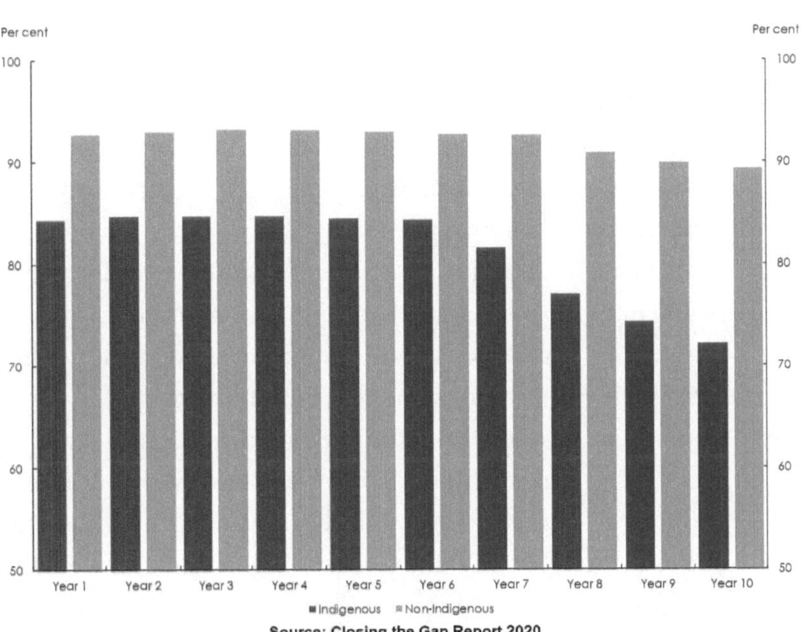


Figure 3: Attendance gap, years 1–10

In contrast, those who live in large cities often have a long journey to school. They may take buses, either the normal community buses or dedicated school buses. Alternatively, their parents or carers may drive them to school, and the impact of this process is clearly visible to anyone who lives near a large school. A long queue of cars disgorging or collecting students clogs up the neighbouring streets for hundreds of metres twice a day.

What is worrying is that the attendance of First Nations students is virtually the same for years 1 to 6 at about 84 per cent, but after that, it drops at a steady rate of about 3 per cent a year, reaching about 72 per cent for year 10. This has implications for year 12 attainment.

## 4. Literacy and Numeracy

The target is to halve the gap for Indigenous children in reading, writing, and numeracy within a decade (by 2018). Here are the key points in the 2020 report:

- At the national level, the share of Indigenous students at or above national minimum standards in reading and numeracy has improved over the past decade to 2018. The gap has narrowed across all year levels by between 3 and 11 percentage points.
- Despite these improvements, in 2018, about one in four Indigenous students in years 5, 7, and 9 and one in five in year 3 remained below national minimum standards in reading. Between 17 and 19 per cent of Indigenous students were below the national minimum standards in numeracy.
- Looking at students exceeding national minimum standards provides a better understanding of how well Indigenous children are placed to successfully transition to further study or work. Between 2008 and 2018, for example, the share of year 3 students exceeding the national minimum standard in reading increased by around 20 percentage points.

The report gives data for reading and numeracy but not for writing. Surely, this is a serious omission. And although there is a wide year-to-year variation, the overall trend is a definite improvement.

Tasmania and the Australian Capital Territory (ACT) do the best, but they were also where attendance was best. Another reason is probably the lower population of First Nations people. There may only be a couple of First Nations children in each class, so they are more likely to socialise with non-Indigenous children, with peer pressure helping them. Queensland also does quite well without these advantages so should be congratulated.

However, remoteness is a major determinant of literacy and numeracy skills, which is hardly surprising – if the students' attendance is poor, they are not going to learn much.

## 5. Year 12 Attainment

The target is to halve the gap for First Nations Australians aged 20–24 in year 12 attainment or equivalent (by 2020). The key points in the 2020 report were as follows:

- In 2018–19, around 66 per cent of First Nations Australians aged 20–24 years had attained year 12 or equivalent.
- Between 2008 and 2018–19, the proportion of First Nations Australians aged 20–24 years attaining year 12 or equivalent increased by around 21 percentage points. The gap has narrowed by around 15 percentage points as non-Indigenous attainment rates have improved at a slower pace.
- The biggest improvement in year 12 attainment rates was in major cities, where the gap narrowed by around 20 percentage points – from 26 percentage points in 2012–13 to 6 percentage points in 2018–19.

Further down in the report is the statement that 'the target to halve the gap in year 12 or equivalent attainment rates by 2020 is on track'. The rates were 45 per cent for First Nations and 85 per cent for non-Indigenous in 2008 and 66 per cent and 91 per cent respectively in 2018–19. So the gap was reduced from 40 per cent to 25 per cent over this period, so it may achieve the target.

It is hardly surprising that remoteness is a major factor in year 12 attainment. For 2018–19, the attainment rate was as follows:

| Major cities | 84% |
|---|---|
| Inner regional | 56% |
| Outer regional | 55% |
| Remote | 50% |
| Very remote | 38% |

Table 1: Year 12 attainment by remoteness

High schools in remote areas are usually only available up to year 10. High schools that go to year 12 are only found in towns with a population of more than about 20,000, apart from those towns built around a mine, like Newman or Weipa. This therefore means that most students in years 11 and 12 who live in remote or very remote areas must attend a boarding school, which is usually located in a large city, sometimes many hundreds of kilometres away.

## 6. Employment Outcomes

The target is to halve the gap in employment outcomes between First Nations and non-Indigenous Australians within a decade (by 2018). The key points in the 2020 report were as follows:

- In 2018, the Indigenous employment rate was around 49 per cent compared with around 75 per cent for non-Indigenous Australians.
- Over the past decade (2008–2018), the employment rate for Indigenous Australians increased slightly (by 0.9 percentage points), while for non-Indigenous Australians, it fell by 0.4 percentage points. As a result, the gap has not changed markedly.

- The Indigenous employment rate varied by remoteness. Major cities had the highest employment rate at around 59 per cent compared with around 35 per cent in very remote areas. The gap in employment outcomes between Indigenous and non-Indigenous Australians was widest in remote and very remote Australia.

The chapter in the report on year 12 attainment points out the effect of completion of year 12:

> Completing high school to Year 12 . . . is a prerequisite for many jobs and is seen as an indicator of aptitude and attitude. Indigenous Australians, who complete Year 12, or a higher qualification, are substantially more likely to be employed. They are also more likely to work full-time and in higher-skilled occupations than early school leavers.

As noted above, year 12 attainment is the only Closing the Gap target that is likely to be achieved. However, the effect of this in improving employment rates will take many years to make a substantial change.

The second of the key points said that 'the gap has not changed markedly'. Looking at the data, it did slightly reduce over the ten-year period. The reduction was 1.3 per cent, but with the gap starting at 26 per cent, at the current rate, it will take a hundred years to halve it.

The other major factor in employment rate is remoteness. For very remote areas, there is a huge difference between the employment rate for First Nations and non-Indigenous people, and it is not difficult to work out why. Non-Indigenous people only live in very remote areas because there is employment there, such as in mines or cattle stations. Firat Nations people live there because that is their country, where they have lived for thousands of years.

## 7. Life Expectancy

Life expectancy is the length of time that a person is expected to live and is generally measured from the time of their birth. It is a hypothetical concept because it does not take into account any future events such as global warming, epidemics, wars, or famine. We all face an uncertain future. Nevertheless, it is a useful concept in assessing the health of a large group of people.

Currently, life expectancy for all Australians is 80.2 years for men and 83.4 years for women. It can also be estimated for people of virtually any age. It may be useful to know what it is at age 65 so you know whether you can expect to enjoy a long retirement or how long your superannuation will last. For non-Indigenous males, it is now 85.3 and for females 88 years. These are average figures, and your personal longevity will depend on how healthy you are at age 65.

In the 2020 Closing the Gap report, the key points for life expectancy were as follows:

- In 2015–2017, life expectancy at birth was 71.6 years for Indigenous males (8.6 years less than non-Indigenous males) and 75.6 years for Indigenous females (7.8 years less than non-Indigenous females).
- Over the period 2006 to 2018, there was an improvement of almost 10 per cent in Indigenous age-standardised mortality rates. However, non-Indigenous mortality rates improved at a similar rate, so the gap has not narrowed.
- Since 2006, there has been an improvement in Indigenous mortality rates from circulatory disease (heart disease, stroke, and hypertension). However, this has coincided with an increase in cancer mortality rates, where the gap is widening.

The report supplied the following graph:

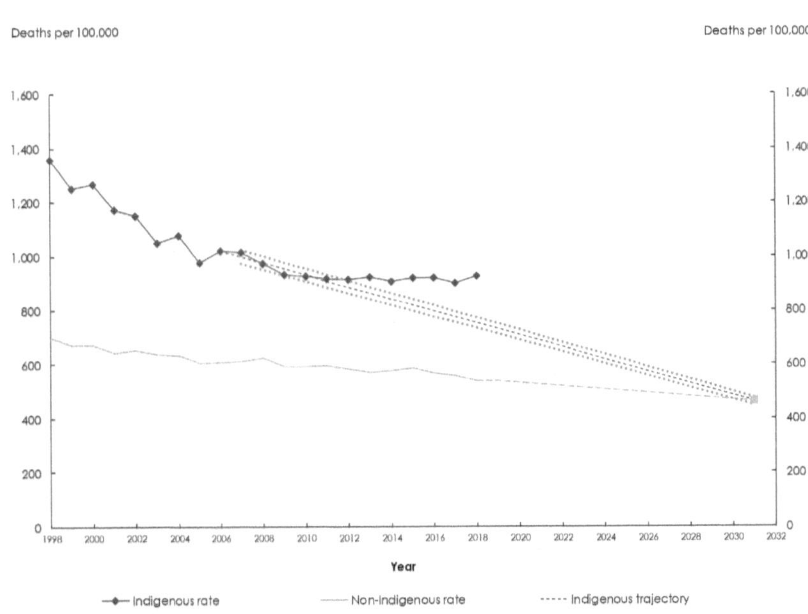


Figure 4: Mortality rate

It looks to me that the mortality rate was coming down nicely between 1998 and 2006 but then slowed down substantially and has been tracking parallel to the non-Indigenous rate since then. I have modified this chart by adding my own trend lines. Had the improvement from 2006 continued at the previous rate, the gap would have closed by about 2015.

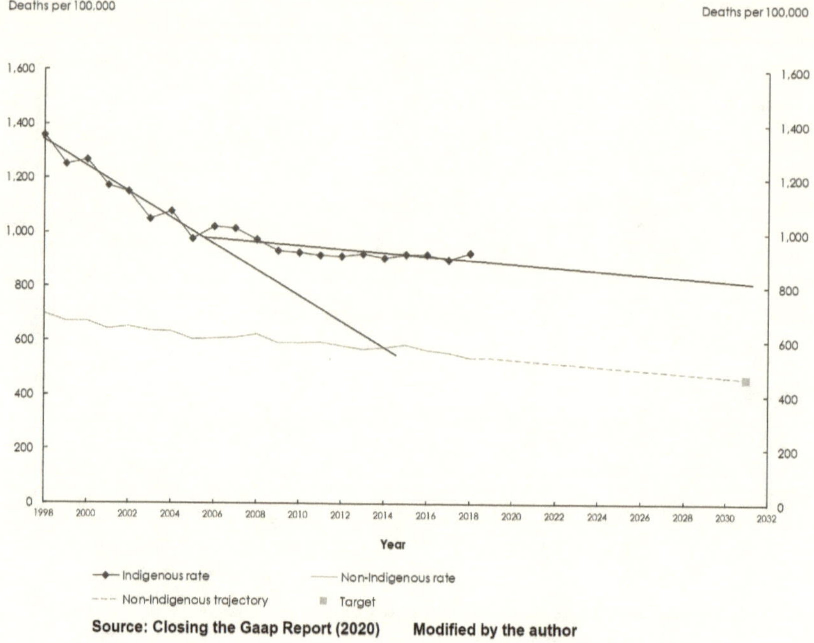


Figure 4a: Mortality rate – modified

The target concerns the gap in life expectancy, but two of the three key points refer to mortality rate. They are closely linked, but the mortality rate is much easier to calculate. Either way, the graph shows that progress stalled just at the time that the Closing the Gap policy started.

## Summary of the 2020 Report

So only one of the seven targets, year 12 attainment, might have been met, but we need more data.

The achievements can be summarised by giving a score for each (out of five):

| Childhood mortality | 0 |
| --- | --- |
| Early childhood education | 3 |
| School attendance | 0 |
| Literacy and numeracy | 3 |
| Year 12 attainment | 4 |
| Employment outcomes | 1 |
| Life expectancy | 0 |

Table 2: Scores for the 2020 report

This gives a total score of 11 out of 35, or 31 per cent, which is abysmal, particularly given the amount of money that has been spent.

## The Changes Which Started in 2020

The whole programme was revamped two years ago, and the Productivity Commission has published two reports. There are now seventeen indicators. I have summarised the 2022 report in the following table, adding my observations and again my numerical assessment:

| | Outcome | Target | Progress | Score |
|---|---|---|---|---|
| 1 | Aboriginal and Torres Strait Islander people enjoy long and healthy lives. | Close the Gap in life expectancy within a generation by 2031. | Gap slowly decreasing but not on track; gap for males 8.6, females 7.8 years. | 3 |
| 2 | Aboriginal and Torres Strait Islander children are born healthy and strong. | By 2031, increase the proportion of Aboriginal and Torres Strait Islander babies with a healthy birthweight to 91 per cent. | Was constant from 2014 to 2018 but then increased a little. | 3 |
| 3 | Aboriginal and Torres Strait Islander children are engaged in high-quality, culturally appropriate early childhood education in their early years. | By 2025, increase the proportion of Aboriginal and Torres Strait Islander children enrolled in year before full-time schooling (YBFS) early childhood education to 95 per cent. | On track, but target is enrolment, not actual attendance. | 4 |
| 4 | Aboriginal and Torres Strait Islander children thrive in their early years. | By 2031, increase the proportion of Aboriginal and Torres Strait Islander children assessed as developmentally on track in all five domains of the Australian Early Development Census (AEDC) to fifty-five. | Decreased between 2018 and 2021. | 1 |

| 5 | Aboriginal and Torres Strait Islander students achieve their full learning potential. | By 2031, increase the proportion of Aboriginal and Torres Strait Islander people (aged 20–24) attaining year 12 or equivalent qualification to 96 per cent. | Possibly on track but no new data since 2016. | 2 |
|---|---|---|---|---|
| 6 | Aboriginal and Torres Strait Islander students reach their full potential through further education pathways. | By 2031, increase the proportion of Aboriginal and Torres Strait Islander people aged 25–34 years who have completed a tertiary qualification (Certificate III and above) to 70 per cent. | Probably on track but no new data since 2016. | 3 |
| 7 | Aboriginal and Torres Strait Islander youth are engaged in employment or education. | By 2031, increase the proportion of Aboriginal and Torres Strait Islander youth (15–24 years) who are in employment, education, or training to 67 per cent. | Possibly on track but no new data since 2016. | 2 |
| 8 | Aboriginal and Torres Strait Islander people and communities have strong economic participation and development. | By 2031, increase the proportion of Aboriginal and Torres Strait Islander people aged 25–64 who are employed to 62 per cent. | Employment rate decreased from 53 to 52 per cent from 2006 to 2016 and no new data since then. | 0 |

| | | | |
|---|---|---|---|
| 9a | Aboriginal and Torres Strait Islander people secure appropriate, affordable housing that is aligned with their priorities and need. | By 2031, increase the proportion of Aboriginal and Torres Strait Islander people living in appropriately sized (not overcrowded) housing to 88 per cent. | Probably on track but no new data since 2016. | 3 |
| 9b | As above | By 2031, all Aboriginal and Torres Strait Islander households within discrete Aboriginal and Torres Strait Islander communities or in a town receive essential services that meet or exceed the relevant jurisdictional standard. | Only one data point in 2018–19. | 0 |
| 10 | Aboriginal and Torres Strait Islander people are not overrepresented in the criminal justice system. | By 2031, reduce the rate of Aboriginal and Torres Strait Islander adults held in incarceration by at least 15 per cent. | Getting much worse over last five years. | 0 |
| 11 | Aboriginal and Torres Strait Islander young people are not overrepresented in the criminal justice system. | By 2031, reduce the rate of Aboriginal and Torres Strait Islander young people (10–17 years) in detention by 30 per cent. | Has come down from 35 to 25 per 10,000 in last ten years. | 4 |

| 12 | Aboriginal and Torres Strait Islander children are not overrepresented in the child protection system. | By 2031, reduce the rate of overrepresentation of Aboriginal and Torres Strait Islander children in out-of-home care by 45 per cent. | Increased from 54.2 to 57.6 per 1,000 in two years. NI rate 5. | 0 |
|---|---|---|---|---|
| 13 | Aboriginal and Torres Strait Islander families and households are safe. | By 2031, the rate of all forms of family violence and abuse against Aboriginal and Torres Strait Islander women and children is reduced at least by 50 per cent as progress towards zero. | Only one data point – from 2018–19, 8.4 per cent of 15+ females experienced harm. | 0 |
| 14 | Aboriginal and Torres Strait Islander people enjoy high levels of social and emotional well-being. | Significant and sustained reduction in suicide of Aboriginal and Torres Strait Islander people towards zero. | Rate of suicide increased from 17 to 28 per 100,000 from 2009 to 2020. | 0 |
| 15 | Aboriginal and Torres Strait Islander people maintain a distinctive cultural, spiritual, physical, and economic relationship with their land and waters. | By 2030, increase by 15 per cent Australia's land mass and sea subject to Aboriginal and Torres Strait Islander people's legal rights or interests. | On track. | 4 |

| 16 | Aboriginal and Torres Strait Islander cultures and languages are strong, supported, and flourishing. | By 2031, there is a sustained increase in number and strength of Aboriginal and Torres Strait Islander languages being spoken. | Number of languages spoken decreased between 2004 and 2018. | 2 |
| 17 | Aboriginal and Torres Strait Islander people have access to information and services enabling participation in informed decision-making regarding their own lives. | By 2026, Aboriginal and Torres Strait Islander people have equal levels of digital inclusion. | No data since 2015. | 0 |

Table 3: Summary of the seventeen new outcomes

This gives a total score of 31 out a of a possible 85, or 36 per cent.

Target 1 shows some improvement, whereas there was none in the 2020 report. However, this one looks at life expectancy as opposed to mortality rates.

Target 2 is totally different from the target for child health in the 2020 report.

There may be some contradiction between outcomes 13 and 10. To reduce the amount of domestic violence (13), it may be necessary to increase the number of perpetrators that are imprisoned, which will cause a worsening of outcome 10.

Here is a little more detail on the first two health outcomes.

## Long and Healthy Lives

Life expectancy has now been restored to the number one position. However, it was the mortality rate which was shown in the previous reports, and this makes it difficult to compare. The ABS only releases life expectancy figures every five years, and these ones are from 2015 to 2017.

Life expectancy for First Nations people is now 71.6 for male and 75.6 for females; the gap is closing from 11.4 to 8.6 years for males and 9.6 to 7.8 years for females over the previous ten years. It is good that they now show the different figures for gender and remoteness. However, it only reports for NSW, Qld, the NT, and WA. It therefore ignores the 148,000 who live in Vic, South Australia (SA), Tas, and the ACT, or 18 per cent of all First Nations people. Life expectancy will be discussed in subsequent chapters. The charts below compare the First Nations life expectancy (the columns) with that of non-Indigenous, shown as a circle with a line through it.

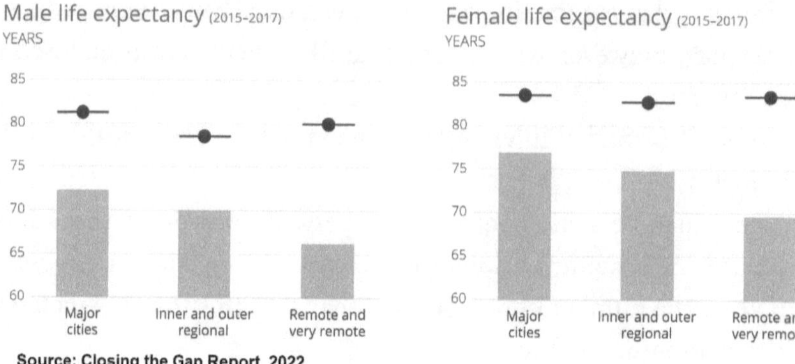



Figure 5: Life expectancy

The overall assessment was that the relevant states (NSW, Qld, and WA) were improving. In the NT, it was improving for females but worsening for males; and overall, there was improvement but not on track. There was no data for Vic, SA, Tas, or the ACT. This improvement does not fit with the mortality rates given in the previous reports, and this will be discussed in later chapters.

A supporting indicator was that, in 2020–21, 271.8 per 1,000 Aboriginal and Torres Strait Islander people (over one in four) had an Indigenous-specific health check, which is an increase from 2016 to 2017. Most people (around 95 per cent) had a health check at a healthcare facility, with the remainder accessing a check via telehealth or in residential aged care. There is no data to benchmark this or explanation on how it improves their health.

## Birthweight

In previous years, childhood mortality was the criterion for childhood health. Childhood mortality is regarded by international bodies as a key indicator of the health status of a nation. Is it no longer important?

The current report states that, in 2019, 89.5 per cent of First Nations



CHRIS GILFORD

babies were of a healthy birthweight, compared with 93.9 per cent for non-Indigenous, up from 88.8 per cent in 2017.

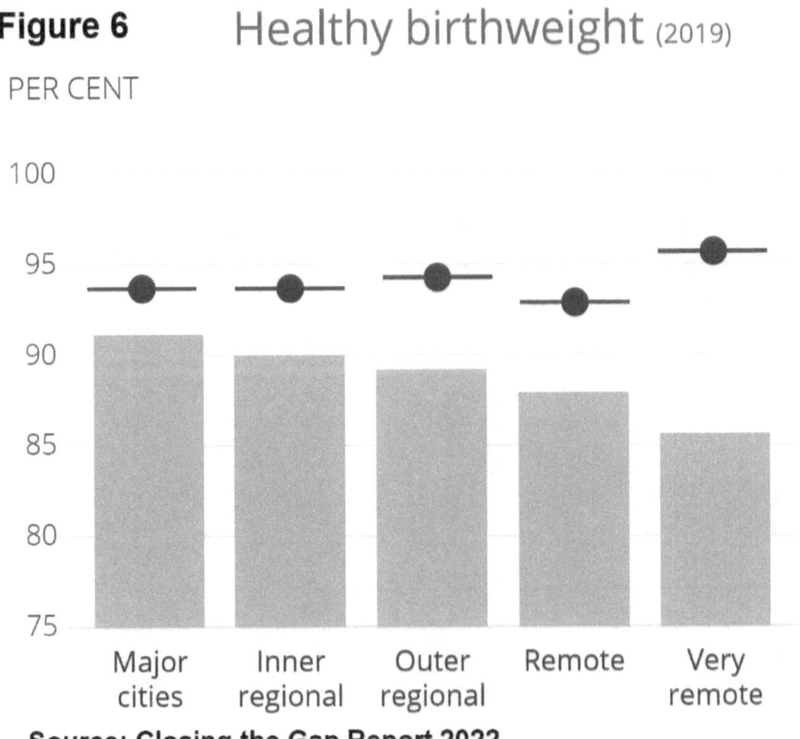


Figure 6: Birthweight

The overall assessment was that this was on track, but there had been no change for NSW and the ACT. This is a rather blunt assessment tool. A mother who smoked and developed gestational diabetes might be lucky in that these risk factors cancelled each other out so she had a baby in the healthy weight range, but the baby would not be healthy.

The supporting indicator was that, in 2019, over two-thirds of pregnant Aboriginal and Torres Strait Islander women attended antenatal care in their first trimester (68.2 per cent), and almost nine in ten attended five or more antenatal visits during pregnancy. These proportions represent an increase from 2017. On average, 79 per cent of Australian mothers had their first antenatal visit in the first trimester, and 95 per cent had five or more antenatal visits according to the Australian Institute of Health and Welfare (AIHW). This at least was useful as there is a standard, but the yardstick for this report has been set rather low. The Australian Pregnancy Care Guidelines (DoH 2020) recommend that first-time mothers with an uncomplicated pregnancy have ten or more antenatal care visits during pregnancy (seven visits for subsequent uncomplicated pregnancies).

For the rest of this book, I will concentrate on the health targets because, as a retired health professional, it is an area that I know much more about and because there is more long-term data.

# CHAPTER 2

# Origin of the Gap

T HE CANADIAN TV series *Air Crash Investigations*, which started in 2003, has produced over 200 programmes. They highlight the work of government authorities such as the National Transportation Safety Board in the USA and the Australian Transport Safety Bureau in trying to discover why aeroplanes crash. They carry out the process of root cause analysis in which they look back, often over many years, for all the problems that contributed to the accident, building on the work of Dr James Reason, a British professor of psychology, rather than just looking at the flight itself.

I will attempt to use the same principles, so we need to go back hundreds or thousands of years. First Nations and non-Indigenous Australians came together in 1788, when the colony of New South Wales was established. It is likely that their life expectancies were similar then. We need to look at the history of both groups to see how their life expectancy differed over time.

We also need to find out why it was Europeans who set out on voyages around the world from the end of the fifteenth century, ultimately colonising Australia and not First Nations people from Australia, sailing around the world to colonise Europe and elsewhere.

**The Hunter-Gatherer Lifestyle**

Until about 10,000 years ago, life in Australia would have been fairly similar to anywhere else in the world, with only minor modifications due to the differences in climate and the different range of plants and animals which could be used as food. People lived in small groups; they inhabited makeshift shelters, particularly if it was cold, and may have worn clothing derived from animal skins or parts of plants.

They obtained food either by hunting for animals, including fish and birds, or gathering seeds, nuts, berries, or other edible parts of plants. There would be virtually no dairy products, processed oils, salt, or caffeine. Both hunting and gathering are inefficient, requiring people to spend most of their time gathering food. Sometimes, though, someone would get lucky and catch a large animal which they could feast on, and it would keep them fed for a few days. Similarly, finding edible plants meant a long walk through the bush. More importantly, the population would remain at a low density, spread out over a large area. There would be custodianship of the land with respect for the neighbours since none would want their neighbours taking over the best hunting areas.

The active lifestyle of the hunter-gatherers together with their varied diet meant that they were physically healthy with heights a little less than people today. Infant mortality was high, but obesity was very rare. Prolonged breastfeeding was the norm due to the lack of domestic animals that could provide milk and no other suitable food for babies and acted as a contraceptive, helping space out births. Common causes of death included accidents such as falls, causing fractures, drowning, and snake bites. They would also suffer from infectious diseases such as bacterial infections from dirty water, wounds, or animal bites but also worms and protozoal infections.

Life expectancy in ancient times was short, generally reckoned to be about 30–35. However, this figure can appear confusing. It is badly skewed by the perinatal mortality rate (death at the time of birth or shortly afterwards), which was high. Probably about 10 per cent of children died before their first birthday and more after that. Those who reached their tenth birthday probably lived to around 50 on average. However, there would have been a wide variation, and the range would be from around 30 to 70 years. Commentators often focus on the upper figure and believe it applies to the whole population. Also, they may be referring to the old biblical phrase 'three score years and ten'. However, one of the main factors to account for the variation



CHRIS GILFORD

in life expectancy is a person's social status. Leaders of a group live longer because they are the leaders, and as a result, their long lives are remembered. Those who did live to 60 or more would have been affected by cancer, neurodegeneration, and arthritis.

## The Transition from Hunter-Gatherer Lifestyle

About 10,000 years ago, there was a change. People found that if they brought back seeds on their long walk, some of them would get spilled on the journey home and start to germinate in the soil closer to their normal gathering points. They then worked out that they could harvest these, keeping some over to plant the next year. Gradually, the amount of food available in an area increased.

Nikolai Vavilov was a Russian/Soviet botanist who worked from 1924 to 1940 on the origin of plants that could be domesticated for food production. He argued that plants were not domesticated somewhere in the world at random but that there were regions where domestication started.

The first was probably the Middle East, an area known as the Fertile Crescent, which includes parts of modern-day Iraq, Syria, Lebanon, Israel, and Jordan. It then started independently in other parts of the world, including the Indus valley of Pakistan, the Yellow River in China, and the Andes in Central America.

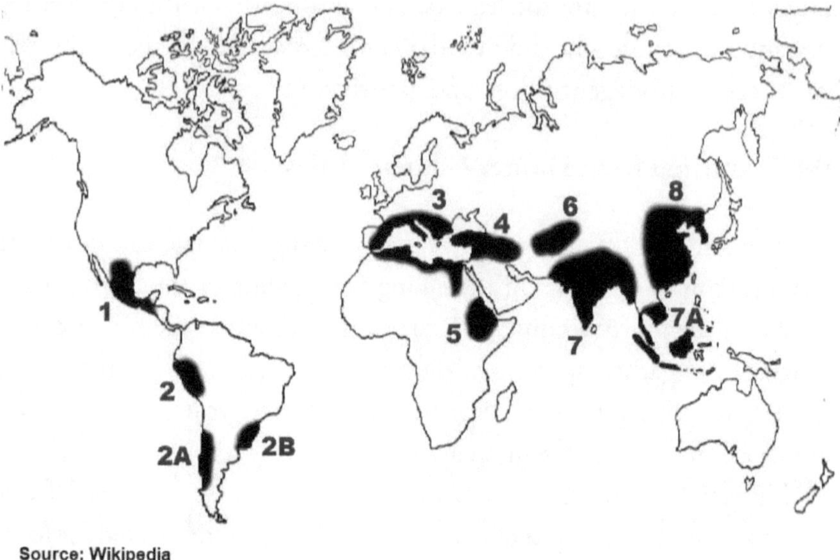

Figure 7: Vavilov centres

Australia does have one native plant that is cultivated today, the macadamia nut, but it was probably considered too insignificant to justify inclusion on this map.

Similarly, the people found that there were some animals that were happy to eat some of the food that had been grown as a crop and were then amenable to domestication. The land could therefore support more people, so rather than a small population spread over a wide area, towns and cities began to form with thousands and then tens of thousands of inhabitants. A map of ancient civilisations that left behind stone buildings shows the same locations.

## The Importance of Cities

To find out why this is important, we need some elementary statistics. Human beings are a diverse group. For example, their height varies around the mean (or average). This variation follows a pattern called the normal distribution. An average adult male is about 175 cm

     CHRIS GILFORD

tall and has a standard deviation of about 7.5 cm. Two-thirds of the population are within one standard deviation and 95 per cent within two standard deviations. This fits with your gut feel as you would probably guess that two-thirds of men are between 167.5 cm and 182.5 cm, and it is rare to find one below 160 cm or above 190 cm.

The same is true for many other characteristics, but I want to consider intelligence. Other relevant characteristics could be used such as motivation or memory, but intelligence has the advantage that it has been quantified by the intelligence quotient, IQ. We now know that it is inappropriate to compare IQs between different populations, but I am considering the distribution of IQ within a population which has shared background and experiences. The average IQ is 100 with a standard deviation of fifteen, so two-thirds of people are between 85 and 115. There are a few below 70 who, these days, would have difficulty reading and writing and would need someone to help look after them. At the other end of the scale are those with an IQ of over 130. In the present time, they go on to get a PhD. However, there are not many of them, only about one in forty. They are the ones in ancient times who would become the leaders of the clan. There are people with IQs beyond that, say, 145, but this occurs only in 1 person in 1,000. When we come up to an IQ of over 160, this only occurs once every 30,000 people. However, this group contains the geniuses who win Nobel Prizes.

If you have small groups of people living together, say, a hundred or two, then the chance of having a genius is very small. Obviously, the occasional group will have one, but they will be seen to be different. They will lie awake at night looking at the stars, trying to make sense of them. They will notice the way the planets move relative to the stars, but others will laugh at them and chastise them for being asleep during the day instead of fulfilling their duties. They won't have anyone with similar intelligence with whom they can network, share their observations, and start wondering about the meaning of it all.

However, once there is a city with a population of tens of thousands, then a few of these geniuses will find one another. Think of Socrates, Plato, and Aristotle with their disciples considering the meaning of life in ancient Athens. As they start to interact, scientific discovery begins and with it civilisation. The word 'civilisation' is derived from the Latin word *civitas*. This means 'city', not in the sense of the buildings but as the social body of the citizens united by law. Therefore, it was the reliable supply of food that triggered the process of civilisation almost everywhere in the world.

The first cities date back to around 5,000 years ago and were found in the Middle East. Since then, the epicentre of civilisation moved westwards into Europe, reaching its first peak with the Greeks, then the Romans 2,000 years ago. However, after the decline of the Roman Empire in the fifth century CE, other parts of the world became dominant. These included China, India, the Ottoman Empire, and Central and South America. By the beginning of the sixteenth century, China was probably the most advanced civilisation. China made enormous technological advances independently from Europe. Other empires left behind huge buildings as indicators of their prowess, including the Incas, Mayas, and Khmer.

However, Europe got its second wind after the Renaissance and quickly surpassed all other parts of the world, launching expeditions to explore and trade with the rest of the world. None of this would have been possible without the efficient production of food and the consequent construction of cities.

## Scientific Progress and Discovery

The increased density of population in the cities enabled scientific discovery to proceed at an ever-increasing rate. After farming and animal husbandry, the next steps were stone masonry and pottery and then metallurgy (the bronze and iron ages), geometry and mathematics, astronomy, physics, and then the Industrial Revolution.

New technology (the practical applications) evolved after these from scientific discoveries. The first step was the creation of a written language, initially by using metal implements to carve symbols on stone or clay tablets. This probably dated from the growth of cities, when traders needed to have some way of recording the amount of grain or other foodstuffs they were transporting from the countryside to the cities. A written language then enabled those with the technology to modify their environment and so improve life for their community. People explored areas of the world further and further from their homes, but from 1000 CE, they were able to take long sea voyages. The main explorers were the Scandinavians from the eleventh century and then mainland Europeans from the fifteenth century. The Chinese also had the same capability and launched a huge fleet of treasure ships for exploration at the beginning of the sixteenth century. Unfortunately, by the time the fleet returned several years later, China was hit with a huge recession due to an epidemic of the plague, thus curtailing further exploration for centuries.

There was a downside to this process of civilisation. There was no improvement in people's health and actually a decline in life expectancy. Even in the initial stages before the growth of cities, infectious diseases became more common due to the increase in population density. The occupational change from everyone being a generalist performing all tasks to specialising in a few tasks repeated continuously resulted in stresses and strains and ultimately deformities. This pattern persisted right up to the Industrial Revolution in the seventeenth to nineteenth centuries.

## Meanwhile, in Australia

However, none of this happened in Australia due to the absence of any useful arable crops. The macadamia nut didn't provide the sustenance required for anyone to move forward. We know that there were eel 'farms' set up in Southern Australia several thousand years ago, but there is no evidence yet of any other type of farming. There were no land animals that could be domesticated.

We know that First Nations people arrived in Australia from SE Asia around 65,000 years ago. For almost all the time since then, they had the whole of Australia to themselves. Dutch and then French and English explorers started visiting Australia from the beginning of the seventeenth century. From their journals, we know a little of the way of life of First Nations Australians. We know that they had dugout canoes and could travel between islands.

We also know that the North West Coast of Australia was regularly visited by fishermen from Malaysia, perhaps for a few hundred years. The Chinese also came. Travellers from Malaysia and the Indonesian archipelago set off across the Pacific from about 1100 to 1200 CE. They only came to fish and perhaps barter a few implements. They did not come to settle, nor did they bring any crops with them, which was a shame because a large number of plants originated in SE Asia, including rice, sugar, and breadfruit.

Therefore, First Nations people could never use all the mineral deposits beneath their feet, a necessary step for going on long ocean voyages.

## Progress in Health

Medicine had been studied since the time of the ancient Greeks and Persians and probably Egyptians. Much of it was in anatomy (structure of the body) and physiology (how it works), but there was very little progress in finding ways of getting patients better. Various treatments were devised such as cupping or bleeding (often using leeches) or even more bizarre treatments like blowing smoke up the rectum. Many herbal remedies were tried with little success for the majority. Most of time, the treatments would only have a placebo effect; but occasionally, they would actually work. For example, a patient with severe shortness of breath from heart failure would get relief from having half a pint of blood removed. However, this would not work for other causes of breathlessness such as asthma and might well make them worse. There were just a handful of drugs in the physician's pharmacopeia. These included digoxin and opium, both of which are derived from herbs.

Surgical operations were performed, but without anaesthetic, this would be a challenging experience for the patient, so no one would consent to it without a very clear benefit. Even then, the risk of dying from the procedure was high. If, though, you were on board ship and had your leg crushed by an incoming cannonball, an amputation might save your life.

The United Nations Population Division maintains a database of mortality through the ages. Extracting the data for Australia and the UK yields the following chart:

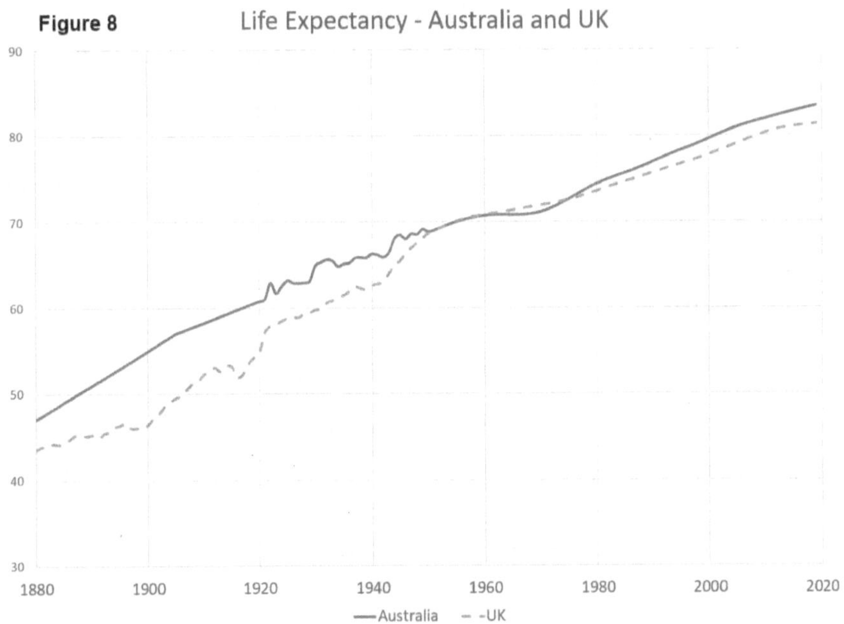


Figure 8: Life Expectancy, Australia and UK

So the average life expectancy in Australia was about 47 in 1880 and then rose steadily to 83 now. Much of this could be attributed to advances in healthcare. However, a trend line shows a slight curve, with the initial increase being about 3.3 months each year in around 1900, falling to about 2.7 months each year in around 2000.

This is more obvious from the figures from the UK. This shows that the life expectancy rose from 46 in 1900 to 68 in 1950 or 5.3 months per year but then to 78 in 2000, a fall to 2.4 months per year. I suppose cynics and conservatives might blame the British National Health Service, which started in 1947.

Therefore, in both countries, there was a substantial slowing in the middle of the twentieth century. Let us have a look at the medical treatments that were available in 1950 or rather the treatments that were not available then. There was no heart surgery or kidney dialysis. There were virtually no antibiotics. None of the drugs used now to treat conditions such as diabetes and heart disease were available. Insulin had become available about twenty years earlier but was in short supply. There was no ultrasound or CT or MRI scans.

So how did people come to live longer without these advances in medicine? The answer is through public health measures and the concept of preventive medicine. Public health means things that are done in the community. Preventive health is things that a person can do to avoid illness and delay death.

## Public Health

The earliest sewer systems were used in ancient Mesopotamia (present-day Iraq) 3,000 to 4,000 years ago. Channels carried the waste into cesspools. Similar systems were found in India, Crete, and Greece. The ancient Romans who ruled Europe for hundreds of years built vast networks of pipes to supply clean water to the cities, erecting huge aqueducts, many of which survive to this day. They also knew about the importance of separating human waste from food and water for consumption. They constructed public toilets which really were public – no screens – so you could chat with your neighbours while you were on the 'throne'.

Unfortunately, at the beginning of the fifth century, the Roman republic collapsed, and Europe entered the dark ages. Much of their achievements were lost. Europe did not start to recover until the end of the fifteenth century with the Renaissance. This was a mixed blessing. There were numerous technological advances, but none of them made any difference to people's health until the nineteenth century.

In the middle of the fourteenth century in Europe, there was an outbreak of the plague known as the Black Death. It was caused by a bacterium which was carried by rats and fleas. It killed half the population of Europe in the fourteenth century. However, public

     CHRIS GILFORD

health measures were gradually put in place. The Italians led the way with preventive measures against the factors which exacerbated the transmission of plague, namely, poverty, filth, bad housing, and dirty water. There were lockdowns, and isolation hospitals were built. Those exposed to plague victims were isolated initially for thirty days and then forty. *Quaranta* is forty in Italian, and so the term 'quarantine' was devised. Despite these measures, it still took 400 years before plague epidemics disappeared, though they had become less severe.

The Industrial Revolution was causing immense social change at the end of the eighteenth century. The cities grew in size to accommodate workers in the factories which produced clothing and other goods. The cities' infrastructure could not cope with the increased population. All the gains of the previous centuries were lost. Rubbish and sewage piled up in the streets. The smell was atrocious, particularly in summer. Houses did not have running water. People only had a bath at most once a week, and there were no showers. People had to collect their water from a well. There was a lot of overcrowding, with many families living four or more people in one room. There was a lot of drunkenness. One of the cheapest forms of alcohol available was gin. It was said you could be drunk for a penny, dead drunk for tuppence. Sometimes dead drunk actually meant dead. Life expectancy dropped in the early nineteenth century, particularly for the working classes in cities like Liverpool and Manchester, where it actually dropped below 20.

So from around 1800, these problems began to be addressed. Sewage treatment plants were built, and running water was piped to every home. In addition, people took pride in their neighbourhood and got rid of the rubbish. The impact of drunkenness was reduced as people started drinking less. More houses were built too, so there were fewer people in each dwelling. Gradually, everyone's health improved.

This was the same period as when most cities and towns in Australia were founded. Town planning became more organised, as can be seen by the orderly design and wide streets of Melbourne and Adelaide, compared with the narrow haphazard streets of Sydney. Essential services for towns could be incorporated in the early stages of building, rather than having to be retrofitted as in European towns and cities.

At the beginning of the nineteenth century, most people got their water from a communal well; but after the outbreak of diseases such as cholera and typhoid, the need to purify water became evident and with it the convenience of piping it into individual households.

Sewerage systems were constructed from the middle of the nineteenth century. Before that, all houses had an outside toilet, and the contents would be taken away by 'night-soil workers'. Initially, the sewerage systems pumped the raw sewerage away from towns and just piped it into natural waterways or directly into the sea. The next step was to pump it into farmland, where it would dry out, and it could be used as fertiliser. Finally, sewerage treatment plants were then developed in which the sewerage was processed to the extent that it could be recycled as drinking water. This seems unnatural to most Australians but is quite normal in England and a lot of Europe.

At the beginning of the Industrial Revolution in Europe, there was a mass exodus of people from the countryside into the towns and cities as that was where the jobs were – in the mines, the cotton mills, and other manufacturing plants. This produced a huge problem of overcrowding. Huge tenement blocks were built, but they rapidly filled up with many families living in a single room. The overcrowding increased the transmission of contagious diseases. This was addressed by a huge expansion of the housing programme until there was room for everyone to live comfortably.

After the urbanisation due to the Industrial Revolution, there was a rapid deterioration in levels of sanitation and the general quality of urban life. The streets became choked with filth due to the lack of waste clearance regulations. Waste collection systems started to appear in cities in the late eighteenth century. By the late nineteenth century, incinerators became widespread.

In the nineteenth and early twentieth centuries, the main method people used for heating their houses in the UK was by burning coal. The smoke that resulted contained large amounts of soot, which settled on all exposed surfaces, blackening the exterior of virtually every building in large cities. It also caused a big increase in the incidence of respiratory diseases such as asthma and chronic bronchitis. The great smog (smoke and fog) of London in December 1952 at times meant that the visibility was less than a metre. It brought London almost to a standstill and resulted in thousands of deaths. Parliament responded by passing the Clean Air Act. The subsequent change in methods of heating has resulted in much cleaner air, and most of the major buildings have been cleaned and are now their original colour. However, in many Asian megacities, like Beijing and Shanghai, air pollution can be severe at times.

Horses were the main method of transport before the twentieth century, either by riding them or by being in a carriage drawn by them. The problem was that they generated a huge amount of horse manure, and those in charge had no control of where they defaecated, and this would often be in the street. As a result, huge amounts, thousands of tons in large cities, accumulated in the street and became a health risk, which was only solved by the invention of the motor car.

### Household Level

The main thrust of these measures is to increase the general level of cleanliness in society. This has also been done at a household level. People are encouraged to leave their dirty boots outside, to wash their hands when they are dirty or have been to the toilet, and to keep their houses clean. It is somewhat surprising to see that some people hardly ever wash, but we see our cats and dogs grooming themselves and each other.

### Personal Level

The first vaccine was developed by Edward Jenner at the end of the eighteenth century against smallpox. Since then, the number of diseases for which a vaccination is available has increased almost exponentially. As well, there are extensive programmes which try and ensure that every human being on the planet is vaccinated against a number of diseases. The planet is now rid of smallpox. Polio got close to being completely eliminated about the year 2000 but has made a comeback. Diphtheria is making a comeback in the UK having been brought in by illegal immigrants. Other diseases for which vaccinations are available are now very rare. Measles is now very rare, but it and smallpox killed many First Nations people when Australia was being settled by pastoralists. Of course, the latest disease to get a vaccine is Covid-19.

Alcohol has been perceived to be a problem for many years. There have been many attempts to deal with the situation. In the nineteenth century, the problems of alcoholism and domestic violence prompted activists in the USA, mainly church leaders, to end the trade in alcoholic beverages. This resulted in the nationwide constitutional ban on the production, importation, transportation, and sale of alcoholic beverages. This was known as Prohibition and ran from 1920 to 1933. It is commonly thought to be a failure as criminal gangs took over the liquor industry. However, there was a general reduction in the amount of alcohol consumed, and it did not reach pre-1920 levels until the 1940s.

Alcoholics Anonymous is an international movement founded in 1935 that helps alcoholics remain sober. It has a twelve-step programme to aid sobriety, and it promotes personal responsibility.

Cigarette smoking was first found to be a health problem in the 1950s. A study of British doctors which started in 1951 had, by 1956, provided statistical proof that smoking increased the risk of lung cancer. Until then, smoking had actually been promoted as being good for one's health. As seen in a recent Oscar-winning film, King George VI was encouraged to smoke to help him relax and reduce his stutter, but he contracted lung cancer, dying from it at the age of 57. Many other diseases have been found to be exacerbated by smoking, and now there is a campaign in most countries to encourage smokers to quit.

Nutrition also improved over the last 300 years. The average daily food intake in Britain in the eighteenth century was about 2,100 calories (8,800 kJ). This was at a time when most people were agricultural workers. To do a full day's work, a man of today's size would need about 4,000 calories (16,700 kJ), a woman 3,500 (14,600 kJ). As a result, they were stunted in growth and would appear to be very thin by today's

     CHRIS GILFORD

standards. By 1850, the food intake had increased to about 2,400 calories (10,000 kJ). By the year 2000, average intake had increased to about 3,000 calories (12,500 kJ), but the average person today has a sedentary lifestyle and only needs about 2,500 calories (10,500 kJ). The sweet spot when intake matched requirements probably occurred in about 1970. The improvement in nutrition until then would have helped people overcome a variety of illnesses, particularly infection, and so contributed to an increase in life expectancy. Since then, it is contributing to obesity, which will likely result in a reduction in life expectancy.

## Modern Medicine

Modern medicine as we know it really took off after the Second World War. The treatment modalities in the first half of the twentieth century included medication, surgery, radiotherapy, and treatments provided by allied health professionals such as physiotherapy.

The first electrocardiographs (ECGs) were developed at the very end of the nineteenth century but assumed their present configuration in 1942.

The first dialysis machine was constructed in the Netherlands during the Second World War. It was first used successfully in a human patient in 1945.

The first heart operations were carried out in the 1940s, but the big breakthrough was the development of the heart-lung machine in the mid-1950s. This enabled the surgeons to use the machine to take over the function of the heart, thus enabling them to operate on the heart valves and coronary arteries while the heart had stopped beating. Surprisingly, much of the early surgery was done without the benefit of images of the heart or coronary arteries. The first coronary angiogram was performed by a German physician on himself in 1929. However, angiography did not become routine until the late 1960s, when suitable plastics and Teflon coating had been devised. The first stents to keep the arteries open became widely used in the late 1980s.

The concept of the intensive care unit began in 1950, when an anaesthetist proposed keeping patients sedated and ventilated in an intensive care environment.

Endoscopes are instruments that allow doctors to see inside the human body. Rigid endoscopes were available in the nineteenth century, but the breakthrough came in 1957 with the flexible endoscope. It consists of a bundle of many thousands of glass fibres which can transmit the image from inside a body cavity. The concept extended to laparoscopic surgery (keyhole surgery) developed by gynaecologists in the late 1960s and 1970s and later by general surgeons.

Joint replacement surgery had been attempted in the first half of the twentieth century, but the first successful total hip replacements were devised in 1962.

The first use of ultrasound to take measurements of body organs was in 1949, but the first handheld scanner became available in 1963.

Kidney transplants were carried out in the 1950s, but the success rate was very poor due to organ rejection. The success rate improved significantly in 1964, when drugs were developed to prevent rejection.

In vitro fertilisation was developed in the 1970s, with the world's first IVF baby being born in 1978.

The first CT scanner was constructed in 1971. The first MRI scanner was used on a patient in 1980.

## Modern Drugs

There were a handful of effective drugs available before the Second World War, such as aspirin, digoxin, morphine, insulin, and cocaine. But scientific advances after that allowed the synthesis of new compounds which could have therapeutic benefits. The following list shows the first drug in each therapeutic class. A few are still used today, but others have been superseded by drugs with fewer side effects or better specificity.

| 1938 | Sulphonamides | First effective antibiotic |
|---|---|---|
| 1938 | Phenytoin | First treatment for epilepsy that did not cause sedation |



CHRIS GILFORD

| 1942 | Penicillin | Although first discovered in 1928 |
|---|---|---|
| 1946 | Streptomycin | First antibiotic against tuberculosis |
| 1950 | Methotrexate | First drug to treat cancer |
| 1953 | Chlorpromazine | First effective treatment for schizophrenia |
| 1956 | Tolbutamide | First oral drug for type 2 diabetes |
| 1957 | Chlorothiazide | First diuretic – causes kidneys to excrete more urine |
| 1958 | Metformin | Still used to treat diabetes but not released in the USA until 1995 |
| 1958 | Imipramine | First tricyclic antidepressant |
| 1960 | Chlordiazepoxide | First benzodiazepine – for insomnia and anxiety |
| 1961 | Anovlar | First oral contraceptive |
| 1962 | Furosemide | First powerful diuretic |
| 1964 | Propranolol | First beta blocker – used in heart disease |
| 1968 | Levodopa | First effective treatment for Parkinson's |
| 1969 | Salbutamol | (Ventolin) first effective and convenient treatment for asthma |
| 1976 | Cimetidine | First treatment for stomach ulcers |
| 1977 | Captopril | First ACE inhibitor – used in heart and kidney disease |
| 1979 | Simvastatin | First statin – used to lower cholesterol |
| 1986 | Fluoxetine | First SSRI – for treating depression |
| 1989 | Omeprazole | First proton pump inhibitor – used to treat gastric reflux |
| 1998 | Sildenafil | First treatment for impotence |

Table 4: Dates when new drugs were introduced

Since then, the majority of drugs that have been developed are for the treatment of cancer and viral diseases, including Covid. A large category of drugs that are used today is in the prevention of diseases. For example, the statin drugs are used to lower cholesterol. High cholesterol itself does not cause disease, but it does increase the risk of someone having a heart attack.

I have included these lists of medical procedures and drugs to show that the biggest advances in medicine took place in the thirty years between the mid-1950s and mid-1980s. However, the increase in life expectancy continued its gradual rise in the last century and then slowed in about 1950. I believe that this shows that the impact of public health and preventive medicine was far more important.

The problem with public health and preventive health is that they take years or decades for their effects to be obvious. On the other hand, with modern medicine, the effects are often noticed straight away or at least within a few days. Surgery is the obvious example. Supposing someone who is crippled with hip arthritis to the extent that they can only walk half a dozen steps has a hip replacement. A few hours after the surgery, they get out of bed with the aid of crutches, and they literally walk out of hospital two days later, covering a greater distance than they have for weeks. Six weeks later, they are walking as well as someone much younger, assuming no other joints are affected.

Vaccinations have been very successful. Smallpox was completely eradicated twenty years ago. Hardly anyone in Australia ever gets tetanus, diphtheria, or polio because of the vaccinations they receive as a child. There are occasional outbreaks of mumps and measles, but they are rare, and sometimes they do occur in people who have been vaccinated. AIHW published a report in 2022 on Australia's health, and it included the following graph:

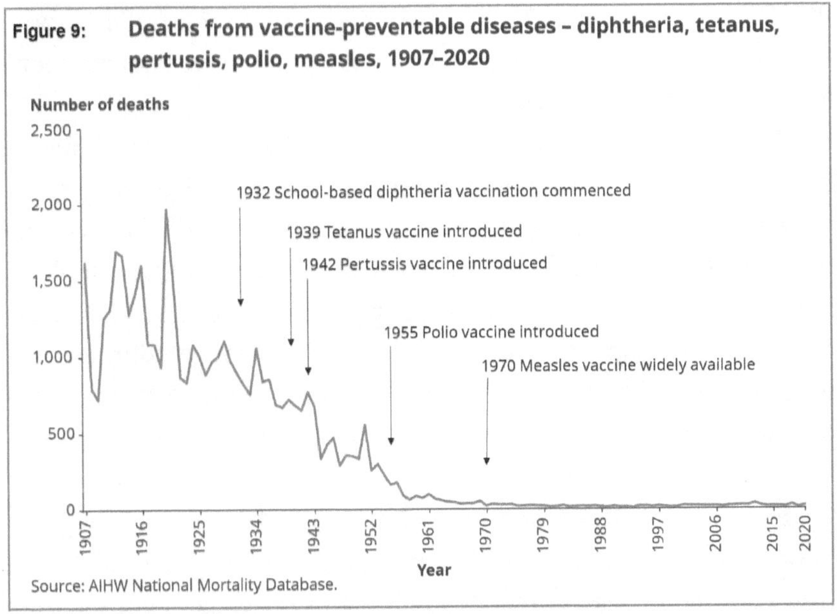


Figure 9: Vaccine-preventable deaths

Since many of the diseases mentioned earlier were largely eliminated in the 1950s, there are few people around who remember the outbreaks, particularly of polio, when there were wards full of people on ventilators. When I was a medical student I went to Sri Lanka for two months to see how medicine was practiced in a developing country. This was the only time I have seen anyone with tetanus and there was a ward full of people with it. This may explain why there has been some opposition to the Covid vaccine in the recent outbreak. I wonder whether publishing this graph might have convinced some of their error. Perhaps vaccinations are a victim of their own success.

## First Nations Health

So finally, we have to ask the question 'Why has First Nations people's health not improved in the last 200 years?'

There have been many changes in the lives of First Nations people over the last 200 years. Their traditional lives have been well documented. An example is the work of anthropologist Herbert

Basedow, who made many trips to remote South Australia between 1903 and 1928, documenting and photographing First Nations people living a traditional lifestyle.

The last pair of First Nations people who lived a traditional lifestyle were found in 1977 in Western Australia. They had been ostracised by their mob for forming a couple when this was against tribal law because they were too closely related. They had succeeded in living completely independently for decades with only sporadic contact with the outside world. An alarm was raised during a long spell of drought, during which time no one had had any contact with them. They were rescued when they were close to death from dehydration and lived the rest of their days in an aged persons' hostel.

First Nations people now live in houses which are grouped together in various ways such as towns or communities or in suburbs of a major city. Each house has water, electricity, and sewerage connected. All communities have a shop where they can buy food, thus eliminating the need to go out hunting. However, many do continue to go out hunting or fishing to improve the variety in their diet. All communities have medical and educational facilities. Every person has a Medicare card, which entitles them to free medical care. Most of them get free medication. If they require medical treatment that is not available in their community, they get free travel to the closest city where that treatment can be provided. Many specialists travel to First Nations communities to hold clinics, so this often avoids the need to go to a city to see a specialist.

Many First Nations people now own cars so they can travel more and see family and friends. Most have mobile phones so they can communicate better.

It appears from the above that First Nations people have rapidly transitioned from a hunter-gatherer lifestyle to a twenty-first-century one.

## First Nations People's Explanation for Their Poor Health

The general consensus among First Nations people is that . . . more than 200 years of dispossession, racism and discrimination have left

First Nations Australians with some of the lowest levels of education, highest levels of unemployment, poorest health and most appalling housing conditions.

These will be discussed in subsequent chapters.

When asked what they want from the Closing the Gap campaign, most First Nations people have two requests – a dialysis unit and a birthing suite in each community. Unfortunately, neither of these will actually help the health indices and may make them worse. They will be discussed in subsequent chapters.

The commonest reasons given by First Nations people for the gap in health indices is the following:

1. Health services are not accessible to many, and particularly remote, Indigenous communities.
2. Mainstream health services often lack cultural sensitivity and remain unwelcoming places for many Indigenous peoples.
3. The Indigenous health workforce remains disproportionately low when compared with the number of Aboriginal and Torres Strait Islanders that make up the Australian population.

These statements need to be addressed.

1. *Health Services Not Accessible*

I am not sure what evidence has been provided to support this assertion, but my own experience disagrees with it. The state governments have been doing their best to provide services for First Nations communities, even the smallest. In Cape York in Far North Queensland, there are hospitals or clinics in all the First Nations communities, apart from the ones that are only a short distance from communities with a clinic. There are five communities with a population below about 700, and they have a clinic with a resident nurse and a visiting doctor. The ten larger communities have a resident doctor and nurses all available 24/7. Thursday Island Hospital is a major referral hospital for the whole area and has about twenty doctors, who also take care of the seventeen clinics in the Torres Strait Islands.

About thirty years ago, I worked for the Royal Flying Doctors Service (RFDS) in Kalgoorlie for a couple of months. Every fortnight one of the doctors would do a three-day tour and hold clinics in the various First Nations communities to the north and east of Kalgoorlie. I did this trip on one occasion. The pilot and I left very early one morning for a three-and-a-half-hour flight to the first clinic at Kiwirrkurra Community. This has a population of about 160 and is described as the most remote First Nations community in Australia. It is in the Gibson Desert, 630 km west of Alice Springs. There is a clinic set up there with a permanent nurse.

After an hour or so there, we got back in the aeroplane to visit about a dozen other communities, with overnight stops at Giles and Warburton. Most of these communities had a population of around 100–200, but each had a resident nurse. About two or three times a week, the doctor on call would have an urgent conversation with the nurse in one of these communities via a two-way radio, the only means of communication; and a lot of the time, a plane would be dispatched to pick up someone who was sick and needed urgent evacuation, often in the middle of the night. The pilots had special training to enable them to find the airstrip, and this was before GPS, and land with only car headlights and a dozen paraffin lanterns to light the strip.

I am sure that there are similar arrangements for First Nations communities in other states and territories. In general, the facilities are greater than for small towns of equivalent size elsewhere in Australia.

A later chapter compares the difference between some aspects of health services provided in remote and very remote areas compared with major cities. There are actually more GPs in the remote areas, and more patients are hospitalised.

2.  *Health Services Unwelcoming*

In fact, health services have now become very unwelcoming for the whole population, not just First Nations people, and Covid has made it even worse. If you phone up a medical centre for an appointment, the first thing you hear is a recorded message saying something like this: 'Medical Centre. If this is an emergency, hang up and dial 000. If you have a cough, cold, sore throat, or fever, hang up and call the government fever line. If you want a Covid vaccination, we don't do them, so talk to the local pharmacist. Did you know that you can make appointments or get your test results on the web? Log into www.yourgp. com.au. If you want to make an appointment, press 1. If you want to speak to a nurse, press 2.' When you finally get through to a human being, the first thing they will ask is, what is your date of birth? They don't want to know your name, just the six- or eight-digit code that usually defines us. Bad luck if you are a twin.

If you do turn up for an appointment, before even saying hello, the receptionist will ask for your Medicare card to confirm your identity with this eleven-digit number. The federal government goes one further. Not content with identifying your health needs with this number, they have devised the Individual Healthcare Identifier number as an adjunct.

3.  *Health Workforce*

Yes, the First Nations health workforce does remain disproportionately low, but it is increasing. The first person who identified as First Nations and qualified as a doctor was Prof. Helen Milroy, an expert in child and adolescent psychiatry who graduated in 1983 and was named WA Australian of the Year in 2021.

There are now about 100,000 doctors in Australia, of whom about 400 are First Nations so 0.4 per cent. As the First Nations population is now about 3.2 per cent, we should now have about 3,200 First Nations doctors to have the right proportion. About 3,800 medical students enrol every year, so to achieve the correct proportion of First Nations doctors in twenty years' time, there should be about 200 First Nations students enrolling in medicine each year. We have not got there yet, but we should do so soon. One hundred twenty-one First Nations medical students enrolled in 2020.

There is a similar situation for nurses and allied health professionals.

There are now about 3,500 First Nations nurses and midwives in Australia, representing about 1.1 per cent of the nursing workforce, so they are well ahead of doctors in achieving the right proportion. Offsetting these figures, there is an occupational category of Aboriginal health worker, and they are similar to enrolled nurses. There are now approximately 1,800 AHWs in Australia, but this number is expected to decline as the number of First Nations registered nurses increases.

Attempts have been made to address all these aspects in the last ten years, but there has been no improvement in the key indicators.

It is impossible to turn the clock back and reverse the events of the past. The prime minister has apologised. What else can be done? Clearly, a new explanation and approach is needed.

# CHAPTER 3

# First Nations Peoples

ACCORDING TO THE 2021 census, the total population of Australia was 25,422,788, of whom 812,728 were recorded as being First Nations, or 3.20 per cent of the total. They are spread throughout the states and territories as follows:

|           | All        | First Nations | % First Nations |
|-----------|------------|---------------|-----------------|
| NSW       | 8,072,163  | 278,043       | 3.44            |
| Vic       | 6,503,491  | 65,646        | 1.01            |
| Qld       | 5,156,138  | 237,303       | 4.60            |
| WA        | 2,660,026  | 88,693        | 3.33            |
| SA        | 1,781,516  | 42,562        | 2.39            |
| Tas       | 557,571    | 30,186        | 5.41            |
| ACT       | 454,499    | 8,949         | 1.97            |
| NT        | 232,605    | 61,115        | 26.27           |
| Australia | 25,422,788 | 812,728       | 3.20            |

Table 5: Population of Australian states and territories

Australia is one of the most urbanised countries in the world, despite the fact that it is one of the largest and almost has the lowest density of population. About 76 per cent of people live in cities of more than 100,000 people. First Nations people are also urbanised, with about 35 per cent of First Nations people living in the capital cities, particularly Sydney and Brisbane. About half live in country towns, and the remaining 15 per cent live in remote communities, mainly in Queensland and the Northern Territory.

Just like the rest of Australians, they are a very diverse group; and by any measure of achievement or behaviour, they are found in a continuous spectrum that runs from leaders and role models down to the low levels of society. It is unfortunate that it is those who are at the lower end that seem to attract most of the publicity.

## A Brief History of First Nations Contact with Europeans

First Nations people first arrived in Australia at least 65,000 years ago when the sea level had dropped, enabling them to travel from South-East Asia. There was never a complete land bridge between what is now Indonesia and Australia, but the gap narrowed to about 80–90 km. It would have been possible for someone standing on the highest point of Timor Island, which is higher than Mount Kosciuszko, to have seen the Australian coastline on a clear day. The oceans were at their lowest levels 90,000, 70,000, 55,000, 35,000, and 18,000 years ago. Australia was connected at times with New Guinea, but the latter was always separate from the rest of SE Asia.

After the end of the last ice age, the sea level rose, and the sea channel increased to around 500 km wide. The next confirmed contact between Australia and the rest of the world probably occurred between AD 1000 and 1500 when Malaysian fishermen arrived, followed by Chinese fishermen and traders. They did not come inland, but they left a few artefacts with the First Nations people.

There is some evidence that Portuguese explorers may have sighted Australia in the 1520s. The Portuguese forged the first global empire. They were the first to round the Cape of Good Hope at the southern tip of Africa, and they formed colonies in southern India and the Indonesian archipelago. However, it was the Dutch in the early sixteenth century who made several expeditions and mapped the northern and western coasts of Australia. The Dutch were mainly interested in trade, so finding little opportunities for this, they did not venture inland. There was little progress in exploration for over a century, until Captain Cook was sent to observe the transit of Venus from Tahiti and then search for the continent of Terra Australis Incognita. He surveyed the whole of

   CHRIS GILFORD

the East Coast of Australia and claimed it for Britain, naming it New South Wales. He described the area around Port Botany in glowing terms when he arrived back in England. This, of course, is well known, but what is less well known is that Cook was disobeying orders.

After Christopher Columbus' voyage from southern Spain to America, various expeditions sailed from England to North America and set up colonies. Convicts were sent there to avoid the cost of building prisons in England to house them. By the early eighteenth century, the new colonists were pushing westwards and seizing the land from the Native Americans. The year 1763 was the end of the Seven Years' War between France and Great Britain, and at the Treaty of Paris, French territory in North America was ceded to Great Britain. King George III issued a royal proclamation in October 1763 which forbade all settlements west of a line drawn along the Appalachian Mountains (and extending north and south of them), which was delineated as an 'Indian Reserve' for the 'Indians'. The royal proclamation continues to be of legal importance to First Nations people in Canada, being the first legal recognition of First Nations title, rights, and freedoms, and is recognized in the Canadian Constitution of 1982.

Cook's first voyage to the Pacific was primarily a scientific one and was sponsored by the Royal Society. The society's president James Douglas, Earl of Morton, successfully lobbied King George III for funds to purchase a ship for the expedition. Lord Morton wrote to Cook and the scientists preparing for the expedition telling them 'to exercise the utmost patience and forbearance with respect to the Natives of the several lands where the Ship may touch . . . They are the natural, and in the strictest sense of the word, the legal possessors of the several regions they inhabit.'

When Cook reached Tahiti, he opened the sealed orders from the lords of the Admiralty. These instructed him to explore the southern Pacific to find the Terra Australis. These orders were quite detailed and asked him to give an account of the native inhabitants, if any, and friendship, alliance, and trade with them; the discoverer was 'with the Consent of the Natives to take possession of Convenient Situations in the Country in the Name of the King of Great Britain; or, if you find the Country uninhabited take possession for His Majesty by setting up proper marks and inscriptions, as first discoverers and possessors'.

It Is somewhat surprising that, in the eighteenth century in Britain, there were two separate documents asserting the legal rights of the people whom Cook might encounter, so where did the concept of *terra nullius* come from?

Back in North America, tensions arose between the colonists and the government in London over trade, colonial policy, and taxation measures. War broke out in 1775, the Declaration of Independence was signed in 1776, and at that point, no more convicts from England were transported there. Another effect was that the proclamation line no longer had any legitimacy in the USA.

The refusal of the new USA to take convicts became a problem in England since transport to the colonies was a common form of punishment for a variety of crimes. With nowhere for them to go, they were housed in 'hulks' moored in the river Thames, east of London. The British government was therefore delighted to hear from Cook about the potential location for a penal colony in New South Wales and, after a delay of a few years, dispatched a fleet in 1787 to form one. The original advice that the views of the existing inhabitants of Terra Australia were to be respected was quietly forgotten.

New colonies were formed around the coast of Australia. However, from early in the nineteenth century, expeditions were sent inland to explore the whole country. During all this period, there was contact between the European explorers and the First Nations inhabitants. There was friction between the two groups as each claimed that the land was theirs. There have recently been questions asked about the role of NSW governor Lachlan Macquarie in the killing of First Nations people in 1816. There were many skirmishes with loss of life on both sides, followed by retribution. The situation deteriorated in the middle of the century when the explorers were replaced by pastoralists who wished to settle on the land so they could use it for running livestock and growing crops.

Estimates of the population of Australia before 1788 vary enormously, from 300,000 to a million. In the eighteenth century,

     CHRIS GILFORD

the First Nations population decreased catastrophically, possibly by as much as 90% per cent in some areas. Similar decimation of Indigenous populations was happening in many other places around the world. Obviously, the Europeans had better weaponry than the First Nations people, but it was the effect of the infectious diseases brought in by the Europeans that was probably much larger. The First Nations people had no immunity to diseases such as measles and smallpox, and large numbers succumbed.

In Tasmania, there was violent conflict between European colonists and First Nations people between about 1825 and 1832, resulting in the near destruction of the First Nations people in that colony.

The colony of Queensland was formed in 1859, and here, the pastoralists found an ally in the new government. The Queensland frontier was more violent than that in any other state. A good account of the violence is found in *Conspiracy of Silence* by Timothy Bottoms. Squads of native police were formed, made up of the First Nations people, who were excellent trackers. There was tacit permission given to the pastoralists that they could kill any First Nations people who blocked their acquisition of land, and they used the Native Police to carry out the dirty work, just making sure that they were deployed away from their own tribal groups. Timothy Bottoms quotes extensively from the *Brisbane Courier*. This one in April 1868 is typical: 'Everybody in the district [Burketown] is delighted with the wholesale slaughter dealt out by the Native Police . . . in ridding the district of 59 [blacks].' As well as being killed by firearms, many First Nations people were killed by systematic poisoning, usually of waterholes.

This genocide continued for over half a century, from about 1860 to 1920. A number of First Nations people did manage to avoid death from disease or murder, but they had to hide in more remote areas.

**Stolen Generation**

In the late nineteenth century, the various colonial governments thought that the First Nations people would eventually die out, and this would solve the 'problem'. However, soon after Federation, it became apparent that this would not happen, and so a new policy had to be implemented. It was observed that there were a large number of children being born to First Nations mothers and non-Indigenous fathers, and there were some reports that the resultant children were being neglected by their mothers. The new policy was to take these children away from their First Nations ancestors and get them adopted by non-Indigenous couples. This process started in about 1920 and continued to the 1960s. The idea was that these children would be brought up in non-Indigenous society and have no interest in their background. These children formed the stolen generation.

The Australian Institute of Health and Welfare has published several reports on the stolen generation. The latest one, dated 2018, reported on the results of Health and Social Surveys conducted among Aboriginal and TSI people in 2012–13 and ran to 144 pages. The estimated total population that had been removed from their families was 24,486. This represents 16.4 per cent of the estimated total First Nations population who were born before 1972.

The report looks at the prevalence of thirteen social outcomes and nine health outcomes and compares the results between those who had been removed, other First Nations people, and non-Indigenous people. In twelve of the social outcomes, there was a very clear trend between the three groups, with non-Indigenous doing the best and those who had been removed doing the worst. For the remaining social outcome, that of how much they felt they had a say in the community on important issues, there was no difference between the two First Nations groups, and they had more of a say compared with non-Indigenous.

In eight of the nine health issues, there was again a clear trend between the three groups, with non-Indigenous doing the best and those who had been removed doing the worst. The greatest differences in prevalence of certain diseases were for diabetes, heart disease, stroke, and kidney disease where the rates for those removed were three to four times higher than in non-Indigenous people. The remaining issue was cancer for which there was very little difference between the groups.

So for almost every indicator by which the impact of removal of

     CHRIS GILFORD

children from their community can be measured, the programme can only be described as a catastrophic failure.

Has this situation been studied elsewhere in other communities?

In 1939, with the threat of war with Germany, the British government implemented a plan to protect children from the effects of war by sending them out from the large cities, especially London, to live in the country where they would be safer. The process was voluntary, but about half the children, about a million in all, were taken away in special trains with only about three days' notice. They stayed away for several years until it was considered 'safe' for them to return home. Shortly after the end of the war, a psychologist talked to over a thousand of them. The results showed that being removed from their parents was more damaging to children than being exposed to enemy air raids. The studies continued for decades and showed that those who had been evacuated as young children were at much higher risk of mental health problems later in life. This was particularly the case for those evacuated under the age of 6 as half the girls and a third of the boys were later diagnosed with depression. Anxiety disorders were also more common in those evacuated at a young age.

In 1948, a federal act made First Nations people Australian citizens. Before that, they had been classified as being part of the flora and fauna of Australia. In 1959, the Social Services Act was amended to extend age pensions and maternity benefits to First Nations people.

In the 1960s, there was a lot of activism by various First Nations leaders to try and gain more recognition for their people. As a result, the Holt government held a referendum on 27 May 1967 which asked two questions: whether Aboriginal people should be counted in the census and whether the government should have the power to make laws for Aboriginal people. The result was an overwhelming majority, about 90 per cent, in favour of making these changes to the constitution.

In 1968, First Nations stockmen were granted equal pay to non-Indigenous stockmen. This decision followed a strike at Wave Hill Station two years before.

In 1982, Torres Strait Islanders, led by Eddie Mabo, took a case to the high court requesting a declaration stating that their traditional rights to land, sea, seabeds, and reefs hadn't been extinguished. The high court found that Australia had been occupied before white settlement and that First Nations people had legal rights to their traditional land. There were further extensions (Wik 1996) to this principle that native title could still exist even if other interests in the land, such as pastoral leases, also existed.

On 6 November 1999, there was a referendum to decide if Australia should become a republic. The prime minister, John Howard, inserted a second question, asking whether there should be a preamble to the constitution. In part, it said, 'We the Australian people commit ourselves to this Constitution . . . . honouring Aborigines [*sic*] and Torres Strait Islanders, the nation's first people, for their deep kinship with their lands and for their ancient and continuing cultures which enrich the life of our country.' However, both questions were defeated.

In 2003, the Queensland government made a settlement to pay First Nations workers for the wages that they had not received.

On 13 February 2008, PM Kevin Rudd addressed the Australian Parliament and apologised for the mistreatment handed out to the First Nations peoples of Australia.

At the end of 2015, a referendum council was appointed by the prime minister Malcolm Turnbull, together with the leader of the opposition, to advise the government on steps towards a referendum to recognise First Nations peoples in the Australian Constitution. The council travelled all over Australia the following year and met with over a thousand First Nations peoples' representatives. This resulted in a consensus document, the Uluru Statement from the Heart, which called for the establishment of a First Nations voice enshrined in the constitution. This was largely ignored by the Liberal-National government but was immediately adopted by the new Labour government in 2022.

Can any of these changes actually reverse all the 200 years of dispossession, the frontier wars, and the stolen generation? Unfortunately, the events of the last two and a bit centuries are historical facts and cannot be changed. The problems of racism and discrimination are currently being dealt with and eliminated, but this process is far too slow.

The Truth and Reconciliation Commission was set up in South Africa in 1996 after the end of apartheid. The Nuremberg trials were held in Germany after the Second World War. In both cases, this was shortly after the end of the previous regime. In Australia, the stolen generation policy finished by about 1967, so no one who made the decisions would still be alive. There may be some people who worked in the relevant government departments who might still be alive but would have been very junior then and would say that they were just following orders and that they were told it was for the children's own good.

There are conflicting views about whether it is helpful to keep dwelling on unpleasant past events. Rape victims find it very distressing to have to keep repeating details of the rape. Sufferers of PTSD have mixed feelings about reliving the past. One of the recognised treatments now is to revisit the precipitating event, and so desensitise them to it, which is helpful for many but others say it makes it worse and occasionally causes more nightmares and flashbacks.

Forgiveness is a method used by some people to come to terms with events where they or someone they care about has been harmed. Occasionally, we see someone whose relative has been murdered but is able to tell the murderer, sometimes in court, that they forgive them. This is often combined with the idea 'forgive but do not forget'. Those who do forgive say that through this process they find peace.

## Life in a First Nations Community

Most Australians have no idea what it is like to live in a First Nations community, so I shall describe some aspects of Mornington Island.

Mornington Island is the largest of the Wellesley Islands, a group of twenty-two islands in the south of the Gulf of Carpentaria. It is the traditional land of the Lardil people, but they have been joined by the Yangkaal, who were from the small islands between Mornington Island and the mainland, and the Kaiadilt, who are originally from Bentinck Island. There are also some Gangalidda and Waanyi people from the mainland. Historically, Lardil people lived around the coast and would move inland only in time of ceremony, hunting and gathering, or shelter in times of inclement weather.

It is about 70 km long and has a maximum width of about 20 km. The township is called Gununa, and it is situated on the coast in the south-west corner of the island. It appears to be on an estuary as there is another island, Denholm, a kilometre offshore. Mornington Island is about 40 km away from the mainland, but there are several small islands in between, so the maximum distance across open sea is about 4 km. This means that people can travel to the mainland in a small boat without losing sight of land.

The weather in Mornington Island is hot for most of the year. The seasons are marked by the rainfall. The wet season runs from the end of November to April, with the dry season after that. In August, there is a unique weather phenomenon. A huge rolling cloud called a Morning Glory forms early in the morning in the southern gulf, travelling southwards, causing a strong, cool breeze. From mid-September, it starts to get hotter and more humid, a period often described as the build-up. The mango trees bear fruit, so it can also be called mango season, but mangoes are not native – they come from NE India, Bangladesh, and Myanmar. In late November or early December, the rain arrives, and it can come down in torrential downpours. Heavy rainfall disrupts communications, especially air services. This is also the beginning of the cyclone season. Daily temperatures in January generally range between twenty-five and thirty-three. In March, the rainfall decreases, usually ending in April. From then on, it is usually completely dry. The temperature drops, and in July, the range of daily temperatures is usually between sixteen and twenty-six. The land dries out completely and looks barren apart from where it is irrigated.

The island is generally flat with a maximum elevation of forty-three metres. Most of the island is low scrub with trees up to five metres tall, but there are she-oaks and mangrove trees on the perimeter. There are no land mammals apart from a few rats, but there are plenty of reptiles, including lizards, skinks, monitors, and snakes (venomous and non-venomous) and several species of frog. The surrounding sea is teeming with fish including barramundi, but there are also plenty of dugong and turtles. There are estuarine crocodiles around the coast.

According to the 2016 census, the total population was 1,136, of which 983 (87 per cent) were First Nations, 130 were non-Indigenous, and 19 did not record their status. However, in 2021, the total population was 1,022, of which 822 (80 per cent) were First Nations. The reason for this drop is not apparent.

These figures may be misleading. More than half the non-Indigenous were in the age range of 25–39 and almost certainly were made up of people on contracts who worked on the island. These would include most of the people working at the school, hospital, shire council, and government agencies. From my observations, about 99 per cent of the permanent residents are First Nations. There are a handful of non-Indigenous people who have settled in Mornington Island and are regarded as part of the community. One was a deserter from the Vietnam conscription and had been there ever since. I think that all are male, living with First Nations partners. The figure of 822 First Nations people is probably an underestimate. Some First Nations people appear not to have a permanent home on the island but drift between different houses so may not have been counted at all. Others move around between different communities, such as Doomadgee on the mainland, and may not have been counted either. Hospital figures suggest that the permanent First Nations population is over 1,200.

Mornington Island has an airport with a commercial service to Cairns and Mount Isa. Flights, though, are expensive. The cheapest return ticket to Cairns is $700 for a distance of about 700 km each way. Compare this travel from Sydney to Melbourne, which is a bit farther, and prices for a return ticket usually start at around $320. There is a barge service from Karumba once a week for the transport of large and heavy goods, but it does not take passengers. Some of the local residents have their own boats – aluminium ‘tinnies’ – and they travel across to the mainland.

If you flew to Mornington Island until this year (2022), you were advised at the check-in desk that there are alcohol restrictions and that no alcohol can be carried on the flight. There used to be a large sign at

Mornington Island Airport advising you of this fact, with a warning that the penalty for being in possession of alcohol was $75,000 and/or confiscation of vehicle and/or imprisonment. However, this sign was considered a bit off-putting and was replaced by a more welcoming one a few years ago. This one was from near the wharf:



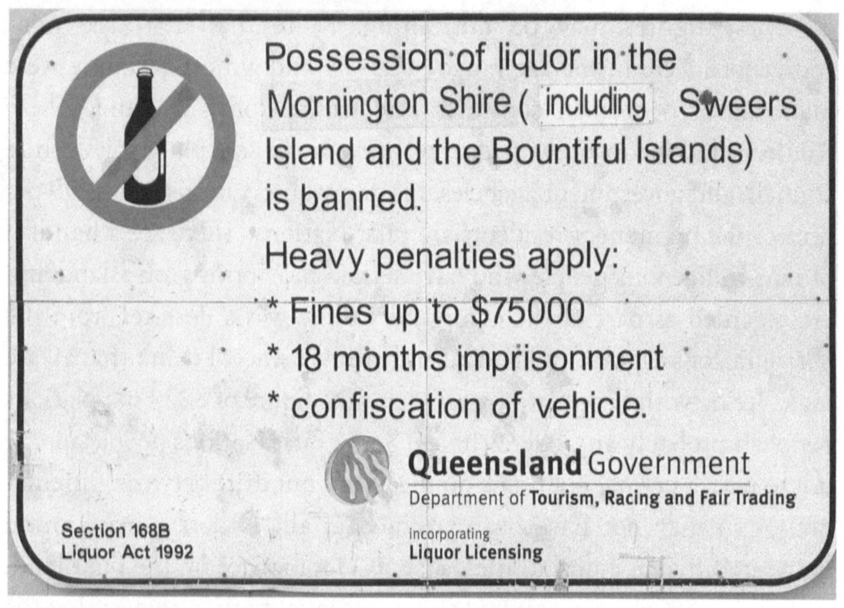


Photo by the Author 2017

Figure 10: Mornington liquor sign

The other thing of interest at the airport is a memorial to five First Nations elders and their pilot who died in 1999 when their aircraft went missing on a flight from Mornington Island to Normanton. The cause of the accident remains a mystery. It was a Cessna 206A, a single-engine aircraft, but there were light showers on most of the route. When he was just north of Bentinck Island, the pilot announced that he was diverting to Burketown due to the weather. The distance over water is only about 50 km, and the sea is shallow, less than 50 ft deep. Although a couple of pieces of an aircraft of that type were found floating in the sea shortly afterwards and some wreckage on the seabed was found in 2002, it was



CHRIS GILFORD

not proved conclusively to be the missing aircraft. The bodies of the occupants were never found.

It remains as much a mystery as Malaysia Airlines flight 370. This was the Boeing 777 which left Kuala Lumpur in March 2014 bound for Beijing but was lost somewhere in the South Indian Ocean. There were six Australians on board. The effort to locate the aircraft was the most expensive in history, with a total bill of around $150 million, of which Australia was a major contributor. So the government was happy to spend tens of millions of dollars looking for MH370, but virtually no search was carried out for the same number of Australians in the plane lost off Mornington Island.

The cemetery is not far from the airport. It is on a gentle slope and has a gazebo where you can rest and enjoy a view of the gulf. The burial plots are in neat rows, and many are well cared for with flowers (albeit plastic) and elaborately carved headstones. If you look closely at the dates on these, you will be struck by the fact that most of the people died at a comparatively young age, often in their forties and fifties.

The airport is right on the edge of the town, so as you drive in from the airport, you can see the residents' houses. The area near the airport was established many years ago, and there are mature trees around the houses. Elsewhere, there are few trees. The houses first built were constructed of weatherboard, but all the more recent ones are made of block since they need to withstand cyclones, which are a feature of life in the tropics during the wet season.

Unfortunately, although there are some exceptions, the majority of the houses do not look well cared for. The backyards are overgrown, and there is lots of rubbish piled up. Broken pieces of furniture are spread round the yard, and there is often a wreck of a car. Even the cars that are mobile have seen better days, often with dents and broken windows. There is no requirement for vehicles that are bought and sold on the island to have a roadworthy certificate. The only cars in a reasonable condition are those owned by government departments and agencies.

As you come closer to the town centre, you pass the two shops in town: one sells food, and the other, called a variety shop, sells toys and household goods. Both are surrounded by a high fence. There is also a small cafe selling pies, burgers, etc.

There are little opportunities for employment. The major employer of the local residents is the shire, which require many workers for maintenance and management of the infrastructure. Some of the locals are employed as trades assistants, but the tradesmen come from elsewhere. Other local residents are employed by the shop, the school (teachers' aides), the aged care facility (personal care assistants), the childcare centre, and Safe House. There is a programme for building new houses and refurbishing existing properties, but I am not aware of any of the local residents being employed as apprentices or trades assistants in this industry. There is a large construction camp which houses all the fly-in/fly-out tradies and other construction workers.

Many of the residents have what they call outstations, but elsewhere, they would be called weekenders.

**Figure 11: Map of Mornington Island with Outstations**

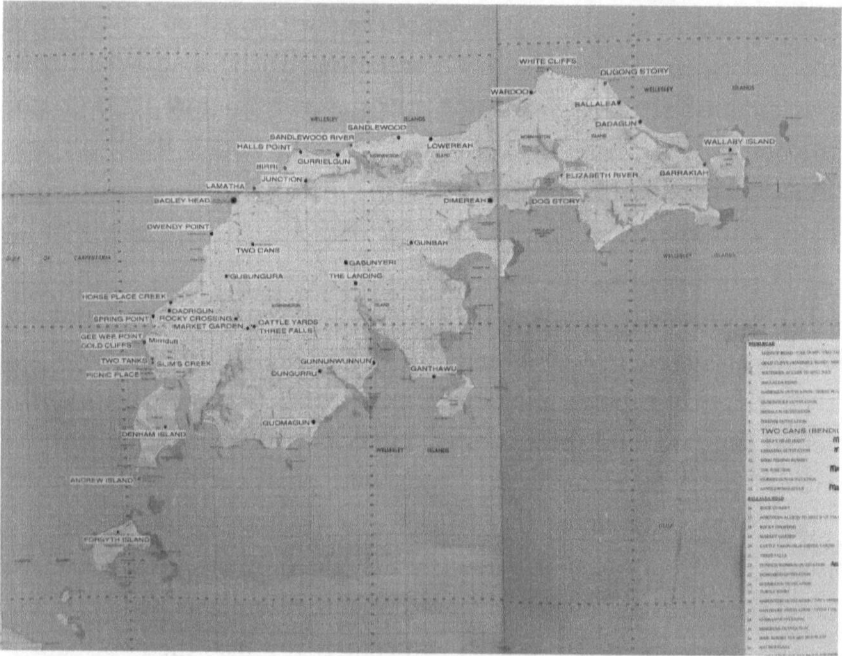

Photo by the Author

Figure 11: Map of Outstations

There are over forty of these small dwellings dotted through the island on the land that have been in their family's traditional hunting and fishing lands. They are not connected to mains water or electricity, so they need generators and a local supply of fresh water. Many of them, though, are equipped with satellite phones which they can use in an emergency and have been supplied under a government programme. Many of the families spend their weekends in these, and they serve as bases for recreation such as fishing.

As you travel round the town, you may see a number of the residents walking around. Many of them seem to wander aimlessly as though they do not have to go anywhere. Sometimes, particularly on the weekends, the whole town seems to be deserted. However, in the evenings, the streets may be full of people, many of whom are intoxicated. Children often wander around in the middle of the night, so there is little chance that they will be at school the next day. You will probably also see a lot of dogs – all cross-breeds – many of them will look as though they are not well cared for. They do seem to have their own code of behaviour. They sit or lie patiently outside the shop while their owners are shopping and never try to enter.

The mood in the town varies over time, and you may become aware of some tension in the air. Every few weeks, this breaks out, and everybody seems to be outside, many intoxicated, yelling and screaming. Fights break out, and they may involve as many as 200 people. The police are often called, but there is little that they can do if there are only three or four officers on duty at the time, other than advising people to go home and cool down.

In contrast, at other times, everyone is quiet and respectful. If one of the elders dies, the whole town goes into mourning. Almost always, it occurs at the hospital. Those who were with the elder help the nursing staff put the deceased in a suitable position in the bed, and then a huge procession of all family and friends, slowly and with hushed tones, file past the bed to pay their respects. It becomes very spiritual. There is some occasional wailing but no pushing, no raised voices. It appears no different, other than in scale, from the procession of mourners past the late Queen's coffin in London. The town shuts down on the day of the funeral. This is often several days later to allow family members to gather.

There is very little entertainment in the town. When I was there, there were no pubs or bars due to the alcohol ban. There is no cinema or theatre. There is no DVD library, but there are a few DVDs for sale in the variety shop. TV stations are available via satellite links – ABC, SBS, Imparja, and Channel 7. Imparja is a First Nations–run TV station based in Alice Springs. It mainly rebroadcasts Channel 9 shows but has some home-grown content. Many of the advertisements are aimed at First Nations people and include health messages such as 'Wash your hands after you have been to the toilet' and 'Wear light-coloured clothing when walking on the street at night.'

There is a mobile phone service (Telstra), and probably about half the population have mobile phones, many of which are smartphones. Those who do are as addicted to them as anyone else, updating their profiles on Facebook and other social media. Many people have discovered that the cheapest way to have a mobile phone service is to keep buying starter packs. These are promoted with incentives of free calls; for example, for $20, you can get $30 worth of calls. The downside is that each time you get one, you have to change your phone number. It makes it very difficult for the hospital and other agencies to contact people if their phone number changes frequently.

There are only a limited number of ADSL connections available, and download speeds are very low, so streaming movies is difficult. According to the 2016 census, only 20 per cent of households have a broadband connection, compared with 85 per cent of homes in the whole country.

There are some organised sports – football is popular for both sexes, and there is a gym. Fishing is a popular pastime, and several families have boats which they use for this. Apart from all the fish such as barramundi, there are many dugong swimming around, and they are highly prized. There are other pastimes which are more of a problem. Many of the houses are referred to as party houses, in which there seems to be an endless supply of home-brewed alcohol, often accompanied by loud music. Other houses are known to be gambling dens, where



CHRIS GILFORD

simple card games are played, with participants contributing to a pool of money. Eventually, someone wins the jackpot, which is often hundreds or even thousands of dollars.

The school takes students to year 10. About 250 students are enrolled, but the daily attendance is only about 70 per cent. Most of the children finish their education at year 10. Those who wish to continue their studies to year 12 have to go to boarding school, usually in the coastal cities of Cairns and Townsville but also Mount Isa or Charters Towers.

The hospital is the major provider of health services, which will be described in a later chapter.

There is a police station with a dozen full-time police officers and a courthouse. Court is usually in session once per week. About thirty kilometres north of Gununa, there was a commercial fishing resort called Birri Lodge. It took guests flown from the mainland for fishing trips but closed in 2017. There are also some pieces of infrastructure run by the federal government. There is a weather radar run by the Bureau of Meteorology, and the Australian Defence Force maintains a building.

**Health of First Nations People**

First Nations writers claim that, before European contact, their health was good. They enjoyed a diet of traditional food, which they obtained by hunting, fishing, and gathering. This type of diet has become fashionable in the last few years, being labelled as a Paleolithic (or Paleo) diet. The food was low in fat and sugar, so they did not have the modern diseases of obesity, diabetes, and ischaemic heart disease. Photographs of First Nations people taken when they first came into contact with Europeans show people in a healthy weight range, but compared with people today, they would be regarded as thin.

Many of the infectious diseases that were common in Europeans only reached Australia in 1788. These include smallpox, measles, chickenpox, whooping cough, influenza, tuberculosis, and syphilis. However, other infectious diseases, particularly those caused by bacteria, would have been more common. Gastroenteritis would have been a serious problem, and probably many children would have died from it. Little treatment would have been available for injuries; so many people would have died from them. Deaths could occur soon after the injury from blood loss or be delayed by days or weeks from infection.

Childbirth is always risky for both mother and baby. Before European contact, the infant mortality, which is the number of deaths of children before they reach 1 year old for 1,000 live births, would have been around 100, or 10 per cent. Maternal mortality, defined as the number of deaths per 100,000 live births, would be at least 1,000 or 1 per cent. For a community of 1,000 people, there would be about 20 babies born each year. Two of the babies would die each year, and one mother would die every five years.

So the current feeling among researchers is that, before 1788, the health of First Nations people was not dissimilar to the rest of the developing world at that time and that their life expectancy was around 30. This may seem low, but it is the figure that the UN Population Division has given. First Nations people might not like it since it may be less than the figure that has been handed down to the current generation. There would have been a few people who lived to the age of 60 or 70, but the average would have been dragged down by a high rate of childhood mortality and also injuries sustained by young adults. If First Nations people want to disagree, they would need to prove a different figure by allowing researchers to examine the bones of any First Nations person who is available for study.

# CHAPTER 4

# Health Problems Commoner in First Nations People

FIRST NATIONS PEOPLE suffer more frequently from a number of chronic diseases, including diabetes and heart and kidney disease. These cause significant morbidity through the later period of their life and a reduction in their life expectancy.

Most of the organs in the body have a reserve capacity. The easiest one to consider is the heart. Normally, when you are resting, your heart is pumping about five litres of blood round your body per minute. If you start moving around, you are using your muscles, and so your heart increases its output to supply extra oxygen and nutrients to your muscles. A young adult who is reasonably fit and healthy can increase their heart's output to around twenty litres a minute, and they need this output to participate in amateur sports. A professional sportsperson can increase it to about thirty litres a minute.

Suppose you develop heart disease, and as a result, your maximum output is reduced from twenty to ten litres a minute. Most of the time, you won't notice it because you don't need the extra output for day-to-day living. However, if you need to play footy at the weekend or run up a couple of flights of stairs, you will get more short of breath than usual. This is what happens in the early stages of chronic diseases.

Like the heart, other organs have excess capacity that you don't need most of the time. Therefore, people can have a chronic disease for years without realising it. However, as time goes by, heart disease gets worse, and the cardiac output gradually decreases. Once it gets down to about six, it becomes really noticeable as even walking to the toilet becomes an effort. The important thing is to acknowledge the problem early and get it treated so that the progression of the disease is reduced.

In this chapter, a number of diseases, particularly those that are commoner in First Nations people, will be discussed in detail. The purpose of this is to demonstrate the way that many of them can be avoided or their impact reduced by taking simple preventive measures.

## Diabetes

'Diabetes mellitus' is a Latin phrase meaning 'sweet fountain'. It was used by physicians hundreds of years ago to describe those who passed a large amount of urine that tasted sweet and contrasted with those with 'diabetes insipidus' who passed a lot of sour-tasting urine. The latter is very rare, so the word 'mellitus' is usually dropped. There are three main categories of diabetes: type 1, formerly known as juvenile diabetes; type 2, formerly known as adult onset; and gestational diabetes, which, as the name implies, occurs in some women in pregnancy. Type 1 is uncommon and usually (but not always) starts in childhood. It is thought that a viral infection causes failure of the cells in the pancreas to secrete insulin. Insulin is a hormone which is needed by most cells in the body to absorb glucose from the bloodstream.

In type 2 diabetes, the pancreatic cells usually secrete enough insulin, but the cells in the rest of the body become resistant to it. A few people may have some of the features of both types 1 and 2.

I am only going to consider type 2 diabetes in this book as it is the commonest and most relevant. The main causes are genetic and lifestyle risk factors, including lack of physical activity and poor diet, but the most important is excess weight. First Nations people have a higher incidence of diabetes than non-Indigenous people. One reason for this is genetic. They do have a different metabolism in that they, in general, still retain more of the characteristics of hunter-gatherers. In the past, good meals were few and far between; so when there had been a successful hunt, everybody ate as much as they could since they didn't know when the next meal was coming. Non-Indigenous people have had several hundred years, so dozens of generations, to adapt to a plentiful and regular supply of food. One reason for the difference may be that plentiful food contributes to gestational diabetes. In this case, the developing baby will grow rapidly and be too big for the mother to push out. If medical science has not progressed to the point of enabling safe Caesarean sections, then mother and baby will both die, thus tending to eliminate that gene.

So type 2 diabetes is largely caused by lifestyle. So lifestyle modification should be the first treatment that is tried. It normally is, but this is rarely more than a token effort. Several studies have shown that when First Nations people abandon their 'Western diet' and live out in the bush eating traditional foods, their diabetes resolves, and they no longer need any medication. People who are morbidly obese and lose a large amount of weight can also reduce their medication substantially.

How is obesity measured? The standard measure is the body mass index, which is calculated by dividing your weight (in kilograms) by the square of your height (in metres). So if someone is 170 cm tall and weighs 80 kg, their BMI is 80 ÷ (1.7 × 1.7), which is 27.7. BMI is discussed at length in a later chapter.

The commonest classification of your body shape is as follows:

| BMI | <20 | 20–25 | 25–30 | 30–35 | >35 |
|---|---|---|---|---|---|
| | Underweight | Healthy weight | Overweight | Obese | Morbidly obese |

Table 6: BMI and weight categories

These classifications are derived from numerous studies which look at health issues and life expectancy for different values for the BMI, but these categories were devised for western European males. The person in the example above is therefore overweight.

A paper published in the *Lancet* in July 2021, titled 'Ethnicity-Specific BMI Cut-Offs for Obesity', looked at the risk of getting diabetes for people with different ethnic backgrounds. These people all came from places that the British had colonised over the last 300 years. The column labelled 'BMI' is the BMI for each group that gave them the same risk of getting diabetes as a white person with a BMI of 30.

On the right is the risk of getting diabetes for a person with a BMI of 30 compared with whites.

| Ethnic background | BMI | Risk ratio |
| --- | --- | --- |
| Bangladeshi | 21.2 | 3.32 |
| Tamil (southern India) | 22.6 | 2.68 |
| Sri Lanka | 23.2 | 2.46 |
| Pakistan | 23.5 | 2.35 |
| Indian and Nepali | 24.3 | 2.12 |
| Black Caribbean | 26.0 | 1.67 |
| Black, other | 26.5 | 1.54 |
| Black African | 29.1 | 1.13 |
| Black British | 29.9 | 1.03 |
| White | 30.0 | 1.00 |

Table 7: Risk of diabetes for different ethnic groups

Their data shows clearly that the risk of getting diabetes varies according to ethnic background. Therefore, there must be also a variation of what BMI or weight range should be considered as being 'healthy' for different races. If the healthy range for whites is 20–25, then this chart suggests that for people from southern Asia, it could be in the range 14–18 and for those from Africa 17–22.

I left Normanton in 2013 but still retain the electronic medical records from the clinic. All the patients had signed a privacy form stating that they agreed that their de-identified data could be used for research purposes. I therefore analysed the data to see where First Nations people fitted into this table. I found that I had sufficient data (height, weight, and diabetic status) on 1,058 adults (defined as those born before 1990) who lived in Normanton in 2012.



CHRIS GILFORD

|               | Diabetic | Non-Diabetic | Total | % Diabetic |
|---------------|----------|--------------|-------|------------|
| First Nations | 149      | 424          | 573   | 26         |
| Non-Indigenous | 48      | 437          | 485   | 10         |

Table 8: Diabetic numbers in Normanton

I first counted the number of non-Indigenous people with a BMI between 27.5 and 32.5. There were 137, and of these, 19 had diabetes, just under 14 per cent. I then did the same for the First Nations people, with BMIs between 16 and 32.

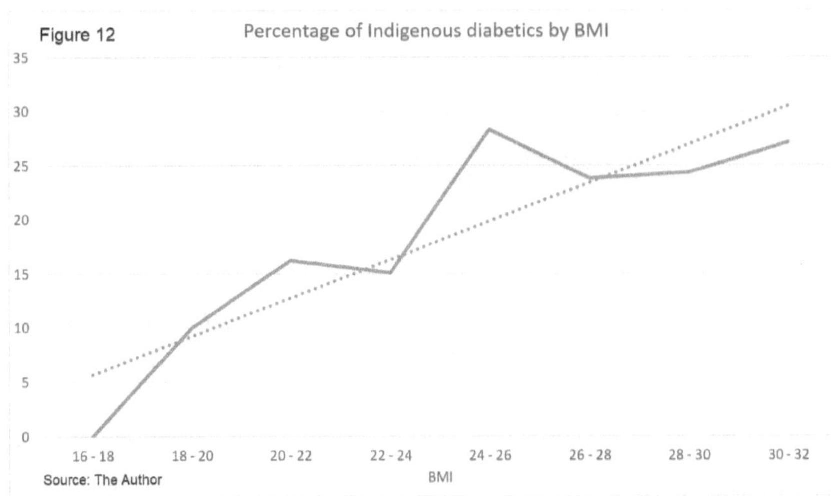


Figure 12: Percentage of First Nations diabetics by BMI

The study in the *Lancet* used the data from nearly one and a half million people. With such a comparatively tiny sample, the Normanton data will be less accurate, but I think that the trend line (shown dotted) shows that First Nations people with a BMI of about 22 have a risk of diabetes similar to that of non-Indigenous people with a BMI of about 30, that is, about 14 per cent, which is considerably better than the figure for all the First Nations people in Normanton (26 per cent). This puts them equivalent to the South Asians in the *Lancet* study. South Asians have an excellent role model in Mahatma Gandhi, who had a

BMI of 17 and died at the age of 78. He also walked around 18 km a day.

A BMI of thirty is the usual cut-off between being overweight and being obese. So for First Nations people, the cut-off between overweight and obese should be a BMI of about 22. The Normanton data further suggests that the ideal BMI for First Nations people is probably between 15 and 19. There were twenty First Nations people in Normanton with BMIs in that range. They appeared thin to our present-day eyes but not unhealthy.

A new study carried out in the USA in 2022, Diabetes Screening by Race and Ethnicity, suggests that people from certain racial and ethnic groups should be screened for diabetes at lower body mass index than non-Hispanic white people. Current guidelines in the USA are for screening for adults between 35 and 70 years old with a BMI of 25 or more. The study now recommends screening for black Americans and Hispanic Americans with a BMI of over 18.5 and for Asian Americans with a BMI of over 20.

Jared Diamond, the geographer and evolutionary biologist, won the Pulitzer Prize in 1998 for his book *Guns, Germs, and Steel*, in which he described how Europeans colonised the rest of the world. They initially subdued the original inhabitants with superior weaponry. However, they inadvertently brought diseases such as smallpox and measles to communities who had no previous exposure to them, with devastating results, with mortality up to 90 per cent. When you add the technological weapons of guns and steel used to make spears, swords, and knives, it is hardly surprising that the colonists were victorious.

However, it now appears that a more insidious weapon is the Western diet. Non-European people have differences in their metabolism. Many have difficulty with milk and other dairy products, but more importantly, they have more difficulty dealing with a Western high-calorie, high-fat, high-sugar diet. They are much more likely to suffer chronic disease from being obese and die prematurely.

When I was in Sri Lanka, I lived with a Sinhalese family and ate the same food as them. This was 'rice and curry' three times a day, not curry and rice as we say here, and meals were eaten with fingers of the dominant hand, not cutlery or chopsticks. Each person would be served a normal-sized plate almost completely filled with rice, and we would share a fish or meat curry and three or four vegetable dishes, but each person would only take about a small spoonful of each dish. The meals were filling due to the quantity of rice and full of healthy nutrients but low in fat and sugar. Now that the big American fast-food companies have set up business in Asia, it is easy to see how obesity is becoming a huge problem there.

Unfortunately, diabetes leads to more problems than just having a high blood sugar. It greatly increases the risk of cardiovascular disease, and this is the reason for the high mortality of diabetics.

In addition, it has some specific effects on various organs. Two of the important ones are its effect on the kidneys and heart. It, firstly, causes the kidneys to leak protein, and the amount of protein which is normally just about zero increases significantly. It can be treated – there is a tablet which reduces the amount of leaked protein, but if not treated, it leads to kidney failure, often requiring dialysis or transplantation. Secondly, it greatly increases the risk of heart disease. Other organs are also affected. It causes abnormalities in the back of the eye which can lead to blindness, and it causes narrowing of the arteries, particularly to the legs, which causes infection of the feet which can be very difficult to treat and may lead to amputation.

In 2015, the Australian Commission on Safety and Quality in Health Care and National Health Performance Authority published the Australian Atlas of Healthcare Variation, a 370-page report on the variation of a large number of health conditions between different parts of the country. In some cases, there was a huge difference between different areas. The highest rate of amputation was found in the outback of the NT with 91 cases per 100,000 population, closely followed by outback Queensland. At the other end of the scale was Sydney with 8 cases per 100,000, a ratio of over 10.

Diabetes is also a major cause of impotence in men. I would have thought that the male preoccupation with sex would mean that the risk of becoming impotent would be an incentive for men to improve their diabetic control. It is perhaps unfortunate that this is a problem for which there is now a drug, thus shifting the emphasis away from prevention.

In view of the seriousness of most of these conditions, most doctors start treating diabetes with medication before seeing whether lifestyle modifications on their own are sufficient. This also means that the diabetic patient is likely to forget about the importance of lifestyle and just take the medication as it is easier. The pharmaceutical industry has been very active in recent years in developing new medication in response to the increased demand. Unfortunately, few of the new medications are particularly effective at reducing blood sugars, despite what their marketing departments might claim. They are really aimed at fine-tuning a diabetic's control.

The main aim of treatment is to lower the blood sugar. If the treatment is too effective, the patient may have an episode of hypoglycaemia (a hypo) when they may feel dizzy and pass out. The control of diabetes is measured through a test called the HbA1c, also known as glycated haemoglobin. This gives an indication of a patient's average level of glucose over the preceding three months. The measurement of HbA1c was formerly given as a percentage of the total haemoglobin. A non-diabetic person has a level of 5 or 6 per cent. An untreated diabetic may have a level of around 15 per cent. A diabetic ideally should have a level of about 7 per cent. Trying to get it lower than that runs the risk of a hypo. There has been a recent change to the way that results are expressed, and it is also given as the actual level to conform to international guidelines. A level of 7 per cent is equivalent to a concentration of 53 mmol/mol.

Insulin and its effect was discovered in the nineteenth century, but the breakthrough came in 1921, when Canadian researchers found a way of isolating insulin from the pancreas of a dog without it being destroyed by digestive enzymes. It was only a few months from these early experiments before insulin was manufactured around the world and used to treat patients. One of its disadvantages is that it has to be given by injection, and so there has been research into finding treatments which can be given orally.

Insulin is the only possible treatment for those with type 1 diabetes. In patients with type 2 diabetes, the main problem is that the patient's cells are resistant to insulin. They may, in fact, have more of their own insulin than non-diabetic people. Treating them with insulin is less effective, and they may need much bigger doses of insulin. Women with gestational diabetes may only need two or three units of insulin a day, but overweight patients with type 2 diabetes may need over a hundred units a day.

The treatments available can be summarised as follows:

| Treatment | Year introduced | Examples | HbA1c drop | Cost per month ($) |
|---|---|---|---|---|
| Lifestyle change | | | 1.0–5.0 | Nil |
| Insulin | 1922 | Glargine | 1.5–3.5 | 80 |
| Biguanide | 1958 | Metformin | 1.0–2.0 | 21 |
| SU | 1966 | Gliclazide | 1.0–2.0 | 24 |
| Alpha-glucosidase inhibitors | 1995 | Acarbose | 0.7 | 31 |
| TZDs | 2002 | Pioglitazone | 0.5–1.4 | 23 |
| DPP-4 | 2006 | Gliptins | 0.5–0.8 | 56 |
| GLP-1 (incretin mimetics) | 2005 | Exenatide | 0.5–1.0 | 90 |
| SGLT-2 | 2014 | *Gliflozins* | 0.5–1.0 | 58 |
| GLP-1 | 2018 | *Semaglutide* | 0.6–1.1 | 132 |

Table 9: Treatments for type 2 diabetes

Most First Nations people know that it runs in families, but this does not always help in trying to get someone to change their lifestyle or take their medication. They may feel perfectly well even if their diabetes is totally uncontrolled. There are also the extra risks of other chronic diseases. So a diabetic often needs a number of different medications – apart from the medication to reduce their blood sugar, they are likely to be on medication to reduce their cholesterol, reduce their blood pressure, and reduce the risk of kidney disease, heart attack, and stroke.

There is a new treatment for diabetes – semaglutide, marketed under the brand name Ozempic, and it is given as a weekly injection. It works by stimulating the secretion of insulin and has been shown to be slightly better than other treatments for diabetes but still nowhere near as good as lifestyle changes. One of the side effects is that it leads to weight loss, and this is further discussed in chapter 8.

## Rheumatic Fever

Rheumatic fever is an immune response that the body makes to certain bacteria, usually the streptococcus, which is a common cause of sore throats and tonsilitis. It generally occurs a few weeks after the initial infection and causes a variety of symptoms including a rash and sore joints. However, it may also affect the valves of the heart, causing rheumatic heart disease (RHD). It generally occurs in young people up to about the age of 25.

The yearly incidence of a first attack of acute rheumatic fever ranges from 80 to 250 per 100,000 in First Nations communities. Identified modifiable risk factors for acute rheumatic fever include poverty, overcrowding, malnutrition, and maternal educational level and employment.

My experience in Mornington Island suggests that the incidence there is at the top end of that range, since we were diagnosing about two new patients a year, in a population of about 1,200. The valves of the heart are involved in about half the cases of rheumatic fever. All children who get rheumatic fever are given a penicillin injection every month to prevent relapses. They also have to be monitored by a cardiologist for decades to ensure that they remain healthy. Unfortunately, some do relapse, and their heart valves are affected. Many of them need to have open-heart surgery to replace their valves. Even so, some develop heart failure. They also need to look after their new valves. They often have to take blood-thinning medication, have regular blood tests, and continue with their monthly penicillin injections. If they don't look after themselves, they may need further surgery.

Open-heart surgery is challenging for the patient. To gain access to the heart, the surgeon cuts through the sternum (breastbone) and puts in a clamp to open up the gap to about ten centimetres so the surgeon can work on the heart. At the end of the surgery, the sternum is joined back together with wire. The patient has essentially a fracture of the sternum, and they experience pain from it and the joints at each end of the ribs. It is painful to breathe, and coughing is terrible. They are also told that they cannot lift anything heavier than a kilogram as there is a risk of the wires breaking. It takes about two to three months for the chest wall to recover. I would have thought that this would be an incentive to try and avoid further surgery, but some do not seem to want to help themselves.

People who have mild damage to their heart valves from rheumatic fever are at risk of further complications, even after they reach the age of 25, when the risk of recurrence of rheumatic fever has disappeared. They can get an infection of the damaged valves, usually from bacteria that cause skin infections. It often develops slowly over several weeks.

A recent (March 2022) *Four Corners* programme on ABC television discussed RHD after the deaths of three people from it in Doomadgee, in north-west Queensland. The programme investigated claims that there were deficiencies in the way that RHD was managed there.

As rheumatic heart disease has virtually disappeared from non-Indigenous Australia, it follows that it must be almost completely preventable. As noted above, the risk factors include poverty, overcrowding, malnutrition, and maternal educational level and employment. These will be addressed in detail in chapter 6.

## Ischaemic Heart Disease

Although the heart has plenty of blood flowing through it, the muscle requires its own blood supply, namely, the coronary arteries, which are small vessels which branch off the aorta, the main artery taking oxygenated blood from the heart. If these get narrowed or blocked, the heart muscle will not get enough blood and therefore insufficient oxygen and nutrients. This is ischaemic heart disease (IHD). If the process is sudden, a heart attack ensues. If the process is slow, the heart muscle gets weak, leading to heart failure.

Several factors contribute to narrowing or blocking of the coronary arteries. They include high blood pressure, high cholesterol, diabetes, smoking, and a sedentary lifestyle. First Nations people have a higher incidence of heart disease largely due to their lifestyle. Like diabetes, IHD may be silent in the early stages. Many people walk around with partial blockages in their coronary arteries. This may weaken the heart muscle.

In March 1965, American forces were dispatched to Vietnam to try and halt the flow of communists as they headed south from North Vietnam. They finally left after the fall of Saigon on 30 April 1975. More than 2.5 million Americans served there, with a death toll of 58,000, most of whom had a full post-mortem examination. Most of them were fit young men, ranging in age from 18 to 30. This was the first time there was a large-scale examination of the hearts of people of that age group. The pathologists were surprised to discover that most of them exhibited signs of coronary artery disease, with plaques of cholesterol lining their arteries. This no doubt reflected their diet of lots of red meat, saturated fats, and drinks laden with added sugar.

**Chronic Kidney Disease**

The kidneys excrete excess fluid and waste products. Various conditions can cause the kidneys to fail, but the commonest are diabetes, infection, and high blood pressure. Also, the kidneys, like any other organ, do depend on a person's general health. They do better if the person has a good diet, takes some exercise, and avoids harmful things like smoking and alcohol. Often, the function of the kidney deteriorates slowly, and the person can be completely unaware of the problem until quite late.

There are a few other causes of kidney disease. Polycystic disease is a genetic disorder causing cysts to grow in the kidneys, thus slowly reducing kidney function. Some drugs are toxic to kidneys; a common one in the past was phenacetin, which was a painkiller used in combination with aspirin and caffeine, commonly taken for migraines. It was banned in about 1980, being replaced by paracetamol. Infections and autoimmune diseases are other causes. Sometimes in children and young adults, the bacteria streptococcus can trigger inflammation of the kidney a few weeks later, and this is known as post-streptococcal glomerulonephritis (PSGN). It is due to the body's immune system reacting to strep throat, scarlet fever, or impetigo. It is much commoner in First Nations communities. It is, in some ways, similar to rheumatic heart disease, and the same risk factors of poverty, overcrowding, malnutrition, and maternal educational level and employment apply. Fortunately, most people recover completely after a few weeks, but a few go on to develop chronic kidney disease.

Kidney function is measured by an indicator called the GFR, glomerular filtration rate. The normal level is above 120. The GFR (strictly the eGFR) is now calculated every time you get routine blood tests done, using a formula devised about fifteen years ago. In the USA, the labs make a correction according to whether the patient is an African American. Here, there is no correction for First Nations people, but there has been debate on whether one is needed. I think, then, that it is reasonable to conclude that there is no significant difference between the way that First Nations and non-Indigenous kidneys behave, unlike the difference in metabolism regarding diabetes.

Like most organs in the body, the kidneys have reserve capacity. If you have kidney disease and the GFR drops to 30, this means that you have lost 75 per cent of the kidney's capacity, but you are unlikely to have any symptoms. If it drops below 30, then you may start to get symptoms such as tiredness. If it gets down to 10, you will feel unwell, and renal replacement therapy – treatment to replace their function – will be planned. There are three options: peritoneal dialysis, haemodialysis, and transplant.

Peritoneal dialysis uses the body's inbuilt membrane within the abdominal cavity to filter excess fluid and waste products. A small tube is inserted into the abdominal wall. Every day the person must connect this tube to large bags of fluid which flow in and then out an hour or two later. It is fairly easy to train a person to do this at home, and it can enable them to survive for several years in this way.

There are disadvantages to peritoneal dialysis. The tube in the abdominal cavity is a permanent fixture. It must be kept really clean as, otherwise, there is a risk of infection. The patient's mobility is restricted. They have to be connected to the bags two or three times a day, and each session lasts an hour or two. They also have an overnight bag of fluid. They get through a lot of fluid, about ten litres a day. This means they receive a delivery of about 300 litres every month. This has to be stored somewhere at their home. This also makes it difficult if they want to go away and stay with relatives somewhere else for a few days.

Haemodialysis is more complicated. A special blood vessel, a fistula, is created in the person's arm and then used when it has matured, which takes about three months. Three times a week, the person connects themselves to the dialysis machine by inserting two cannulas into the fistula. Their blood is pumped from their body to the machine for a few hours so that their excess fluid and waste products are removed. Training for this is more complicated, and it does not suit everyone to do this at home. Some people, therefore, attend dialysis centres where trained staff do it for them.

The dialysis centres are not located in First Nations communities but in large towns and cities. In northern Queensland, they are in Townsville, Cairns, and Mount Isa. The kidney units in these cities have a large community of people living nearby who come in for haemodialysis three times a week. This means that if someone needs dialysis and can't manage it themselves, they have to move permanently to a big town or city. The social impact is huge. It means leaving their friends and family behind. One patient who was in Townsville on haemodialysis could not cope with the isolation and chose to come back to their community and die there within a week or two rather than stay isolated in the big city. When I started in Mornington Island, there were seventeen residents on dialysis, most of whom had relocated to Townsville since they could not manage it themselves.

Although dialysis does prolong lives, it is never as good as having real kidneys. There are restrictions on the amount of fluid they can drink. Anyone diagnosed with early stage kidney disease should do their best to try and maintain their remaining kidney function by making lifestyle changes like losing weight, getting their diabetes better controlled, and stopping smoking and alcohol. A couple of patients in

Mornington Island said to me, 'What's the point of stopping the things I enjoy if I'm going to be on dialysis in a few months anyway?' They obviously didn't understand the concept of preventive medicine.

Life expectancy on dialysis is much shorter than most people realise, particularly if they don't do it well. In Mornington Island, patients on home peritoneal dialysis on average only lived for two to three years, from starting on dialysis to when they died.

The last option is transplant where a normal kidney is taken either from a living donor, usually a relative, or from a deceased person. This is probably the best option, but there is a shortage of donor organs, and a person may wait years for one. I have often thought that one way of increasing the number of donor organs would be to legislate that no one can be a recipient of a donated organ unless they have declared themselves to be an organ donor continuously from the age of 18.

The other main disadvantage with transplants Is the body's response to the transplanted organ since it tries to reject it. Powerful drugs are used to stop the rejection, but it still can happen. These have to be taken for the rest of the person's life. If all goes well, a transplant recipient can live an almost normal life without many of the restrictions that dialysis patients have.

According to AIHW, the incidence (the number of new cases per year) of ESKD (end-stage kidney disease) among First Nations Australians was almost seven times the rate for non-Indigenous Australians (63 and 9 per 100,000, respectively).

One reason for the high incidence of kidney disease in First Nations communities is diabetes. However, the main problem is that people with diabetes do not look after themselves. Their compliance is poor, and they do not follow the advice they are given. When told that their kidneys are failing and that they may need dialysis, a common response is, 'I'll just go on dialysis then', as if it were no inconvenience.

If the rate of kidney failure among First Nations people was reduced to that of non-indigenous people, very few would require dialysis, and so most communities would not have anybody who needed to relocate to a large town or city for this.

It is somewhat surprising that the thought of having to go on dialysis with the attendant disruption to their lives does not seem to be a sufficient incentive for people to change their lifestyle, even though such a change will help postpone or even completely avoid dialysis. There is a push for clinic-based dialysis to be made available in rural clinics and hospitals. In a rather twisted logical argument, I wonder whether people in the early stages of kidney disease are actually jeopardising their own health to increase the demand for dialysis and so pressure the government to start dialysis in rural clinics. This is akin to obese people not losing weight but waiting for a cure for diabetes. This notion was put forward many years ago by the Nobel laureate and economist Gary Becker, who said that the obesity epidemic could be explained by people's belief that a cure for diabetes will soon be available.

## Sexually Transmitted Infections

It is possible that STIs arrived in Australia in the seventeenth century from the Dutch and later other explorers such as Cook. However, we do know that STIs were carried on the first fleet in 1787–88. There were ten cases on the *Lady Penrhyn*, all caused by interactions between female convicts and the male crew. During the first fleet re-enactment in 1987–88, the health team on the fleet had to treat some of the participants for STIs. Some things never change. Since 1788, STIs have spread throughout Australia.

STIs are now commonly found in First Nations people. There are several different STIs including syphilis, gonorrhoea, chlamydia, trichomoniasis, herpes, hepatitis B and C, HIV, donovanosis, and mycoplasma genitalium. Monkeypox, which only became a health emergency in 2022, is not transmitted sexually but between people who have close skin-to-skin contact, which, of course, happens during sex. They can all be spread by sexual activity, but some – hepatitis B and C and HIV – can be spread in other ways, for example, among intravenous drug users. One of the problems with them is that, often, someone with the infection does not have any symptoms to begin with. Gonorrhoea in men is the exception – it tends to cause a yellow discharge from the penis a few days after contracting it, and so the sufferers usually seek medical attention.

There are no vaccinations against any of the STIs, except hepatitis B. All the infections are notifiable – the various state health departments collect data on them to try and eradicate them. There are four components in the eradication process: promoting 'safe sex' including the use of condoms; screening the 'population at risk', which means anyone who is having sex and is not completely monogamous; using single-dose treatments for STIs whenever possible; and trying to trace the contacts of those who have acquired an STI.

In Mornington Island, the hospital supplies vast numbers of condoms – there are dispensers at the hospital entrance which are restocked every day. Screening is done by checking for STIs whenever anyone in the community has a blood test for any reason. Treatment is usually a single dose, but sometimes it is difficult to find a person who has been found to have an STI and persuade them to come in for treatment. Contact tracing is more difficult. Some people are reluctant to tell the hospital the name of the person who might have given them an STI. It is considered a 'shame', which has connotations in First Nations society. A commoner problem is that they might not know the other party's identity. Common reasons given are that they were drunk and cannot remember who they had sex with or that they were away from the community and had a one-night stand and only know their first name.

Other than abstaining from sex, the best way of preventing STIs is by using condoms, until members of a couple know each other well enough to trust each other. This was demonstrated in the early years after the AIDS epidemic when condoms became much more widely used, resulting in a significant decrease in all other STIs.

*Syphilis*

The STI of most concern in First Nations communities is syphilis. It was present in North America before European contact and brought back to Europe by Columbus' crew. For the next 300 to 400 years, it became a huge public health burden and was given the alternative name the Great Pox, in contrast to smallpox. It affected people of all walks of life, including one former British prime minister who died at the age of 45 from it. It is caused by a small bacteria called *Treponema pallidum* and is now easily treated with three injections of long-acting penicillin given at weekly intervals.

**Figure 13: Notifications (n) and notification rate (per 100,000) of infectious syphilis* reported, by Indigenous status, sex, quarter and year, 2010 – 2022 (to 31 March)**

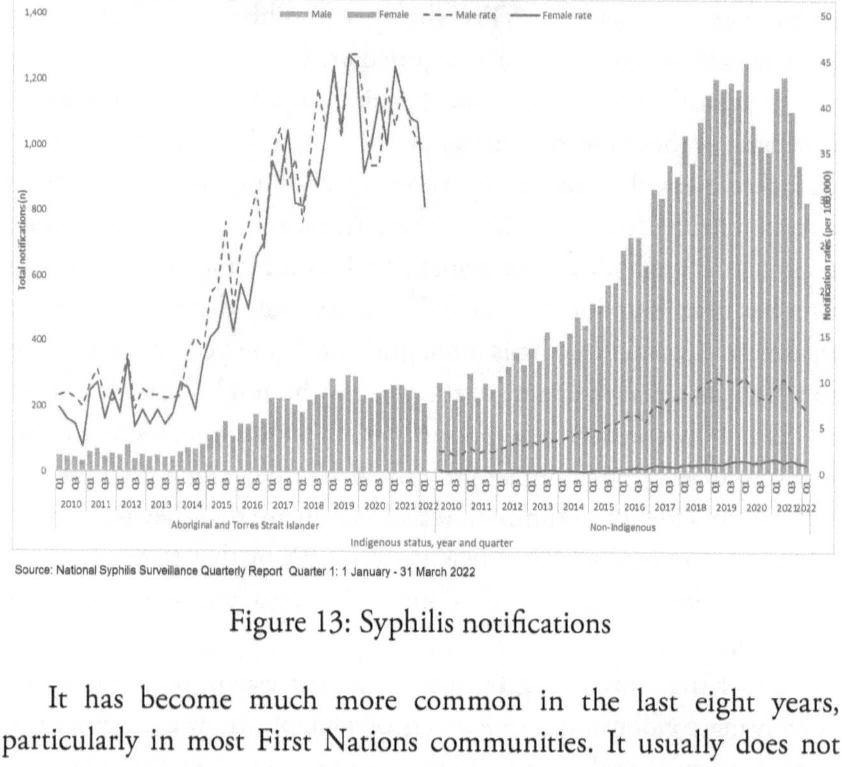


Source: National Syphilis Surveillance Quarterly Report Quarter 1: 1 January - 31 March 2022

Figure 13: Syphilis notifications

It has become much more common in the last eight years, particularly in most First Nations communities. It usually does not cause any specific symptoms for a few months or years, apart from a rash at the point where the organism entered the body, usually the genitals, but this may be ignored as it generally does not last long. It is particularly dangerous for pregnant women as it can cause death or disfigurement of the foetus. Left untreated, it remains dormant for many years but can then cause heart disease and neurological problems like strokes and dementia late in life. Usually, the only way to detect it is by a blood test.

This chart shows the incidence of syphilis in Australia from 2010 to 2022 as recorded by the Federal Department of Health and Aged Care. It is probably easier to look at the lines rather than the columns: males are the dashed lines, females the continuous lines. The left half is First Nations people, the right half non-Indigenous, but the columns are the other way round.

In non-Indigenous people, the rate is much higher in males than females, and it is mainly found in men who have sex with men. In First Nations people, it is about the same in both sexes and about five times the rate for non-Indigenous males and forty times the rate of non-Indigenous females. Fortunately, there are indications that the present outbreak is resolving. There was another outbreak in the 1990s in First Nations communities, and this resolved after a few years.

The most alarming aspect is that there have been some children under the age of 14 who have contracted syphilis.

## Gonorrhoea

Gonorrhoea causes a yellow discharge from the penis in men, usually starting about five days after it has been contracted, but it is usually asymptomatic in women. It is caused by a bacteria which can easily be treated by a single dose of an antibiotic but is now becoming resistant to some of them. Left untreated in women, it may cause pelvic inflammatory disease, which is a serious infection and may be life-threatening. In men, it can infect the testicles and, after a long period, cause a urethral stricture, which can stop the flow of urine completely. In both sexes, it can spread to joints, causing a septic arthritis. It is easily prevented with condoms. If a mother giving birth has gonorrhoea, she may pass it on to her baby, often causing conjunctivitis.

## Chlamydia

Chlamydia is caused by a small bacteria and is often asymptomatic in women but in men often causes a severe burning pain when passing urine. In women, it can lead to pelvic inflammatory disease if untreated.

This may cause blockage of the fallopian tubes and is a major cause of infertility. It is easily treated with a single-dose antibiotic and can easily be prevented with condoms. Like gonorrhoea, it can cause conjunctivitis in babies. It can also cause trachoma, an eye infection, at any age and was once a leading cause of blindness throughout the world.

*Trichomoniasis*

*Trichomonas vaginalis* is a protozoal parasite which is commonly transmitted sexually. Again, it is usually asymptomatic in men; but in women, it causes a smelly, watery discharge that may be green and frothy. Again, it is easily treated with specific antibiotics and can be prevented with condoms.

There are other STIs, including herpes, hepatitis B and C, HIV, donovanosis, and mycoplasma genitalium, but these are less common in First Nations communities.

## Skin Infestations and Infections

Scabies is a skin condition caused by a tiny mite called *Sarcoptes scabiei*. It is less than half a millimetre in size but can be seen with a good magnifying lens. It is very contagious and can move by direct contact from one person to another in a matter of minutes. It burrows under the skin and, assuming that a pair get together, lays eggs. The first symptom is a severe itch, often occurring only a few hours after acquiring it, followed by a rash. It is usually just an inconvenience as it is easily treated in its early stages with a topical insecticide. But this has to be applied to the entire body, not just the itchy areas.

Although the itch is a good stimulus to get treatment, this does not seem to apply to those who live in substandard, overcrowded housing or who drink alcohol to excess, and so the entire household will probably get it. Untreated, it spreads to the whole body, and then the outer layer of the skin gets much thicker and contains a rabbit warren of burrows containing the scabies mite. If the person has poor immunity, they can get a secondary bacterial infection. This can travel to the heart,

  CHRIS GILFORD

particularly in someone with pre-existing rheumatic fever, with very serious consequences.

Many children get skin sores, usually on their limbs. They are often called school sores or impetigo. They are caused by bacteria – either streptococci or staphylococci. They are best treated by good hygiene practices and using an antiseptic ointment, but antibiotics may be required. There is a big risk of the bacteria getting resistant to antibiotics if they are not used correctly. Some of these bacteria are the ones that cause rheumatic fever or PSGN, which affects the kidneys, so it is another example of a problem which at first appears fairly innocuous but may have serious consequences.

## Sepsis

Sepsis is an overwhelming infection, a serious complication of what would otherwise be a localised infection. Meningococcal disease is an example of one that can progress very rapidly and is notable for the fact that it seems to affect young adults who are otherwise fit and healthy. There is a different infection with probably worse prognosis that affects people in remote northern Australia. It is worse in those with impaired immunity, who drink alcohol to excess, or who are diabetic. It is called melioidosis, and the organism is found in the black soil in wetland areas.

There is a vaccine for meningococcal disease, but melioidosis is preventable by looking after your general health, especially if diabetic; minimising alcohol consumption; and examining your skin for any cuts or abrasions if you have been wading through black soil wetlands.

## Mental Health – Suicide

This is an emotive subject, so I am not dealing with it other than acknowledging that it is a very serious problem but one that the federal and state governments are trying to address, and despite spending billions, the numbers are getting worse.

The only comment I will make is that the amount of interpersonal antagonism that seems to be pervasive now is increasing, and this can be seen in 'sledging' on the sports field or derogatory comments on social media.

# CHAPTER 5

# Childhood Health and Mortality

WHEN I WAS a medical student, we studied all the various specialties such as general medicine and surgery, cardiology, paediatrics, obstetrics and gynaecology, orthopaedics, dermatology, etc. in turn. I remember the first seminar from a paediatrician. His opening question was, 'What do children die from?' It is something few people think about until a tragedy strikes their own family. The reality was brought home to me soon after I qualified.

I worked in the emergency department of a hospital north of London, and in my first week, two deceased 6-year-olds were brought in by ambulance, a couple of days apart. One was the victim in a motor vehicle accident; the other most likely had had an epileptic seizure. It affected me deeply at the time, and I wondered how I would cope. By the end of my six-month secondment, I had not encountered any more deceased children, so it was a statistical anomaly.

The process of giving birth and raising the resultant babies is a natural process. Midwives started to get involved a few thousand years ago, but medical intervention only began in the last 200 years or so. Unfortunately, childbirth is hazardous, and there is a substantial mortality. This mortality is not confined to humans as anyone who has tried to breed dogs or cats or has worked on a farm knows. This is the reason that, in virtually every species, extra pups/kittens are born in excess of the two required to replace the parents.

If there is no intervention, as in much of sub-Saharan Africa, about one in ten children die before their tenth birthday. The cost, not so much in dollar terms but in the social implications of having adult females go through the latter half of pregnancy and then five years of devoting much of their time to bringing up a small child who then dies, is enormous. Human beings have therefore done their best to try and reduce the attrition rate, but this has resulted in the medicalisation of the whole process. It is hardly surprising, then, that childhood mortality is one of the key indicators to assess the performance of a country's health system.

As we saw in the first chapter, the 2020 CTG report stated that the First Nations child mortality rate in 2018 was 141 per 100,000 – twice the rate for non-Indigenous children (67 per 100,000). There were 117 First Nations child deaths from 21,928 births.

The population of Australia in 2018 under the age of 5 was about 1.56 million, of whom about 83,000 were First Nations. This means about 1,100 children died before their fifth birthday. Although the report defines 'childhood mortality' as the number of deaths of children under 5 per population of 100,000, this is not the usual definition. The 'child mortality rate' is defined internationally, for example, by the WHO and UNICEF, as the mortality of children under the age of 5, expressed as the number of deaths per 1,000 live births. In 2018, there were 315,147 births in Australia, of whom 21,928 were First Nations. So by the international definition, the First Nations child mortality rate was 5.52 per 1,000 live births and compares to 3.39 for non-Indigenous and 3.53 for the whole population.

There are two other statistics used in this subject, but again, there may be differing definitions. The WHO defines 'perinatal mortality' as the 'number of stillbirths and deaths in the first week of life per 1,000 total births, the perinatal period commences at 22 completed weeks (154 days) of gestation, and ends seven completed days after birth'. The infant mortality rate is the rate of deaths of children under 1 year of age per 1,000 live births.

The World Bank publishes figures of childhood mortality (deaths per 1,000 live births) for every country, and they include these:

| Scandinavia, Japan | 2.5 |
|---|---|
| Italy, Spain | 3.1 |
| Australia | 3.6 |



CHRIS GILFORD

| United Kingdom | 4.3 |
| New Zealand | 4.7 |
| United States | 6.5 |
| China | 7.9 |
| India | 34.3 |
| Sub-Saharan Africa | 50.0 – 120.0 |

Table 10: Childhood mortality in certain countries

The reasons that young children die can generally be divided into two periods. The first is from twenty weeks' gestation up to four weeks of age, and the reasons are generally a problem that occurs before birth or shortly afterwards. This is the stillbirth rate, plus the neonatal mortality rate. In 2019 in Australia, there were 2,183 stillbirths and 714 neonatal deaths. The second period is from four weeks to five years, and the number of deaths is similar to the neonatal mortality rate, even though they occur over a period of almost five years, not about a month or two.

The leading causes of death in the neonatal period are preterm birth, low birthweight, complications during birth, birth defects, and infection. To deal with these, we need to go right back to before conception takes place.

As I have argued in other chapters, the shortened life expectancy of First Nations people is primarily due to the poor lifestyle of young adults. So to reduce childhood mortality, it is important to look at risk factors that are present even before the time of conception.

## Family Planning – In the Broadest Sense

There is often discussion about the most significant things in life, whether it is finding your dream job, buying your first home, or finding your life partner. However, I think that it is the decision to create a new member of the human race which is the most important since you will want this new person to have a long and healthy life, even after your own demise, so you need to make sure you do your best for them. It is therefore very important that you make plans for this.

Selection of partner is important. You need one who is going to share your concerns that the child is brought up in a good environment. It is important that you are not too closely related to your partner. There are a number of genetic disorders in children that are commoner in couples who are closely related. This has been known by First Nations people for thousands of years.

Girls should consider carefully the age at which they want to get pregnant, for too many just take the view 'if it happens, it happens, and I will deal with it'. Before contemplating pregnancy, a girl should evaluate her own health to make sure that is as good as it can be. She should stop smoking and drinking and get her weight into the ideal weight range. She needs to check her vaccination status to make sure she is immune to rubella. She should look at her employment and financial status and make sure she can look after a new baby. It is far better if she waits until she is at least 18. Once the pregnancy is confirmed, she should attend the local clinic so she knows how often she should get a check-up or get blood tests or scans done.

**Preterm Birth**

'Preterm birth' is defined as birth before thirty-seven weeks' gestation, three weeks before the forty weeks which is regarded as full term. It is the most common cause of death among infants worldwide. Although people generally talk about the stage of pregnancy in months, with birth usually occurring at about nine months, health professionals always use weeks as the unit of measurement. Gestation is measured from the date of the beginning of the mother's last period. Conception usually occurs about fourteen days after that. The result is known as an embryo until eight weeks and then a foetus. The embryo, at first, looks a very strange organism, but the foetus looks recognisably human with all its normal anatomical parts. The heart starts pulsating at about six weeks, and the limbs start to appear. The mother's uterus starts to be palpable (a baby bump) at about fourteen weeks. This is an important time for the mother to attend antenatal clinic since time-critical tests are done then. Between sixteen and twenty weeks, the mother will start to feel her baby's movements. The time at which the foetus is viable is gradually being pushed back and is now below twenty-four weeks, but the mother does need to be in a tertiary centre with a neonatal intensive care unit for the baby to have any chance of survival.

The best environment for a baby before thirty-seven weeks' gestation is almost always inside the mother's uterus. If the mother starts to get contractions and go into labour, she is given medication to halt the labour but also other medication to help the baby's lungs develop more quickly. Hopefully, labour can be delayed by a week or two, which will improve the survival chances. Survival rates are now about 40 per cent at twenty-four weeks, 80 per cent at twenty-seven weeks, and 90 per cent at twenty-eight weeks. Having a baby at less than thirty weeks is a very stressful time for the mother and the whole family. It is bad enough if you live nearby, but if you live in a remote community a thousand kilometres away, it is really difficult being cut off from all your family and support for weeks. Moreover, babies born before twenty-eight weeks have a high risk of disability such as cerebral palsy, among others.

**Low Birthweight**

The normal birthweight is usually defined as being between 2.5 and 4.5 kg, with the median at 40 weeks' gestation being 3.4 kg for girls and 3.55 kg for boys. Low birthweight is usually caused by prematurity, so the median is 1.85 kg at 32 weeks and 2.7 kg at 36 weeks (average for boys and girls). However, there are some risk factors and medical problems which cause a reduction in the growth rate of the foetus. This can be detected at routine ultrasound scans at twenty-eight and thirty-six weeks. The ultra-sonographer estimates the waist measurement and other parameters and can calculate the weight.

Overall in Australia in 2020, about 6.5 per cent were classified as having a low birthweight; but in the NT, the figure was 9.4 per cent. Almost 12 per cent of babies born to First Nations mothers were of low birthweight compared with 6.2 per cent for babies of non-Indigenous mothers. The reason for the difference is not due to racial background but due to the higher incidence of risk factors which could be modified. These include harmful behaviours such as smoking or alcohol consumption, poor nutrition during pregnancy, poor antenatal care, and low socio-economic position. Even the latter could be modified, for example, if the mother's partner works at a nearby mine site he could be bringing home a substantial pay packet.

Tobacco smoke reduces the flow of blood and therefore oxygen to the placenta and exposes the foetus to a number of toxins. If the placenta does not function well, the foetus' growth rate will be reduced. This is analogous to the effect of smoking on the heart in adults, increasing the risk of heart attack. Smoking also affects the health of the baby for years or decades afterwards as it increases the risk of sudden infant death syndrome, cancer, high blood pressure, asthma, obesity, and lowered cognitive development.

If a mother drinks alcohol while she is pregnant, the alcohol passes through the umbilical cord to the foetus, and the concentration of alcohol in the foetus' blood is similar to that of the mother. The alcohol causes undernourishment of the foetus and poor brain development and may cause some changes to the appearance of the face. It also increases the risk of a stillbirth. This combination of effects results in foetal alcohol spectrum disorder. It is a lifetime condition affecting learning and behaviour.

The risk factors that cannot be modified include illness during pregnancy, multiple pregnancy, maternal history of spontaneous abortion, and the mother being under the age of 18 or above 35. Teenagers sometimes get ideas that there is something romantic about having children before the age of 18. There may be some benefits like the baby bonus or finding it easier to get a house, but it really is difficult to raise a child, and it becomes more difficult for her to complete her own education. It is far better to make use of the widespread availability of contraception and wait until 18 or later before she thinks about getting pregnant.

## Complications during Birth

The birthing process in humans is a complex, risky process compared with other mammals. We have all seen videos of wildebeest giving birth on the run during their migration across the Serengeti. The newborn calf immediately stretches its legs and starts running to catch up with its mother. In contrast, human babies have a relatively large head, so the birth takes several hours, not under a minute, and the baby is completely helpless at birth and remains so for years.

The female pelvis is larger than the male for it to accommodate the baby's head and is described as a canal with an inlet and outlet, both of which are oval shaped. The inlet at the bottom of the abdomen is larger from side to side, but the outlet is larger front to back. Therefore, the baby's head enters the canal on its side but then turns through ninety degrees, so it is facing backwards, relative to the mother, to complete its journey.

The uterus is normally a small organ weighing about 60 g. During pregnancy, it expands until it weighs approximately 1.2 kg, about three times the weight of the heart; and like the heart, it is very muscular. The muscle is much slower to contract compared with the heart, taking about three to five minutes for one cycle of contraction and relaxation. It needs regular contractions firstly to open the lower end of the uterus, which is normally completely closed, until it is wide enough to let the baby out, and then provide the force to push the baby through the birth canal. During contractions, the pressure in the uterus is very high and stops the blood flow through the umbilical cord. The baby needs the relaxation time between contractions to get the blood flow from the mother again.

Many things can go wrong during delivery – these are just a few of them. The baby may be the wrong way round – known as a breech presentation. The baby's head may be too large to fit through the birth canal. The placenta may be too low down and block the exit. Labour may not start spontaneously and may need to be treated by giving the mother uterine stimulants. The baby's head may get stuck halfway down. Blood flow through the umbilical cord may stop for too long, resulting in damage to the baby's brain. There is normally a fair amount of bleeding from the uterus after the birth as it has a large blood supply. The mother is given drugs to reduce this blood flow, but a number of mothers still have a substantial loss of blood, some requiring a transfusion.

The solutions to these problems may be a C-section, or the baby can be pulled out by using a suction cap on the baby's head. However, there is a lot of evidence that babies who are born naturally have a better development than those born by C-section. It is often a tough judgement call by the obstetrician.

## Gestational Diabetes

This is a type of diabetes that occurs during pregnancy, usually during the last three months, but it may start earlier. It is caused by insulin resistance, as in type 2 diabetes, or a relative lack of insulin due to the increased weight of the mother or a combination of both of these. It generally does not cause problems in the mother, but the babies are at risk of being large as the increased sugar level makes them grow more, and so they are more likely to need a caesarean section. If untreated, it may result in a stillbirth or jaundice, or the baby may have low blood sugar immediately after birth. As they grow older, they are at increased risk of being overweight or getting type 2 diabetes.

Risk factors for the mother are being overweight, previous gestational diabetes, and a family history of type 2 diabetes. Most cases resolve after delivery, but for some, it is the start of type 2 diabetes; but if not, they are at increased risk for it over the following decades.

It affects up to 10 per cent of pregnancies but is commoner in First Nations women. This may be due to First Nations people having a higher risk of diabetes at the same BMI compared with women with a European background.

**Birth Defect**

This is defined as any abnormal condition that is present at birth. There are enormous number of these, and they vary in severity from very mild, such as a skin rash or having an extra toe or finger, to the most severe in which it is not compatible with life, so the baby dies soon after birth. There are two main causes: firstly, anatomical, in which an organ does not grow with the correct structure, and secondly, biochemical or metabolic, when a body part does not work correctly, for example, when a critical enzyme is missing. Birth defects may result from chromosomal or genetic disorders, exposure to chemicals during pregnancy, or factors in the mother's lifestyle, such as alcohol abuse, poor diet, or diabetes.

The main groups of structural defects are as follows:

| Group | Number per 10,000 births | Notes |
| --- | --- | --- |
| Brain/spinal cord | 8 | If the brain fails to develop or spina bifida is severe, it will be seen at the thirteen-week scan, and termination can be offered. |
| Heart | 50 | Screening allows planning. Some conditions need surgery immediately after birth, but others can wait months or years. |
| Cleft lip/palate | 18 | Early surgery enables baby to suck. |
| Alimentary tract | 8 | Some need urgent surgery. |
| Limb defects, e.g. club foot | 36 | Depends on condition. |
| Eye defect | 2 | Depends on condition. |

| Chromosomal abnormality | 21 | Seen at thirteen-week scan, and termination can be offered. Parents may be willing to have a Down's syndrome baby (the commonest), but other chromosomal abnormalities may cause death after a few days. |

Table 11: Structural birth defects

Almost all these problems can be detected by good antenatal care, and most of these can be avoided, or their impact can be reduced. Good antenatal care means attending the midwife or GP every four weeks from when the pregnancy is confirmed up to twenty-eight weeks and then with increasing frequency. It also means having the various blood tests and scans done at the right time.

Many First Nations women have a great desire to have their baby 'on country', meaning in their own community, preferably in their own home. They know that if the health services in their community find out about someone being pregnant, they will go to great lengths to find them and 'medicalise' the birth. So they know that they have to hide in the community and get looked after by friends who will keep their secret. This is all right provided that they know the risks, which will be the same as someone giving birth in sub-Saharan Africa. There will be about a 10 per cent chance that the baby will die at birth or soon afterwards. There will also be a risk of a mother dying, which happens about 1 in 200 births. For a community of about a thousand people, about one mother would die every fifteen years.

To avoid this death rate, the whole process of giving birth has been medicalised. Since the last chance of salvaging a birth which is going badly wrong is a C-section, births have to take place in a town with a hospital where C-sections can be done. So all pregnant women must travel to such a town or city for the final weeks of their pregnancy.

Women who live in a town with a hospital providing obstetric services may be able to find a midwife who is prepared to do a home delivery. However, there is a very strict checklist that they must follow before agreeing that a home birth is safe. The checklist includes criteria such as between second and fourth pregnancies, attended all antenatal visits, all tests normal, not overweight or obese, never ever smoked, never drank alcohol after pregnancy contemplated, and several more, but being First Nations is not one of them.

## Neonatal Infection

Unless it has a major birth defect, once the baby is born, it has overcome nearly all the obstacles to its existence. One hurdle, however, remains – the risk of infection.

At birth, the baby transitions from a relatively sterile environment in the uterus to the outside world, where it is suddenly exposed to a range of pathogens, including viruses, bacteria, and fungi. The baby's immune system is relatively weak and may not be able to cope. The baby can be infected before birth, particularly by viruses including rubella, HIV, and cytomegalovirus (CMV) but also by some bacteria including syphilis and listeria. Rubella and CMV can cause birth defects.

The baby may get infected during the birth process, picking up the infections as it passes through the vagina. The most common of these is the bacteria GBS (group B streptococcus) but also staphylococcus and E. coli.

Most of these can be prevented by the normal screening that is done at antenatal clinics. All children are routinely vaccinated against rubella, and it is best to get this repeated before pregnancy is contemplated. Similarly, mothers with HIV or CMV can be given antiviral treatment throughout pregnancy to reduce the risk of transmission to the baby. Syphilis can cause congenital defects or stillbirth and so is tested a couple of times during the pregnancy so the mother can be treated with penicillin if necessary. Listeria is a bacteria that can survive in a refrigerator and is sometimes found in soft cheeses and salads that have not been freshly prepared. It can cause stillbirth or listlessness in the newborn and can be fatal if not treated promptly. Prevention (avoiding these foods) is the best plan. GBS and other bacterial infections can be prevented by the mother being swabbed a couple of weeks before delivery and given antibiotics if necessary.

Infections that occur after the age of one week are, in general, not caused by the mother or the birth but by the environment. It is particularly important that good hygiene is practised. Breastfeeding is also important as the baby is able to use the antibodies present in the mother's milk.

## Mortality after Four Weeks

Unless there is some serious problem like being severely preterm, the vast majority of babies will have gone home well before four weeks of age. They will gradually start to interact with other family members, including siblings if they have them. The different environment means that there is a change in the types of problem that can lead to their demise.

Worldwide, the leading causes of death in children between four weeks and five years include gastroenteritis, pneumonia, malaria, and malnutrition. In Australia, the leading cause of death in children of this age group is injuries (including drowning), followed by cancer, birth defects, nervous system disorders, respiratory disorders, infections and circulatory disorders, and a big group labelled 'other'.

A significant cause of death in children under 1 year is a sudden death while the child is asleep. The two components are SIDS (sudden infant death syndrome) and SUDI or sudden unexpected death of an infant, also known as fatal sleeping accidents. SUDI occurs when babies suffocate or get trapped or strangled by things in their sleeping environments.

AIHW publish figures for causes of infant (<1) deaths by First Nations status, NSW, Qld, WA, SA, and NT, 2010–2014 and 2015–2019. An extract from the table shows the following:



CHRIS GILFORD

| | 2010–2014 | | | | 2015–2019 | | | |
|---|---|---|---|---|---|---|---|---|
| | Deaths | | Rate per 1,000 births | | Deaths | | Rate per 1,000 births | |
| | First Nations | NI | First Nations | NI | First Nations | NI | First Nations | NI |
| SIDS | 49 | 214 | 0.6 | 0.2 | 25 | 88 | 0.3 | 0.1 |
| SUDI | 47 | 137 | 0.6 | 0.1 | 51 | 178 | 0.6 | 0.2 |
| Total SIDS & SUDI | 96 | 351 | 1.2 | 0.3 | 76 | 266 | 0.8 | 0.3 |

Table 12: Deaths from SIDS and SUDI

SIDS and SUDI are more common in First Nations infants. It was discovered a long time ago that the rate of SIDS could be reduced significantly by making sure that the baby had their own space for sleeping and that they were placed on their back and definitely not on their tummy. It is obviously very convenient for breastfeeding in the middle of the night for the baby to share the bed with its parents but quite dangerous. First Nations families may not have a cot for the baby, and so the Pepi-Pod has been devised for this purpose. This is a portable baby bed which can be placed in the parents' bed or near it. It was first developed in New Zealand over ten years ago because Maori babies were seen to be at risk and is now available on this side of the Tasman. It looks as though the Pepi-Pod is already making a difference, with the rate of SIDS halving over a period of five years. It should be possible to get the rate of SIDS and SUDI down to the same level as non-Indigenous infants, and this would save many babies over a five-year period.

For children up to the age of 5, the AIHW publish tables comparing the causes of death between First Nations and non-Indigenous children. I have extracted the data for injury and poisoning as this is where the biggest differences are:

| Underlying cause of death and ICD-10 code | Deaths | | % First Nations | Rate per 100,000 | | Ratio |
|---|---|---|---|---|---|---|
| | First Nations | NI | | First Nations | NI | First Nations/NI |
| Injury and poisoning (V01–Y98) | 45 | 205 | 47.4 | 13.6 | 5.0 | 2.72 |
| Transport accidents (V01–V99) | 15 | 66 | 15.8 | 4.5 | 1.6 | 2.81 |
| Pedestrian injured in transport accident (V01–V09) | 8 | 43 | 8.4 | 2.4 | 1.0 | 2.40 |
| Car occupant injured in transport accident (V40–9) | 7 | 18 | 7.4 | 2.1 | 0.4 | 5.25 |
| Other injury and poisoning (W00–X59) | 24 | 116 | 25.3 | 7.2 | 2.8 | 2.57 |
| Accidental drowning and submersion (W65–W74) | 9 | 75 | 9.5 | 2.7 | 1.8 | 1.50 |
| Other accidental threats to breathing (W75–W84) | * | 16 | * | * | 1.4 | |
| All other causes (medical causes) | 50 | 396 | | 14.1 | 9.6 | 1.47 |
| Total | 95 | 601 | 100.0 | 28.7 | 14.6 | |

Table 13: Deaths of young children from injury and poisoning

Of this group, the biggest difference for First Nations and non-Indigenous children was injuries from 'car occupant injured in transport accident'. Almost certainly, this is where the child has been unrestrained in a car. I think that a reason for this may be the difference in car ownership between First Nations and non-Indigenous people. Families who own a car know that they have to use a car seat or capsule for their young children, as well as seat belts for all occupants. But it is more difficult for those without a car. Many First Nations people use taxis and rideshare cars to do their shopping and take their children with them. However, unlike drivers of private cars, these drivers are exempt from prosecution for not providing children's car seats. It is impractical for taxis to supply child seats. Perhaps there is room for compromise, taking a lead from the airline industry. Would a seat belt extension similar to those found in aircraft provide a solution and save some lives?

Poisoning does not refer to a child getting hold of a substance used to kill weeds or rats but getting hold of medication that has been prescribed for other people living in the same house. If a child of 10 kg takes a single dose of a medication prescribed for an adult of 70–100 kg, they may be getting ten times the therapeutic dose, which may be fatal for them.

Overall, injury and poisoning was 2.7 times as common in First Nations people. Bringing that ratio down to 1 is not a health issue. It just requires that parents and carers who supervise children should monitor them closely and make sure that the guidelines are followed. In addition, if they are delegating childcare responsibility, then they need to make sure that whoever is doing it will be conscientious and not get distracted, for example, by looking at their phone. Forty-five young First Nations children died from injury and poisoning between 2015 and 2019. If the rate was the same as for non-Indigenous children, that number would be reduced to seventeen, a saving of twenty-eight children in five years, and this would produce a significant reduction to the total childhood mortality.

## Gastroenteritis

The number one cause of death worldwide in children under 5 is gastroenteritis. This is due to drinking or eating something that is infected with certain bacteria or viruses. It is often associated with poor hygiene, not washing hands after going to the toilet, and in other countries a polluted water supply. The suffix '-itis' means inflammation, so the lining of the gut gets swollen and red and cannot absorb fluid but instead secretes fluid. The symptoms are vomiting and diarrhoea.

A newborn baby drinks about 720 ml of milk a day. This is about 20 per cent of its weight (typically 3.5 kg). If it has gastroenteritis, it cannot take any fluid by mouth, so it is losing out on a lot of fluid relative to its weight. In contrast, an adult of 70 kg consumes about 2.5 litres of fluid a day, or about 3.5 per cent of their weight. So the effects of gastro in an infant are far more profound. The mainstay of treatment is rehydration. Giving milk at this stage can make the problem worse, but the infant may be able to absorb clear fluids. This is best given by passing a fine tube up through the nose and so into the stomach. A sterile fluid with glucose and salts is trickled in slowly, and often, this will work. If not, an intravenous catheter must be inserted and the baby rehydrated in this way.

*Failure to Thrive*

A baby puts on weight normally by consuming firstly milk and then solids. To begin with, its weight gain is quite rapid, about 25–30 g a day from birth, but this decreases gradually to about 15 g daily at 6 months and 10 g at 12 months. The baby's weight is checked regularly and plotted on a chart, known as a percentile chart, and this is standardised to show the normal weight gain. The nurse or doctor can then see whether the baby is putting on weight at the correct rate or whether it is falling behind, and if it continues to do this, it is diagnosed with failure to thrive.

The main cause is inadequate food intake. For example, the mother's breast milk may not be adequate, or she may be unable to source enough powdered milk or not know the correct amount to give. Alternatively, the child may have a medical problem in that they cannot absorb the milk. This problem is commoner in First Nations families, and often, the mother and child need to be admitted to hospital.

An associated problem is iron deficiency. Babies have difficulty in getting enough iron from milk. It is an important mineral as it is a component in blood and is also needed for brain development. It may also be due to worm infestation, which may need treatment. Again, it is commoner in First Nations families and is treated with iron supplements, which may be given by mouth or injection.

*Ear Infections*

These are much commoner in First Nations children. The important one is otitis media – infection of the middle ear. Anatomically, the ear is divided into three parts, firstly the outer ear, which is separated from the middle ear by the eardrum. The middle ear contains the three tiny bones which amplify sound, and the inner ear, filled with fluid, contains the cochlear, which turns sound waves into nerve impulses which our brains interpret as sound. The middle ear contains air and is connected to the throat by the auditory tube so the pressure across the eardrum can be equalised. This is a conduit for infection getting in.

There are many risk factors that contribute to the high rates of ear disease in First Nations people. They include overcrowding, passive smoking, premature birth, bottle feeding, and malnutrition. Another factor is that First Nations children tend not to blow their noses, preferring to just wipe them.

It also appears to be a more serious type of infection in First Nations children. Non-Indigenous children seem to get over an infection easily, but in First Nations children, it often causes the eardrum to rupture, and then pus can be seen dripping from the ear. Once this has started, it is very difficult to stop it, and it may destroy the whole eardrum. When this happens, it can affect the child's hearing to the extent that they need hearing aids. This affects their speech and so their education and development.

To summarise, just like in adults, the risk of many of the health problems that affect babies and children can be prevented by the parents following the instructions of health professionals, avoiding risk factors, and being vigilant with their offspring.

# CHAPTER 6

# Lifestyle and Risk Factors

B EFORE 1788, FIRST Nations people led a fairly healthy lifestyle. They had a varied diet that was mostly plant based. They did not consume much fat, sugar, salt, caffeine, or alcohol. They had smoking ceremonies but did not deliberately inhale the smoke. They had an active lifestyle, walking long distances. This gradually changed as Europeans spread through the country. Unfortunately, the Europeans brought with them a lot of unhealthy habits, chiefly smoking tobacco and drinking alcohol to excess. Their diet was rich in fats, sugar, and salt. They introduced crops and farm animals, thus increasing the amount of food available. This meant that obtaining food was no longer the main activity, so a more sedentary lifestyle was possible. This led eventually to obesity.

The Australian Institute of Health and Welfare publish regular reports of health risk factors. The figures from 2018 to 2019 show the following percentages of people who did <u>not</u> comply with the guidelines:

| Health behaviour | Standard | First Nations | Non-Indigenous | Ratio |
| --- | --- | --- | --- | --- |
| Inadequate fruit and vegetable intake | 2 fruit and 5 veg daily | 97.2 | 94.8 | 1.03 |
| Below physical activity guidelines | ½ hr 5 days/ week | 89.0 | 85.1 | 1.05 |
| Overweight/obese | BMI<= 25 | 76.8 | 66.3 | 1.16 |

| Risky alcohol consumption | <10 drinks/ week | 48.5 | 41.6 | 1.17 |
| --- | --- | --- | --- | --- |
| Current smoker | Nil | 41.4 | 14.4 | 2.88 |

Table 14: Non-compliance with guidelines

Obesity is a huge topic to deal with, so it has its own chapter.

## Nutrition

From the table above, it appears that hardly anybody eats the recommended quantity of fruit and vegetables, despite numerous campaigns to change this behaviour.

Another AIHW report breaks down the amount of fruit and vegetables eaten by age. The age range that does best is 0–3, with over 95 per cent having adequate fruit and 20 per cent adequate veg. These numbers drop to about 50 per cent and 5 per cent at age 18 and then rise slowly to 60 per cent and 10 per cent at age 65.

The National Health and Medical Research Council (NHMRC) publishes guidelines for the minimum recommended number of serves of fruit and vegetables per day at different age groups. The well-known phrase 'two fruit and five veg' is good for adults, except the NHMRC recommends 5½ or 6 serves of veggies for teenage boys and men.

### Malnutrition

How can a community have an increased incidence of both malnutrition and obesity? It seems like a paradox, but malnutrition refers to an excess of food of poor quality, not a lack of calories. Poor-quality food means high in sugars and high in saturated fats, is excessively refined, and contains few raw ingredients. Processed food is known to be associated with a lower life expectancy. The problem is getting worse as more people move away from home cooking to getting takeaway meals or, if they do cook at home, using sauces, pastes, or processed foods that have been manufactured in an establishment that resembles a factory rather than a kitchen. All processed food is labelled with its ingredients. For example, I looked at the ingredients in a bottle of soy sauce and found terms such as 'preservative' (202), 'flavour enhancer' (635), and 'sweetener' (635). These are typical of the additives that food manufacturers use. Why does soy sauce need a flavour enhancer? Why does it need a sweetener? Surely, this would stop it tasting like soy sauce. The answer is that they are responding to the change in our taste buds, which they and other companies, particularly the purveyors of sweet drinks, have created.

There has been a recent move to replace meat with something that looks like meat but is made from plants. It is processed in a factory, and the manufacturers do not give us the full list of ingredients. There may be some benefits for us and for the environment in giving up meat, but processed food is known to have an adverse effect on our health. It is too early to know the long-term consequences.

There is debate about introducing a sugar tax as a reduction in sugar consumption would aid everyone's health. This would probably result in increased sales of drinks using artificial sweeteners. It is surprisingly easy to give up sugar in drinks. Just stop adding sugar to your tea or coffee. For a few days, it will taste sour, but your body soon gets used to it, and you find you don't need it.

**Physical Activity**

The Department of Health and Aged Care publishes guidelines for physical activity. The current ones for adults include the fact that adults should be active most days, and each should do 2.5 to 5 hours per week of moderate-intensity physical activity – such as a brisk walk, golf, mowing the lawn, or swimming – or vigorous activity for half that time. They should also include muscle-strengthening activities twice a week. There are similar guidelines for other groups: birth to 5 years; 5 to 17 years; pregnancy, 65, and older; and people with disability and chronic conditions. Their website includes recommendations for all groups of people.

From the table above, over 80 per cent of the population are not doing enough exercise. Most people say they have an interest in sport, and for an awful lot of people, this means just watching their favourite team participate in football, basketball, netball, tennis, etc. or watching the Olympics every four years. Unfortunately, the benefit that the elite players are getting does not travel over the airwaves to your body. Even worse, if you get an adrenaline rush when your team scores, it might actually be harmful.

When I was in Normanton, I used to ask patients what sort of exercise they did, and the commonest response for every age group was 'I walk a bit.' Just walking on the flat is all right if you are elderly, but for everyone else, you need to do something that raises your heart rate and makes you sweat. There are some cities that have a convenient hill for this purpose. Cairns has Mount Whitfield, Townsville has Castle Hill, and Brisbane has Mount Coot-tha. Lots of people do these every day; some of them run. One of the common excuses for avoiding exercise is that 'gym memberships are too expensive'. However, there are options which cost very little. Jogging only requires a pair of suitable shoes, and these can be used for other activities. Swimming in the sea is free, and there are some free pools, but you do need to do some laps, not just splash about.

Jogging is also good and needs no special equipment, but it may be hard for people who have some joint problems but not as problematic as sports using balls, pucks, or shuttlecocks as sudden twisting movements can tear ligaments and tendons. Cycling is easier as it involves smooth movements. If you are not planning to race, then there is no need to get an expensive bike. A cheap one on which you can go 10 km in half an hour will be just as beneficial as an expensive one on which you can go 15 km in half an hour.

Governments around Australia have invested heavily in cycling to make it both safer and easier. They have assigned traffic lanes on roads to cyclists and built dedicated cycle tracks. Despite this, the number of cyclists who use them is comparatively small. This is in marked contrast to many of the big cities in Europe, such as Paris and Amsterdam, where bicycles outnumber cars. In contrast, many Australians have embraced the use of e-scooters, which convey no exercise benefit to the rider but seem to be causing an increasing number of accidents.

## Maternal Education Level and Employment

This was not listed in the AIHW report quoted at the beginning of this chapter but is an important risk factor for some diseases found in First Nations people, such as rheumatic fever. As noted in an earlier chapter, school attendance in a First Nations community is low. In Mornington Island, it was about 70 per cent, and most teenagers left school at year 10. Therefore, most did not have much of an education. Employment opportunities in a First Nations community are limited. Generally, the only employers are the council, the school, and the hospital. There is little incentive for teenagers to continue their education.

Elsewhere in the world, there has been an increase in the educational level that girls reach. Going back only 150 years, girls throughout the world were deprived of the educational opportunities that boys had. Even in 'advanced' countries, their education was aimed at seeing that they could perform domestic duties or run a household and so supervise their staff.

In the UK, a school in London in 1850 was the first in England to offer girls the same educational opportunities as boys. In Australia, universities started accepting women undergraduates in 1880, and the first woman to graduate did so in 1883 from the University of Melbourne.

When I started medical school in 1973, only 26 per cent of the students were female, but this was an improvement from four years earlier, when the figure was 8 per cent. Now it is over 50 per cent.

Girls' education became more available during the twentieth century, starting in westernised industrial countries and gradually spreading down to developing countries. One of the tragedies of the Taliban retaking Afghanistan is that they have prohibited girls' education.

It was uncommon for women to work when they married, until the 1970s. It has now become the norm for all women to work except for a period of maternity leave, resulting in the huge growth of childcare centres.

## Alcohol, Tobacco, and Other Drugs

Recreational drugs are used all over the world and often cause problems in society. I have used the heading above as Queensland Health groups them together as ATODS, employing staff to help communities deal with the problems. Modern terminology is to use the word 'substance' instead of 'drug'.

## Alcohol

Chemists use the term 'alcohol' to refer to an organic compound that carries a hydroxyl group, which consists of an oxygen and hydrogen atom. The one that is relevant here is ethyl alcohol, also known as ethanol. Other common alcohols include methyl alcohol, found in 'metho' or methylated spirits; isopropyl alcohol, known as rubbing alcohol and also used as a disinfectant; and ethylene glycol, found in antifreeze. The rest of this chapter is about ethyl alcohol, and it will be referred to simply as 'alcohol'. It is a simple chemical substance with the formula $C_2H_5OH$. It is produced in nature as a by-product of the breakdown of sugars to release energy without needing oxygen. It requires enzymes which are usually found in yeast or bacteria.

It has a number of uses apart from being in drinks. It can be used as a fuel additive, and we are being encouraged to use petrol mixed with 10–20 per cent alcohol in our cars. It is also a good disinfectant, killing bacteria, fungi, and viruses, but it does not kill bacterial spores. However, it is almost useless below a concentration of 50 per cent. We have all seen movies where someone tries to sterilise a wound or the instruments they are going to use on it with a bottle of whisky, but this is far too weak to kill any germs.

Its effects on the animal kingdom predate the arrival of *Homo sapiens*. Birds such as lorikeets which regularly eat fruit are at risk if they cannot find fresh fruit but have to rely on fruit that has started to decompose and ferment as they therefore consume some alcohol. They can become intoxicated, most of them only mildly, but a few get completely inebriated. When birds are drunk, they lose mobility, making them helpless in the presence of predators. And if they can manage to fly while under the influence, their lack of coordination may have devastating consequences, much like those affecting humans who drink and drive. There is also evidence that larger mammals such as orangutans, apes, and elephants seek out rotting fruit to try and get high.

So it should be no surprise that early man experimented with producing alcoholic drinks. Archaeologists have found evidence of alcohol production in several countries dating back over 10,000 years, including Israel, China, Iran, Egypt, Mexico, and Sudan. It even gets a mention in the Bible as being useful in palliative care but with warnings for others:

> It is not for kings to drink wine; nor for princes strong drink: Lest they drink, and forget the law, and pervert the judgment of any of the afflicted. Give strong drink unto him that is ready to perish, and wine unto those that be of heavy hearts. Let him drink, and forget his poverty, and remember his misery no more. (Proverbs 31:4–7) Authorised (King James) Version

The New Testament tells how Jesus turned water into wine at the wedding feast at Cana (John 2:7–9), so presumably, he approved of its consumption.

As noted earlier, alcohol is produced during the fermentation of sugars. This is accomplished by certain yeasts. Yeasts are single-cell organisms, members of the fungus kingdom. The other main kingdoms are plants and animals. There are hundreds of species of yeast, but the main one which causes fermentation is *Saccharomyces cerevisiae*, which contains the enzyme zymase. Yeasts are widespread in the environment and are often isolated from sugar-rich fruits such as grapes but also many other plants. It is not airborne but is carried around by insects.

Yeasts are living organisms as those who bake their own sourdough bread know since they observe that their supply keeps regenerating.

The same fermentation process takes place in both baking and brewing. The chemical equation is

$C_6H_{12}O_6$ (glucose) $\rightarrow$ 2 $C_2H_5OH$ (ethyl alcohol) and 2 $CO_2$ (carbon dioxide).

In baking, carbon dioxide is the required product so that the bread rises, and alcohol is a by-product, but this evaporates or boils off while the bread is being baked. On the other hand, in brewing (or winemaking), alcohol is the required product, and the carbon dioxide may be required, as in beer or sparkling wine, or it is a by-product. There are different strains of the yeast which have been developed to assist in reaching the desired outcome.

Alcohol releases energy when it is broken down by the body. A standard drink in Australia contains 10 g of alcohol. So 260 ml regular-strength beer releases 75 calories or 313 joules. The current alcohol guidelines recommend no more than ten standard drinks a week. This means an average of about 110 calories (460kj) a day which is not going to make much difference to a person's calorie intake, but for those people who drink in excess of the recommendations the alcohol may increase the risk of obesity.

Alcohol that has been consumed is metabolised by the body, mainly in the liver, into acetaldehyde, then acetate, and finally carbon dioxide and water. A small amount of alcohol is eliminated unchanged in urine, breath, and sweat, and this is how the police find out whether you have been drinking and driving.

Alcohol has been used in medicine in the past, apart from as a disinfectant. The side effects, of course, are intoxication, but the main problem is that the lethal dose is not much greater than the toxic dose, which is also not much greater than the therapeutic dose. Before modern agents for general anaesthesia became available, it was used widely in emergency situations, such as doing amputations on the battlefield or on board a ship. It was also found that it could stop premature labour in pregnant women, but they had to be given enough to make them quite intoxicated. Fortunately, there are more effective treatments now.

It is, of course, the use of alcohol as a recreational substance that is the most important consideration. It is used recreationally because, in the short term, it causes happiness, decreased anxiety, increased sociability, and euphoria, but these effects vary widely between different people. It also causes sedation, which may be desirable or a disadvantage. Unfortunately, it also has negative effects including impairment of cognitive, memory, motor, and sensory function, particularly dizziness and disorientation, and generalized depression of central nervous system function. There may also be behavioural effects such as disinhibition and increased risk-taking. Non-neurological effects include nausea and vomiting.

Excessive alcohol can also cause a hangover, usually the morning after a heavy drinking session. The effects include headache, dizziness, light sensitivity, depression, sweating, nausea, and anxiety. The effects usually last a few hours. They are due to the increased concentration of acetaldehyde, one of the breakdown products of alcohol.

People get conditioned to the adverse effects by gradually increasing the amount they drink. The liver responds by making more of the enzymes that metabolise it. They are then able to tolerate more and more alcohol. An additional problem occurs if a habitual heavy drinker suddenly stops drinking alcohol. They can get a condition called delirium tremens, or the DTs, but also called 'the horrors'. This usually starts about three days after their last drink and consists of mental confusion including hallucinations, shaking, shivering, sweating, and sometimes seizures. It can be a life-threatening emergency.

Alcohol is also a diuretic, meaning that it makes your kidneys excrete more urine than would be expected from the water content of the beverage. This is not a problem if you drink a low-alcohol drink such as beer, but drinking wine or neat spirits causes you to excrete a volume of urine that is higher than the volume of the drink you have consumed. You therefore paradoxically become thirsty and need to drink more fluid. This is a problem if you continue to drink fluid with a high concentration of alcohol. You will probably fall asleep but then wake up feeling very unwell and dehydrated, which is part of the hangover. The solution includes drinking plenty of water. This dehydration problem is similarly found in shipwrecked sailors who may be tempted to drink seawater when their supplies of fresh water are exhausted. The sailors cannot produce urine that is more concentrated than seawater, and so their dehydration is made worse.

Alcohol has long-term effects on the body. It has deleterious effects on virtually every organ and increases the risk of many cancers. A severe alcoholic tends not to eat as much as they should. They do not eat much protein or vitamins, and this contributes to ill health. Some of the important adverse effects are as follows:

*Liver.* It causes alcoholic hepatitis, swelling, and inflammation of the liver. The early stages can be detected by a simple blood test. Normally, the liver can only be felt (palpated) under the right-sided ribs when you take a deep breath in, but when it swells, it can easily be felt there and may extend ten or more centimetres downwards. Routine blood tests can easily show the extent of the inflammation. However, as the inflammation progresses, the liver then shrinks, a condition called cirrhosis, and will not be palpable at all. When the liver fails, there is jaundice, or yellowing of the skin, and there may be swelling of the whole abdomen from fluid retention called ascites. There may also be a tendency to bleed more than normal and then mental deterioration.

*Heart.* It causes swelling of the heart muscle, called cardiomyopathy, the muscle becoming weaker than normal. Their exercise tolerance is reduced, and they get breathless on minimal effort. Their blood pressure usually increases, putting more strain on the heart. They can also get atrial fibrillation, in which the atria, the upper chambers of the heart, beat fast and erratically, reducing the heart's efficiency at pumping blood round the body.

*Brain.* Alcohol is toxic to nerve cells, so brain function deteriorates. It can cause epileptic seizures either when the person is intoxicated or when they are withdrawing from alcohol. There are also specific syndromes in heavy drinkers. Wernicke's encephalopathy is caused by a deficiency of vitamin $B_1$ (thiamine), which is invariably caused by alcohol. It consists in disorders of eye movements, ataxia (lack of coordination of limb movements), and mental confusion. The other syndrome is Korsakoff's syndrome, in which the sufferer has severe loss of memory for recent events, but they may retain their memory from their early life. They may try to cover up the memory loss by inventing false memories, a process called confabulation. Both of these syndromes are irreversible.

*Blood.* Alcohol causes red blood cells to increase in size, so their alcohol dependence can again be diagnosed with a simple blood test.

These pathophysiological effects result in broader changes with someone's health. Alcohol makes people incapable of looking after themselves properly, such as taking their tablets or turning up for appointments. People don't seek treatment when they are drunk, so their illnesses which would be easily treatable early then progress and become untreatable. It makes people more aggressive, and therefore confrontations more easily progress to violence, particularly domestic violence; people who are intoxicated are also more likely to become a victim of violence. They may say things they wouldn't if they were sober, and they are less able to avoid the punches when they come.

These social effects result in a huge economic cost for society. Those affected by alcohol are much less likely to work or contribute in other ways to the community. They require friends to assist them or look after them and reduce the potential for harm. This may well have a negative impact on the friends' other obligations. The community will require more health support and more police and justice resources to deal with the legal problems that arise.

Community groups started to try and deal with the problems over 200 years ago, known as the temperance movement. The groups were often based around a church, particularly Protestant ones and their more Puritan offshoots such as Methodists, Calvinists, Mormons, and Seventh-Day Adventists. Other religions banned alcohol consumption, notably Muslims. Governments were lobbied, and in the USA, there was an amendment to the constitution in 1920 which prohibited the production and sale of alcoholic drinks, and it lasted until 1933. It was a partial success in that some health indices such as the rates of liver disease and infant mortality did improve, but there was little change to the levels of crime and violence. One of the reasons for this is that criminal gangs gained control of the beer and liquor industry in many cities.

Another movement with some success is Alcoholics Anonymous, which started in 1935 and now has a worldwide membership of over two million. Their twelve-step programme is well known and starts with the person admitting their powerlessness over alcohol and acknowledging its damage. They advocate the goal of complete abstinence since few alcoholics are able to become 'social drinkers' and just have one or two drinks and then stop.

*Alcohol in Australia*

Alcohol was an integral part of the colony of New South Wales from its inception in 1788. Indeed, it was known as a rum colony. Three of the ships in the First Fleet that set off from Portsmouth were store ships, carrying enough supplies to keep the new colony going for two years, but the Marine Corps who accompanied them to keep law and order insisted on having enough rum to last them for four years. The provisions included 5 puncheons of rum and 300 gallons of brandy. A puncheon is about 100 gallons. The first governor, Arthur Phillip, kept a tight rein on the distribution of rum (the word was used generically to include all distilled spirits) with the assistance of the marines. However, in 1789, the Marine Corps was relieved by the NSW Corps, a permanent regiment of the British Army, who took over the distribution of rum. Rum became a prized commodity, and as there was no real alternative, it also became a de facto currency.

First Nations people living in the vicinity of Sydney Cove would have observed the white settlers drinking the rum and have seen the effect it had on them, but did First Nations people use alcohol before 1788? The answer is 'yes' but only in small quantities as they did not grow any crops. They were good observers and so would have seen the birds eating decaying fruit that was fermenting. They produced alcohol from a variety of plants including pandanus, coconut palms, and banksia cones and from fermenting honey. In addition, there were traditional rules which controlled how and when it was used.

The first pubs in Sydney Cove opened soon after the arrival of the First Fleet. Many First Nations labourers were often paid in alcohol or tobacco. In the early 1800s, the white settlers in Sydney found it amusing to ply First Nations men with alcohol and encourage them to fight each other, often to the death. White settlers also gave alcohol to First Nations people to pay for sex. Alcohol-induced prostitution harmed child rearing and accelerated the birth rate of mixed descent children, usually rejected by their European fathers.

The whole social structure of First Nations communities deteriorated during the nineteenth and early twentieth centuries. It is hardly surprising that alcohol became a way for many of them to cope, survive, and resist.

*Alcohol Consumption by First Nations People Today*

Contrary to the general view of most Australians, fewer First Nations people drink alcohol than non-Indigenous, and this is backed by data from multiple sources. The National Drug Strategy Household Survey 2019 published by AIHW found that

- abstinence among First Nations Australians has increased from 25 per cent in 2010 to 29 per cent in 2019, and
- after adjusting for differences in age, First Nations Australians aged 14 and over were more likely to abstain from drinking alcohol than non-Indigenous Australians.

On the other hand, 48.5 per cent of First Nations adults drank more than ten drinks a week, compared with 41.6 per cent of non-Indigenous.

Anyone who lives in a town or city with a large First Nations population will have seen intoxicated First Nations people wandering around the streets, shouting out to one another, and assume that this is their normal state. This is not a good look in cities with many international tourists like Cairns or Darwin. It is nowhere near a good representation of First Nations people. The problem is that those First Nations people who do drink alcohol drink it in large quantities. The

          CHRIS GILFORD

reason that they are more conspicuous is that First Nations people spend more of their time outside. This is particularly the case in the hotter parts of Australia, again Cairns and Darwin, where non-Indigenous people spend more time indoors in air conditioning.

There have been many attempts to try and control the alcohol consumption of First Nations people, usually at the community level, backed up with state legislation. Several communities in the Northern Territory and the north of Queensland and Western Australia have an alcohol management plan. In most cases, the communities are declared to be 'dry', in which case there is prohibition on the sale or possession of alcohol. Some are partially dry in that they allow beer but not wine or spirits. Others allow someone in a dry area to get a permit which allows them to purchase alcohol for their own consumption.

Often, there is some initial improvement in the health and well-being of the community members after restrictions are introduced; but often, this deteriorates after months or years of the prohibition. This also depends on how well the policy is policed.

When I arrived in Normanton in 2000, there were no restrictions on the amount of alcohol that could be purchased. At that time, the favourite drink for First Nations people was cheap cask wine, the casks being four litres in volume. The commonest brand was a sweet wine called Fruit Elixir, but this was always abbreviated to 'Fruity'. Many people were drinking a cask each in a day. It was often left out in the sun in the belief that the fermentation process would continue and the alcohol content increase. As well as making them drunk, as explained above, it also made them dehydrated. The health of many of them suffered irreversibly.

I soon found that alcohol was making a huge difference to people's lives. Alcohol management plans were introduced in nearby First Nations communities in 2003. In early 2005, I was asked by the police for a report on the effects that alcohol was having in Normanton. I looked at the records of all the people who had died during the five-year period up to the end of 2004. I found eighty-one cases, of whom fifty-seven were First Nations people. Of the First Nations people, twenty-one had been heavy drinkers. The median age of death was 67 for the non-Indigenous, 62 for the non-drinking First Nations people, and 41 for the drinkers. I looked at the cause of death in the drinkers. The commonest cause of death was sepsis – overwhelming infection. This occurred in about a third of them. It commonly followed a period of self-neglect. The person had been drinking heavily with very little food intake. They became weaker, and so they lost the ability to fight infections. Their poor state of hygiene made them prone to contracting infections, usually from wounds in the skin. They then stayed at home and refused any care or to be taken to hospital. By the time they were, it was too late.

In June 2005, an alcohol management plan was introduced in Normanton. It prohibited the sale of cask wine and any fortified wine. If you wanted to buy more than five cartons of beer (twenty-four cans each), then your name and address were recorded. These restrictions seem quite mild, but they did make a significant difference to the health of the community, at least from the perspective of everyone working at the hospital. On the other hand, according to the ABC, it provoked a backlash from civil libertarians.

> Civil libertarians say the new license conditions placed on a group of far northern Queensland pubs are an insulting invasion of privacy.
>
> Seven publicans in Normanton, Karumba and Chillagoe now have to record the personal information of customers buying more than 45 litres of takeaway alcohol.
>
> The Queensland Council for Civil Liberties says alcohol is a legal product and the conditions discriminate against people in nearby First Nations communities.
>
> Council president Terry O'Gorman says they are disturbingly similar to requirements for people buying the drug Sudafed.
>
> 'Well, I think most people in the community would be insulted that they're being required to provide as much personal details to buy alcohol as people are to

buy Sudafed when the Sudafed restrictions are directed at trying to cut down the amphetamine manufacturing trade,' he said.

In Mornington Island, the 2003 plan allowed a canteen to sell beer for consumption on the premises. However, in 2009, the state government, with little consultation with the community, imposed a complete ban on the sale and consumption of alcohol. Large signs were put up at the airport and on the jetty announcing that there were heavy penalties for bringing alcohol into the community: fines of up to $75,000, eighteen months' imprisonment, and confiscation of vehicle. This was relatively easy to enforce as Mornington Island is an island. Anyone boarding an aeroplane to go there had to make a declaration that they were not carrying any alcohol. There is a weekly freight service, with no passengers, by barge, but all goods are inspected. It is possible to go there in a small boat, but this can be hazardous.

So there was some improvement in people's health. However, after a couple of years, many of the community discovered how to make home brew. The important ingredients are yeast, sugar, water, and flavourings, and there are no restrictions about how much of these you can buy or own. If you are making beer, you use malted barley (or malt) as your source of sugar and use hops as the main flavouring. Home brew on Mornington Island usually used fruit as a flavouring. The best sugar to use is glucose, but it is much easier to obtain sucrose, a combination of glucose and maltose, and called simply 'sugar' which is normally used to sweeten your coffee or make a cake, and of course, it can be bought in any supermarket. The one in Mornington Island used to stock vast quantities of sugar, far more than a large supermarket in Cairns, and I don't think much of it was used for baking cakes. Brewer's yeast cannot be purchased in Mornington Island, but you can get it over the internet. A common brand is turbo yeast, which has been formulated to produce a high concentration of alcohol quickly.

In 2017, I was asked by Mornington Shire Council to make a report on the impact of home brew alcohol on the workload of Mornington

Island Hospital. They hoped to use it in an application to the state government to get the alcohol ban lifted. This was it:

Introduction

Theoretically Mornington Island is a 'dry community' as the importation and manufacture of alcohol has been prohibited for over ten years. However during that time a large home industry of home-brewing has been established. The 'home-brew' has been manufactured from Turbo-Yeast purchased on the internet and sugar purchased from the local shop, possibly with other substances to give it some flavour, and it is sold in containers of ten litres. These are sold at a price of around $250, and there is no shortage of people willing to pay this amount. Some batches of the home-brew have been analysed and found to contain between 4 and 14% alcohol, mostly in the upper part of that range. Other substances have been found but it is the alcohol which is important. The concentration of alcohol is the same as that found in wine. Each container is drunk in one sitting by a small number community members. Each person may well be drinking about 2 litres in one sitting, or about 28 units of alcohol. Current guidelines are to limit alcohol to 14 units in one week. Most of the people who drink home-brew do so at least once a week.

Impact on the hospital

The hospital normally sees patients in the Emergency Department, in the GP Clinic and in Community Health. It is the patients who present to the ED who are relevant here. The figures given below refer to the Calendar year 2016. They have been collected by me by systematic analysis of the charts, and may differ from 'official' figures.

There were 2,245 presentations to the ED. This figure is the number of patients with new problems; it does not include re-presentations such as wound dressings or removal of sutures.

Of these 2,245 presentations, the patient was recorded as being intoxicated in 35.4% of the total. This is probably an under-estimate, as minor degrees of intoxication are rarely recorded, and some nurses are reluctant to record the fact that a person is intoxicated.

These figures are broken down as follows:

|  | Intoxicated | Not Intoxicated | Total | % Intox. |
| --- | --- | --- | --- | --- |
| Presentations | 794 | 1451 | 2245 | 35.4 |
| Admitted | 78 | 115 | 193 | 40.4 |
| Transferred | 10 | 80 | 90 | 11.1 |
| Victim | 198 | 120 | 318 | 62.3 |
| Perpetrator | 16 | 34 | 50 | 32.0 |
| Other trauma | 19 | 51 | 70 | 27.1 |
| EEO | 36 | 17 | 53 | 67.9 |

Table 15: Alcohol and presentations at Mornington Island Hospital

'Admitted' means that the person was admitted to the ward. A large number of other intoxicated people may be kept in the ED up to 4 hours and then allowed to go home when they have sobered up sufficiently.

'Transferred' means that they have a medical condition that we cannot handle here and so they have been transferred to Mount Isa or Townsville by RFDS, at a cost in excess of $10,000. For the intoxicated patients, all of the transfers were required because of an injury that occurred because they were intoxicated.

'Victim' means someone who has been assaulted

and received an injury as a result. The high proportion in those who were intoxicated is no doubt due to them saying something that they would not have said if they were sober, and then being too intoxicated to avoid the assault when it came.

'Perpetrator' means someone who has assaulted another person and have themselves been injured as a result. An example is a tooth-knuckle injury in which the person who punched someone has an infected wound on their finger as a result.

'Other trauma' means an injury when no one else was involved, such as falling over, or when they were fighting and it is not possible to say whether they were victim or perpetrator.

'EEO' means an Emergency Examination Order. This is when someone has threatened suicide or self-harm and have been brought to the hospital by the police or ambulance. The vast majority of these are in people who have been in an argument, and make the threat of suicide as part of attention-seeking behaviour. In very few cases is it a person with a mental illness such as depression or psychosis. We have been fortunate in Mornington Island that there has been a dramatic reduction in the number of completed suicides in the last few years.

Five years after writing this, on 16 April 2022, the alcohol ban was lifted, allowing the consumption of beer or pre-mixed spirits, with an alcohol concentration of up to 4 per cent, in either case. However, when I telephoned the hospital six months after this, I was told that this had made little difference to the situation.

## Tobacco

Tobacco is the common name of several herbaceous plants and shrubs in the genus *Nicotiana* of the family *Solanaceae*, which is native



CHRIS GILFORD

to the Americas, Australia, South West Africa, and the South Pacific. 'Tobacco' is also the general term for any product prepared from the cured leaves of these plants. More than seventy species of tobacco are known, but the chief commercial crop is *N. tabacum*, which is native to the Caribbean.

*Tobacco Smoking*

Tobacco smoking dates back several thousand years in the Americas. The most common form was in pipes, usually done for religious or social purposes. Sometimes it was part of a truce between warring tribes who would smoke a peace pipe. In some Native American cultures, tobacco is seen as a gift from the Creator. After Europeans arrived in both North and South America at the end of the fifteenth century, it became a widespread recreational activity and was also used as currency.

It was first brought to Europe in 1559 on the orders of King Philip II of Spain. The seeds were planted in an area of Spain near Toledo called Los Cigarrales, from which we have the words 'cigar' and 'cigarette'. From there, it made its way to France and then England. It became popular for its alleged medicinal properties, but it also launched the debate into whether its introduction was a curse or a blessing. From there, it spread to every country. Tobacco was grown in Australia, mostly near Mareeba, west of Cairns, and the Australian government subsidised the construction of Tinaroo Dam in 1920 to increase the amount of water for irrigating the tobacco fields.

Tobacco smoke contains thousands of different chemicals. One is nicotine, which is responsible for the addictive properties of cigarettes, but it is also toxic in high doses. There are also many other chemicals which can cause cancer.

Tobacco smoke has been found to have numerous adverse effects on the human body. The link with lung cancer is well known, but it causes an increased incidence of almost all cancers but especially of those parts of the body that come into direct contact with smoke, including lips, tongue, mouth, nose, oesophagus, throat, larynx (voice box), and stomach. The cancer-causing chemicals can be absorbed in the lungs or stomach and travel throughout the body, causing cancer in the breast, liver, kidney, pancreas, bladder, blood, cervix, vulva, penis, and others.

Nicotine causes narrowing of the veins and arteries. This can result in a heart attack or stroke if the blood vessels to the heart or brain are affected. Sometimes the blood vessels to the arms or legs are narrowed, and this can result in pain, loss of function, and then gangrene in the hands or feet. I have seen patients who have had all four limbs amputated due to smoking.

Smoking is a major cause of chronic obstructive lung disease (chronic bronchitis and/or emphysema) and makes asthma worse. Smoking also has adverse effects on almost every part of the body.

Smokers say that it helps them relax, but this is a fallacy, which has actually become more plausible in the last two decades. Smoking is not allowed at work, so smokers have to have a cigarette break to indulge. They have to leave their workplace and go outside. It is the ten-minute break from work and the process of going outside, being distracted by looking at the traffic, or smelling the roses that helps them relax, not the nicotine or other components of the smoke.

In the last couple of years, many people have been working from home due to Covid restrictions, but some are resisting pressure to return to the office. Is this because when they are at home they can smoke whenever they like? Has this been studied?

The AIHW publish regular reports of the prevalence of smoking. The 2021 report shows that 11.6 per cent of adults smoked daily in 2019, and this had decreased from 25 per cent in 1991.

Rates were even higher before that. After the Second World War, over 70 per cent of males and about 25 per cent of females smoked. The rate for men dropped virtually in a straight line to the present levels. Half of them managed to stop smoking before the bad effects were known and without any help from counselling or medication. The rate at which women smoked increased after WWII, peaking at about 33 per cent in the mid-1970s. If you watch movies from the latter half of the twentieth century, smoking seems to be ubiquitous. It was seen to be 'cool'. The mortality rate for lung cancer peaked in men in the early 1980s and for women in about 2010, in each case a lag of about thirty-five years from the peak consumption. A similar lag is found in other diseases linked to smoking.

The AIHW report also showed that the age group with the highest numbers of smokers is now 40–49 in men and 50–59 in women. Pleasingly, the number of young people (18–24) who smoke is low at 8.5 per cent for women and 10 per cent for men. Breakdown by other demographic factors shows that the highest proportion of smokers are found among those from low socio-economic areas, remote and very remote locations, unemployed, and people unable to work. That particular report does not break down the numbers by First Nations status, but another of their reports, quoted earlier, stated that 41.4 per cent of First Nations people smoke, compared with 14.4 per cent of non-Indigenous people.

A 2015 study showed that the life expectancy among smokers is ten years less than the general population. If the average life expectancy is now 80, then for non-smokers it is about 82 and for smokers 72. This assumes a smoking rate of 20 per cent which was the case around the year 2000.

If the gap between First Nations and non-Indigenous people is 15 years, then their life expectancy is about 65. If 40 per cent of First Nations people smoke, then the life expectancy of smokers is about 61 and non-smokers 71. In other words, about 40 per cent of the gap is due to smoking.

*Quitting Smoking*

It is therefore vital that the smoking rates among First Nations people be reduced to zero. With alcohol, there is debate about whether there might be some benefit to drinking a glass of red wine daily. The current thinking is that doing this may reduce the risk of cardiovascular disease, but it will not reduce your cancer risk and may increase it. With tobacco smoking, there is no debate – the goal must be zero consumption.

The government has been trying to help people stop smoking for decades. The main tools have been increasing the tax on cigarettes, restricting the places where people can smoke, and subsidising medication to assist quitters. Nicotine replacement therapy was introduced in 1984 in the form of chewing gum. Initially, it was only available as a prescription drug, but this restriction was gradually eased. Also, other forms of delivery were used including patches, nasal spray, and lozenges.

Two drugs have been developed to help smokers quit. The first was bupropion, marketed with the name Zyban. Originally, it was developed as an antidepressant but found to help with smoking cessation and introduced in 1997. Varenicline (Champix), which has greater efficacy, was introduced in 2006.

Electronic cigarettes or e-cigarettes were developed in the 2000s and were originally designed to help smokers quit smoking. They contain nicotine which satisfies the smoker's addiction to cigarettes but replaces it with addiction to e-cigarettes, now called vaping. Unfortunately, now they have created a new generation addicted to nicotine. What is worse is that vaping has been found to be unsafe. The number of research studies which confirm this is rapidly increasing. Vaping has been shown to increase the risk of heart attack and stroke. Many of the chemicals present in vapours damage DNA, and this will lead to an increased risk of cancer.

## Other Drugs

There are, of course, a huge number of other drugs which can be used recreationally, and they almost invariably cause social problems. They include cannabis (in marijuana), opiates, cocaine, amphetamines, methamphetamine (crystal meth or ice), MDMA (ecstasy), LSD, gamma hydroxybutyrate (GHB), and tranquilisers. Opiates are some of the oldest known drugs and are very good painkillers and so are legally prescribed by doctors. They are ideal for use for short-term pain, for example, after an injury or heart attack. For long-term use, they are normally only prescribed for patients with cancer; but about ten years ago, there was a push by American pharmaceutical manufacturers to prescribe them for other problems such as back pain, and this has resulted in huge numbers of people in the USA getting addicted to

 CHRIS GILFORD

them, to the extent that it is now reducing the average life expectancy. Fortunately, the problem is not nearly as bad over here. One problem is that some patients are saying that they need higher doses and then selling their excess supply to people for recreational purposes. Similarly, tranquilisers, usually members of the group known as benzodiazepines, are very good at alleviating anxiety but have huge potential for addiction. They can also cause some short-term memory loss, so one of the more powerful ones, flunitrazepam, is used as a date rape drug.

I am only going to discuss two drugs here, cannabis and amphetamine, as these are the ones that are causing most problems in First Nations communities.

## Cannabis

*Cannabis* is a genus of flowering plants in the family *Cannabaceae*. It is widely accepted as being native to and originating from Central and South Asia. The plant is also known as hemp and, with this name, has been grown for industrial hemp as it was one of the first plants to be spun into a usable fibre. The fibre is processed from the stems of the plants. It is used as a building material, including insulation, and can be combined with plaster as in fibre cement. Hemp oil can be used as a varnish on wood and hemp leaves as vegetables and as juice. Industrial hemp products are made from cannabis plants selected to produce an abundance of fibre and minimal amounts of psychoactive constituents.

Cannabis plants produce scores of chemicals called cannabinoids, one of which, tetrahydrocannabinol (THC), has psychoactive effects when consumed. Cannabinoids are secreted by hairs 'pistils' and resin glands 'trichomes' that occur most abundantly on the flowers and adjacent leaves of female plants. Some strains have been selectively bred to produce a maximum of THC, the strength of which is enhanced by curing the fruits. These are harvested and dried, and the buds are then known as marijuana, but a resin called hashish can also be produced. As a drug, it usually comes in the form of dried infructescences ('buds' or 'marijuana'), resin (hashish), or various extracts collectively known as hashish oil. During the twentieth century, it became illegal in most of the world to cultivate or possess cannabis for sale and even sometimes for personal use.

Cannabis users claim that it is harmless, but unfortunately, it can be associated with psychosis in some people, and this can be quite severe. It is unclear whether the cannabis causes the psychosis or whether the psychosis makes people want to take up cannabis smoking.

*Medicinal Cannabis*

Some of the drugs used today have their origins as herbal medicines. The most notable ones are morphine and its derivatives as painkillers, cocaine as a local anaesthetic, and digoxin, obtained from the foxglove as a medicine for heart disease. There are numerous studies which demonstrate their effects. Practitioners who practise herbal medicine use a number of herbal treatments. Many of them have been subjected to controlled trials. They include echinacea and St John's Wort, but cannabis was rarely used in traditional herbal medicine.

Cannabis has been promoted by a large number of people as having a number of therapeutic benefits, particularly in the relief of pain and nausea. There are two problems here. Firstly, most drugs that we use today have been fully investigated by biochemists who can state exactly what their mode of action is, for example, how they bind with receptor sites in the body or how they interrupt particular biochemical pathways. This information is lacking for cannabis.

Secondly, controlled trials have failed to show that it has a therapeutic effect in any condition apart possibly from the treatment of some rare types of childhood epilepsy. The problem is with trying to have a controlled trial. Normally, any drug is compared to a placebo, a substance like a sugar pill which has no active ingredient. Neither the subject nor the experimenter knows whether the subject has received the active drug; hence, this is called a double-blind trial. The problem with cannabis derivatives is that subjects will know from the psychological effects whether they have received the active drug. It is important to do controlled trials because about 30 per cent of the effect of any drug is a placebo effect.

                    CHRIS GILFORD

My own feeling is that if it did have any definite therapeutic effect, this would have been known about for decades or centuries.

## Methamphetamine

Amphetamine and methamphetamine are derived from ephedrine, which has been a component of traditional Chinese medicine for over 2,000 years. Ephedrine is obtained from the plant *Ephedra sinica*, which is native to China, Mongolia, and eastern Russia. About 30,000 tons of the plant are processed every year. Ephedrine is a central nervous system stimulant that can be used to prevent low blood pressure during anaesthesia and for asthma, narcolepsy (excessive sleeping), obesity, and nasal congestion. It is on the WHO's list of essential medicines, even though there are better drugs for all conditions for which it is indicated.

Amphetamine was first synthesized from ephedrine in 1887, and methamphetamine followed in 1893, but it was not until 1935 that the psychological effects were discovered; the reported effects were 'a sense of well being and a feeling of exhilaration' and 'lessened fatigue in reaction to work'. During the Second World War, both sides gave the drugs to their troops for their stimulant and performance-enhancing effects. During the 1950s and 1960s, they were taken by truck drivers to enable them to stay awake. Recreational use started after that, and governments around the world started to restrict their use.

Methamphetamine hydrochloride (crystal meth or ice) is a volatile derivative of methamphetamine which can be vapourised by heat which enables it to be inhaled or smoked from glass pipes. Australia now has the highest methamphetamine addiction rate in the world, with double the rate found in other Western countries, including the UK, USA, NZ, Sweden, and France, according to an article in the *Economist* in 2017.

After being inhaled, ice gives the user pleasurable sensations – an intense 'rush' that can make a person feel confident and energetic. They may get a raised heartbeat and sex drive, and the effects can last up to about twelve hours. It is easy to see how it can become addictive. There are, though, some downsides. They may get itching and scratching or a dry mouth and may grind their teeth or sweat excessively, which are just seen as side effects.

However, they may get some more serious psychiatric problems, particularly with repeated use. Initially, they can get strange thoughts, memory loss, and difficulty sleeping, but it can progress to paranoid delusions, hallucinations, and aggressive or violent behaviour. If they continue to use ice, they can develop physical problems as their whole life revolves round trying to get more of the ice as they try and avoid the unpleasant features of withdrawal.

More and more studies are being carried out to investigate the risks associated with using methamphetamine and other drugs. A new one in the *European Heart Journal* found that chronic use of cannabis, cocaine, methamphetamine, and opiates all increased the risk of atrial fibrillation, a type of irregular heartbeat which can cause strokes.

## Social Status and Employment

Michael Marmot is an epidemiologist based in London who has analysed numerous studies on the social determinants of health and written two books on the subject – *The Health Gap* and *Status Syndrome*. He has found a clear gradient linking mortality with characteristics such as social status, education, and wealth. An increase in any of these variables was associated with greater life expectancy. He initially worked on studies of British civil servants but found exactly the same results from numerous different studies around the world.

Before these studies were reported in the 1980s, it was generally believed (and taught) by medical practitioners that heart attacks, stomach ulcers, and some other medical conditions were mainly a problem with middle-class people, such as managers, since they were the ones under the most stress. All the studies showed the complete opposite. The lower down someone is in the hierarchy, the more likely they are to have a heart attack, stomach ulcer, or virtually any other illness.

It is easy to see how increased wealth reduces mortality. You own your home so you don't have to worry about rent or that you might be thrown out. The house is not overcrowded, there is good sanitation, you don't have to worry about having money for food, heating, or medication. You can afford a better diet and private healthcare, so you can get elective surgery done when you want. Similarly, good education means that you can get a better-paid job. You can probably also get a desk job away from the back-breaking and dangerous work at the coalface or on the workshop floor.

But how does your social status fit in with this? Marmot found out that even after adjusting for income, education, and other risk factors, your status or socio-economic position is an important predictor of your health outcome. Marmot argues that this comes from the psychological benefits of 'being in control' of your life.

As an example, Marmot looked at the age at which Oscar winners died, compared with the age of Oscar nominees. The winners' lifespans were on average four years longer than the nominees. This may not sound much but is more than many other risk factors. It happens because of the extra control they have on their lives. They can choose what movies they make, they can tell a director how they want a scene played, and they can have a tantrum whenever they want.

Coming back to more mundane occupations, the higher you are in an organisation, the more freedom you have. You do not have to ask permission to have family time, you do not have to explain your expenses, and you rarely have to think about job security. On the other hand, near the bottom of the hierarchy, you often have huge difficulty balancing the demands of your job and your responsibilities to your family, which can cause huge stress at home.

There are often stories in the media about people who have left the rat race and either gone for a sea change or started their own business. The number doing this has increased in the last few decades, and I think we will see the participants enjoying health benefits.

**Housing**

Poor housing is known to be associated with poor health, being named specifically in the section on rheumatic fever, but how did the housing get to be poor? In the past, it might have been built as a low-cost temporary structure, but the houses constructed in First Nations communities in the last fifty years are often constructed of concrete blocks so they can withstand tropical cyclones. In contrast, the houses for hospital staff on Mornington Island are constructed of weatherboard on a wooden frame. Overcrowding is one reason. Most of the houses in Mornington Island are in the range 120–180 sq. metres, and have three to four bedrooms. This should be adequate for most families, and in fact, the houses are larger than many in Cairns, other than in the wealthy suburbs. The size becomes a problem if a family has six or more children, which is not uncommon, or if it contains a blended family or even two families. Some houses have as many as a dozen people listed as living in one house. Another issue is that there are a number of people who would be described as being 'of no fixed abode' and exist by 'couch surfing' between various houses in the community.

The second problem is that the houses have been allowed to deteriorate. This can start as a simple problem of them just not being cleaned or that any defects either are not reported to the owner or are not acted on. The situation should be no different from that in the private rental market anywhere else in Australia. There are duties for both parties. The First Nations tenants should keep the houses clean, ensure that the number of occupants is within the agreed capacity, and report any defects. They should keep the garden tidy and dispose of any rubbish. The landlords, who may be a government body or a community organisation, must ensure that the houses are safe and adequately maintained and make sure that any defects, particularly electrical or plumbing, are repaired promptly.

An AIHW report in 2018 looked at the access to functional housing. It found that 33 per cent of First Nations households were living in houses with major structural problems. The rate showed the usual gradation of problems from major cities to very remote areas, where it was 50 per cent. In the latter case, 17 per cent had major cracks in walls/floors, 16 per cent had walls or windows not straight, 20 per cent had major plumbing defects, and 13 per cent had major electrical defects.

There are four major features of a dwelling that are important for

  CHRIS GILFORD

health. The proportion of houses in very remote areas with deficiencies were storing/preparing food (27 per cent), washing clothes/bedding (20 per cent), washing people (11 per cent), and sewerage facilities (8 per cent).

So why have they deteriorated? The possible factors include:

- normal wear and tear, which has accelerated due to the harsh environment – extreme heat and rainfall;
- poor construction, such as rain leaks from poorly constructed joints;
- failure to carry out routine maintenance, such as not checking for termite damage;
- failure to carry out timely repairs, which could lead to the tenants trying to make amateur repairs, with their inherent dangers;
- vandalism can be an issue. I mentioned this earlier, saying that some people vent their anger by punching the wall rather than their partner, which from the health point of view is preferable. However, they may, in fact, have done some damage to the building itself.

Whatever the cause, the owners of the building should be ensuring that they are fit for purpose. I appreciate that this may present challenges in very remote areas. If, for example, there are no tradies, especially plumbers or electricians, in the community, they have to be flown in from a nearby town. However, repairs should not be delayed as a form of punishment for not paying the rent on time or vandalising the property.

Overcrowding is the second risk factor. When I left Mornington Island in 2017, the First Nations population was about 1,200, and there were about 220 houses on the island that were inhabited by First Nations people. This makes an average of 5.5 people per dwelling. The average dwelling had three bedrooms. However, there was a wide variation in the number of people per household. Some dwellings only had a single occupant, whereas at the other extreme, there were several with ten or more inhabitants. Therefore, to bring the occupancy down to an average of four per house and allowing for the fact that there will be some dwellings with only one or two inhabitants, around a hundred new houses are needed.

It is very expensive to build in Mornington Island. All the construction materials need to be brought to the island on a barge. There is already a construction camp, an area of two hectares with twenty to thirty 'dongas' or cabins. Construction workers are flown in like mine workers on a fly-in-fly-out basis. A typical three-bedroom, one-bathroom home costs about a million dollars to build. So what would be the result of spending $100 million on housing on Mornington Island over, say, five years? Mornington Island would be seen as a desirable place to live, and so the population would increase. It could easily go up by a hundred and so require another twenty houses.

This calculation is only for Mornington Island. There are probably a hundred other communities that require a similar level of investment.

It is not just the number of people living in each house that is the problem. The general level of cleanliness in the house is a problem. I have been in houses in Mornington Island and Normanton that are disgustingly dirty. I have also been in houses inhabited by non-Indigenous people that are disgustingly dirty. This really is important in the prevention of RHD as where there is dirt, there are bacteria which can lead to RHD. People who live in a house of ten people and only one bathroom can probably not shower or change their clothes every day. This is particularly a problem in the tropics when temperatures are in the thirties every day for most of the year, it is humid, and everyone sweats a lot.

If you rent a house anywhere else in Australia, then every few months you have a 'rent inspection', in which the agent will come round and see that the house is clean and being looked after. Why doesn't the same apply in First Nations communities?

**Poverty**

Poverty appears to be worse in First Nations communities. However, the income of an First Nations family should theoretically be the same as



CHRIS GILFORD

the income of a non-Indigenous family living in the same circumstances. There is no racial discrimination in Centrelink benefits or pay scales for those with a job. There is theoretically no gender discrimination either, but female earnings are always less than male. Unemployment is high in First Nations communities largely because of the lack of employment opportunities. Food prices in remote communities are much higher than in major cities.

Another factor is that many First Nations people live off the grid. They do not have a permanent home but move around different houses in the community, usually those of family members or friends. They may therefore have difficulties with their registration with Centrelink, and their benefits may be stopped. Further, those who are unemployed need to try and obtain jobs, or show proof that they have tried, to continue to receive benefits. This is difficult when there are probably few opportunities for work.

Alcohol was banned in Mornington Island, resulting in the home-brewing cottage industry. Those who manufacture it charge an excessive amount, around $250 for ten litres of a brew that is 10–15 per cent alcohol, like a fortified wine. This is often the first thing that someone buys when they do get a payment, rather than food or rent.

Many First Nations people gamble. There are, of course, no casinos or poker machines in First Nations communities. The gambling occurs in people's homes by playing simple card games. About a dozen people put money in a pot, and then cards are drawn, with the winner taking the pot, usually several hundred dollars.

Transport is more expensive in remote communities. People do need to go to a major centre at times for shopping or business matters. Return journeys are often 1,000 km, so that is $150–200 on fuel, plus the cost of staying overnight at the major centre. Commercial flights in the regions are very expensive, many times costlier than flights between Sydney and Brisbane or Melbourne. Flights from Cairns to Mornington Island (740 km) often cost more than flights from Cairns to Perth (5,000 km via Brisbane).

Wealth is the opposite of poverty. One of the features of First Nations culture is the concept of community ownership of property, something no doubt that Marx and Engels would approve of. The Australian Antarctic bases operate on a similar principle – if you want anything from the shop/store, it is all free; you just take it – and I imagine the same is true on the International Space Station. Unsurprisingly, the American Antarctic bases operate on a capitalist principle, so you have to pay for your personal food and supplies. First Nations people have learned to transition and understand how this works. However, many of them retain the idea that if someone is earning a lot of money, then they should let the whole family share in their wealth. The size of the family may then increase substantially, beyond what will normally be described as an extended family. The most famous First Nations painter was apparently supporting about 350 'relatives' when he died in 1959.

The idea that someone who makes a lot of money should share it out is not confined to First Nations culture. Most people who buy lottery tickets tick the 'no publicity' box to avoid being approached for donations. Some keep their win completely secret, not even telling close relatives about it.

Wealth does increase life expectancy and other health indices, but it is not necessarily the amount you have but how you spend it. An obvious example is people who spend a fortune on recreational drugs.

First Nations people need to reject the idea that giving money away will help the recipients. It may help their short-term problems but will do nothing to increase their social status, which is a more important predictor of life expectancy. Helping someone get a job, or a better job, is a much better way to assist them.

## Footwear

Most people like the idea of walking barefoot on the beach, feeling the sand between their toes. In the distant past, everyone walked barefoot all the time because there were no shoes. The soles of their feet became thicker and harder so they could not be penetrated by sharp thorns, spines, or shells. Despite this, there is an additional risk to walking barefoot. Hookworm is a parasitic worm that may be found in soil so can be picked up by walking barefoot. The larvae can penetrate the skin of the foot, and from there, it travels to the intestine. It can cause gastrointestinal symptoms, but it also causes blood loss, leading to anaemia. It is a major cause of anaemia in First Nations people.

*Homo sapiens* has created additional hazards to walking barefoot such as glass and metal fragments on the ground. They can cause cuts and contusions to the feet. There is a risk of getting infected, and this is much worse in diabetics. People with diabetes often lose sensation in their feet, so they are unable to feel any injury that they may get. They also have a poorer blood supply to the feet, which slows down the healing process and makes infection more likely. Unfortunately, this can result in gangrene for which the only treatment is amputation.

The best treatment for foot problems is prevention, which means wearing shoes, particularly for diabetics, and for checking the feet daily and getting any cuts treated properly.

**Remoteness**

In the first chapter, analysis of the performance of the Closing the Gap programme, taken from the 2020 report, showed that remoteness was a major factor in determining almost all the health and educational indicators. Remoteness was not discussed as a factor in child mortality, but it is notable that the rate is highest in the NT.

Australia is the sixth largest country in the world by area. Its population is comparatively small, and therefore, the density of population is almost the lowest among the 193 countries that are members of the United Nations; only Namibia and Mongolia are lower. Australia is also one of the more urbanised countries with about 86 per cent of us living in urban areas.

The Australian Bureau of Statistics divides the country up by remoteness with five labels: major cities, inner and outer regional, and remote and very remote, and these can be seen on the following 2016 map.

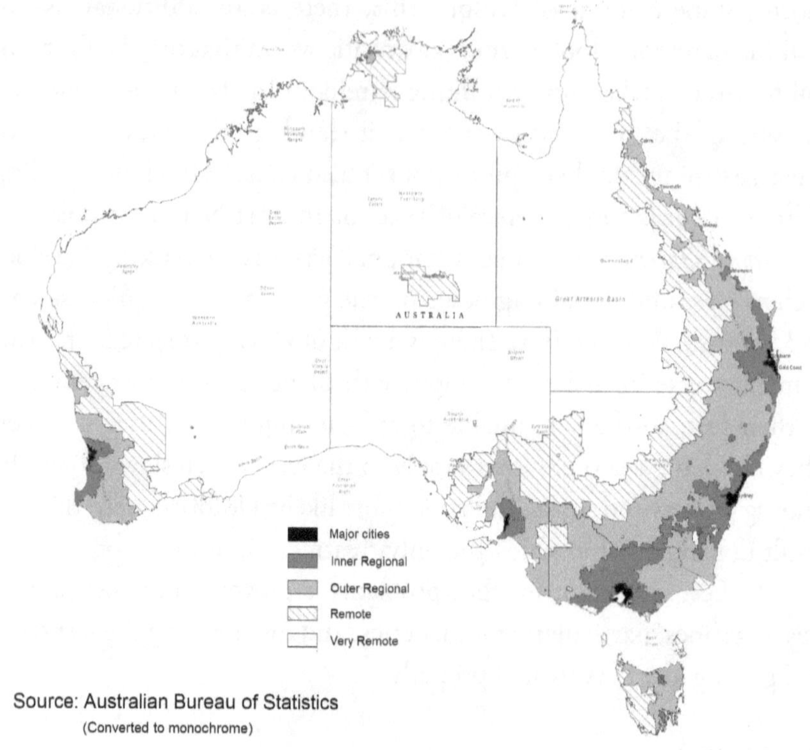


Figure 14: Remoteness map

The AIHW produces a biennial report on the health of Australian people. There are slightly different topics in each edition. In 2018, they looked at the impact of remoteness using data from the 2011 census. They deduced that the proportion of people living in these areas was as follows:

|  | Major cities | Inner regional | Outer regional | Remote | Very remote |
|---|---|---|---|---|---|
| First Nations | 35% | 22% | 22.0% | 7.7% | 14.0% |
| Non-Indigenous | 71% | 18% | 8.7% | 1.2% | 0.5% |

Table 16: Proportion of people by remoteness



CHRIS GILFORD

These figures may be misleading. The total population was then 21,507,717, of whom 548,369 were First Nations. Therefore, the actual numbers in each category were (thousands) as follows:

| | Major cities | Inner regional | Outer regional | Remote | Very remote |
|---|---|---|---|---|---|
| First Nations | 192 | 121 | 121 | 42 | 77 |
| Non-Indigenous | 14,881 | 3.773 | 1,823 | 252 | 105 |
| % First Nations | 1.27 | 3.1 | 6.2 | 14.4 | 42.3 |

Table 17: Numbers of people by remoteness (thousands)

All the lifestyle risk factors (smoking, overweight, inadequate exercise, and risky alcohol consumption) increased moving from major cities to remote areas. This is true also for non-Indigenous people, who outnumber First Nations people in all towns, including remote and very remote ones but not in First Nations communities. Chronic conditions, particularly diabetes, also increased in the same way.

Statisticians talk about the burden of disease, expressed as disability-adjusted life years (DALYs), which is a measure of the health impact of disease on a population in a given year, both from dying and living with disease and injury. Again, this increases progressively from major cities to very remote.

The median age of death, which is easier to calculate than life expectancy, decreased gradually from eighty-two in major cities to sixty-seven in very remote.

As regards access to healthcare, the number of healthcare professionals per head of population decreases between major cities and remote areas. The ratio (no. in major cities to no. in remote or very remote) was 3.5 for psychologists, 2.6 for dentists, and 1.6 for pharmacists. For medical specialists, the figure was 4.6, but this is not surprising since some like cardiothoracic surgeons never set foot outside major cities. On the other hand, for GPs, the figure was actually less than one.

The number of hospitalisations, while virtually the same in major cities and inner and outer regional areas, was considerably higher in remote (20 per cent more) and very remote (80 per cent more) areas. What the report doesn't examine, as far as I could tell, is how much the difference in health outcomes between cities and the bush, is a function of distance and how much due to ethnicity.

There are some medical conditions for which the treatment is time critical. A good example is stroke. If you live in a major city and have a stroke, for example, losing all power in a limb, you call an ambulance and then are rushed through the nearest emergency department to the CT scanner where the diagnosis is made. Most of the time, it will be due to a clot in one of the arteries to your brain; but in about 10 per cent of cases, it is due to a bleed in the brain. If it is a clot, you will be given a clot-busting drug. If this is given within a couple of hours of the onset of the stroke, it should reverse the effects, and you regain much of the use of your arm. However, if it is a bleed, the clot-busting Drug would kill you. So it is imperative you get a CT scan first. So if you are not within an hour's drive from a CT scanner, the treatment choices are limited. CT scanners are usually found in towns of about 10,000 or more. People who live in outer regional areas may have access, but those in remote or very remote areas don't and so have to accept the risk of a lowered standard of care.

The RFDS and other aero-medical transport organisations do an excellent job in bringing a mobile intensive care unit to all parts of Australia, but there are limits to what they can do. The cabin is quite cramped. They are starting to introduce jet aircraft for the longer distances, such as in WA.

First Nations people need to weigh up their desire to live in their traditional lands with their desire for a life that is as long as that for someone living in a city.

# CHAPTER 7

# A Weighty Issue

I WANT TO DEVOTE a chapter to discussing a subject that affects the entire population of Australia, and indeed the rest of the world as well, and show how the cause is exactly the same as the cause of the inequality in health between First Nations people and non-Indigenous. The problem, of course, is obesity. Its importance has been stressed by a new report (November 2022) from Health and Wellbeing Queensland, an agency of the Queensland government.

What do you do if you suddenly feel hungry in the middle of the night? These days, if you live in a city, you literally do not even have to move a finger to get some food, assuming that there is nothing appetising in the fridge. You call out to your smartphone to wake it up. Ask it to contact the nearest twenty-four-hour pizza shop which delivers, arrange payment from your credit card, and sit back and wait. Half an hour later, the doorbell rings, so your smartphone can open the door for the pizza delivery boy or girl; and for a joke, you can ask them to put the first slice in your mouth. The sad thing is that the hunger pangs which woke you up have probably gone away, and you might even have gone back to sleep, but having ordered the pizza, you have a couple of slices anyway.

Going back a few thousand years, life was different. If you were hungry in the middle of the night, it would not be safe to go out in the dark, so you would just lay there and wait until morning. Since then, one of the key driving forces for progress has been to make it easier to eat, and another is to make it easier to travel, and both have had a negative impact on people's health.

Up to 10,000 years ago, everyone was a hunter-gatherer. If you were hungry, then you had limited choices. Either you went on a walk or jog to chase after a wild animal which you would try and kill by throwing a spear at it or you would go for a long walk and try and gather fruit, nuts, or seeds. Then in the fertile crescent of the Middle East, some plants that could be cultivated were discovered, and others found that there were some large mammals which could be domesticated. The increased abundance of food meant that no longer did the whole settlement have to contribute to the production of food, and so a significant portion of the labour force could then, for example, construct buildings.

The yield from crops gradually improved over the next few thousand years as did the ability to transport the food. Various methods were devised to prolong the storage life of food such as pickling food or using salt. However, the next major advance was the invention of the refrigerator. It was first used on a commercial scale in ships in the 1880s and enabled frozen meat to be exported from New Zealand to Europe. Refrigeration plants slowly decreased in size, and domestic refrigerators became available early in the twentieth century. The motor car and telephone also became widespread over the next few decades.

Food itself has also changed. We eat more processed foods, and these contain large amounts of fat and sugar. Food has now become tastier to eat. Perhaps TV cooking shows and celebrity chefs are contributing to the obesity problem. Finally, the smartphone enabled the scenario I presented earlier.

It has been this dramatic change in the opportunity to satisfy one's hunger that has been a major contribution to obesity. Ten thousand years ago, it required a real effort to obtain food, so we needed the hunger stimulus as motivation. These days, we can satisfy our hunger without any expenditure of effort.

## How Is 'Obesity' Defined?

This was discussed in chapter 5, but here it is again. The standard measure is the body mass index, which is calculated by dividing your weight (in kilograms) by the square of your height (in metres). The commonest classification of your body shape was given earlier:

| BMI | <20 | 20–25 | 25–30 | 30–35 | >35 |
|---|---|---|---|---|---|
| | Underweight | Healthy weight | Overweight | Obese | Morbidly obese |

Table 6: BMI and weight categories

The BMI has been getting increasing criticism over the past few years. One article even described it as being 'racist' because it was originally applied to European men. How can a mathematical formula be racist? The fact that different ethnic groups might have different ideal ranges of BMI does not make it racist either.

The BMI was originally devised in the 1830s for western European men. The instigator was Adolphe Quetelet, a Belgian statistician who was interested in defining obesity for residents of his country. Few paid attention to it until the 1970s, when obesity began to be a problem. There has been little research into BMI and ethnicity until recently. The chapter on diabetes discussed recent papers on this subject. Despite all the criticisms, it is acknowledged that mortality risk increases substantially as BMI increases. There is obviously much more work to be done, but there is nothing yet to dispute the hypothesis that there is an optimal BMI for least mortality, around 25 for white males, with a small increase for people with a BMI of 20 or below and a huge increase for those with a BMI over 30. The figures suggest that the optimal BMI is lower in many races compared with whites.

Limited data from the WHO would support this for Asia-Pacific people since they classify those with BMIs of <18.5 as underweight, 18.5–22.9 as normal, 23–24.9 as overweight, and >25 as obese.

The other common indicators use the waist measurement as a parameter. However, some just use the waist measurement, some use the waist/hip ratio, and others use the waist/height ratio. It is true that the waist measurement is important as fat around the belly, as tends to happen to men who get overweight, is more dangerous than fat on the buttocks and thighs, as tends to happen to women. The problem is the way the waist is measured as there is a big potential for observer error. In people who are slim and particularly women, the waist is easy to identify as it is the narrowest part of the torso. However, for assessment of obesity, the standard measurement is taken at the level of the umbilicus, and this may be quite a lot bigger than their trouser measurement.

The waist/hip ratio is used to categorise weight as follows:

| WHR Women | <0.8 | 0.80–0.84 | >0.85 |
|---|---|---|---|
| WHR Men | <0.9 | 0.90–0.99 | >1.00 |
|  | Normal | Overweight | Obese |

Table 18: WHR and weight categories

I have not been able to find a similar classification for non-European people. Experts argue about which classification is more important. This is unfortunate because the message this gives out is that the experts cannot agree about how people's weight should be classified, and so they are all wrong. This is, of course, incorrect. Most people will have the same classification using either method, but a few people may, for example, be at the top of the overweight group in one measure but the bottom of the obese group in the other or vice versa. Nobody who is obese by one measure will be regarded as normal in the other and vice versa.

These indices may seem a bit complicated, and most people would need a calculator to work them out. However, the common question 'What is my ideal weight?' is very easy to answer. If you are 175 cm tall or over, just subtract 100 cm from your height. If you are below 175 cm, you can make a small correction – you can add 1 kg for every 5 cm you are less than 175 cm. This simple calculation gives the weight in kg that coincides with a body mass index of 25 or a little under. So this should be the maximum weight that you should aim for.

One reason for the criticism of the BMI is that professional sportspeople have high BMIs but are very healthy despite this. For example, the New Zealand All Blacks forwards have an average height of 1.91 m and weight of 111.5 kg, which gives them a BMI of 30.5. They are larger than heavyweight boxers. The South Africa Springboks are a little bigger with a BMI of 31.1. They are therefore obese according to the classification above. However, their extra weight is almost all muscle.

The problem for them is that they rarely lose weight when their sports career is over. Their muscle turns gradually to fat, and they then have the health problems of obesity. A few continue to exercise hard and claim that their weight is healthy. This is probably untrue. A recent study of bodybuilders has shown that their mortality is 34 per cent higher than the normal age-matched population according to a study presented at the American Urological Association's 2016 annual meeting. Some of this excess mortality may be due to the use of steroids, but it is likely that their weight itself is a significant factor.

A second group whose BMIs give a false picture of their health risk is pregnant women. When they are nearing full term, they obviously have the baby on board, and the baby may weigh 3.5 to 4 kg. They also have a placenta, and their uterus and blood volume are also larger than normal. Obstetricians recommend that women in the healthy weight range before pregnancy should have an increase in weight of around 14 kg. An average woman of 162 cm weighing 60 kg before pregnancy will see her BMI increase from 23 to 28.

## How Common Is Obesity?

A note on terminology – the incidence of a disease is the number of new cases that are diagnosed every year; the prevalence is the cumulative total of all those who have been diagnosed with it.

AIHW reported on obesity in 2020.

> The problem now is that two thirds of adults in Australia are either overweight or obese. It has become the new normal so it will need a National Strategy to deal with the problem. Otherwise the health consequence will just keep increasing and eventually it will bankrupt the country.

I have taken the data from a 2020 AIHW report and created a new chart which combines the data from children and adults and also First Nations and non-Indigenous. It may appear a bit confusing at first because the data classifies all First Nations people over the age of 55 as that, whereas for older non-Indigenous they are classified as 55–64, 65–74, 75–84, and over 85. It is interesting to note that there is a steady decline of obese people after the age of 74. Either a lot of them died or they lost weight.

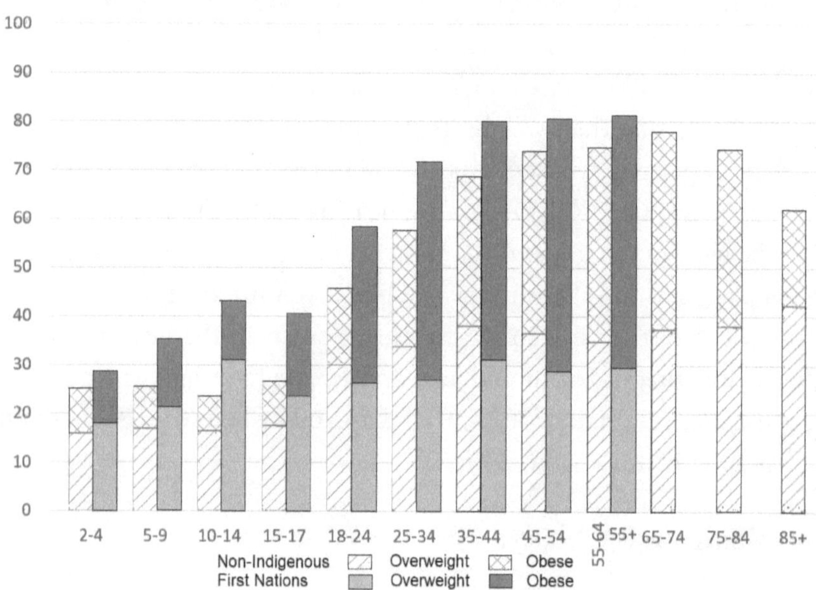


Figure 15: Prevalence of obesity by age and ethnicity

The report also notes how the prevalence is highest in the lower socio-economic areas, thus demonstrating Marmot's observation that the burden of disease falls on those who can least afford to deal with it.

Here are the findings from this report:

In 2017–18, 38 per cent of adults in the lowest socio-economic areas were obese, compared with 24 per cent in the highest. Two in three (67 per cent) adults were overweight or obese in 2017-18: 36 per cent were overweight but not obese, and 31 per cent were obese. Australia had the sixth highest proportion of overweight or obese people aged 15+ among twenty-two OECD member countries. In 2019, 60 per cent of men and 66 per cent of women in 2017–18 had a waist circumference that indicated a high risk of metabolic complications.

Here are some international comparisons:

| Country | Obesity % | Average BMI | | | Diabetes |
|---|---|---|---|---|---|
| | | Male & Female | Male | Female | Rate % |
| Tonga | 48.2 | 31.9 | 30.4 | 33.5 | 15.0 |
| United States of America | 36.2 | 28.5 | 28.5 | 28.5 | 10.7 |
| New Zealand | 30.8 | 25.4 | 25.9 | 25.0 | 6.2 |
| Canada | 29.4 | 27.2 | 27.6 | 26.8 | 7.7 |
| Australia | 29.0 | 27.2 | 27.6 | 26.8 | 6.4 |
| United Kingdom | 27.8 | 27.3 | 27.5 | 27.1 | 6.3 |
| Indonesia | 6.9 | 23.9 | 22.4 | 23.4 | 10.6 |
| China | 6.2 | 23.9 | 24.2 | 23.6 | 10.6 |
| India | 3.9 | 21.9 | 21.8 | 22.1 | 9.6 |

Table 19: Prevalence of obesity by country

The nine countries with the highest prevalence of obesity and diabetes are all Melanesian and Polynesian. The next group are Arab states including Saudi Arabia, Jordan, and Libya.

It is interesting that Australia, Canada, New Zealand, and the UK have comparatively low rates of diabetes, given their high rate of obesity, whereas China, India, and Indonesia have increased prevalence of diabetes despite lower rates of obesity. I think that this shows further proof that the Western diet is to blame for the high rates of obesity elsewhere.

This graph below shows how the problem continues to get worse even though there has been enormous publicity on the subject.

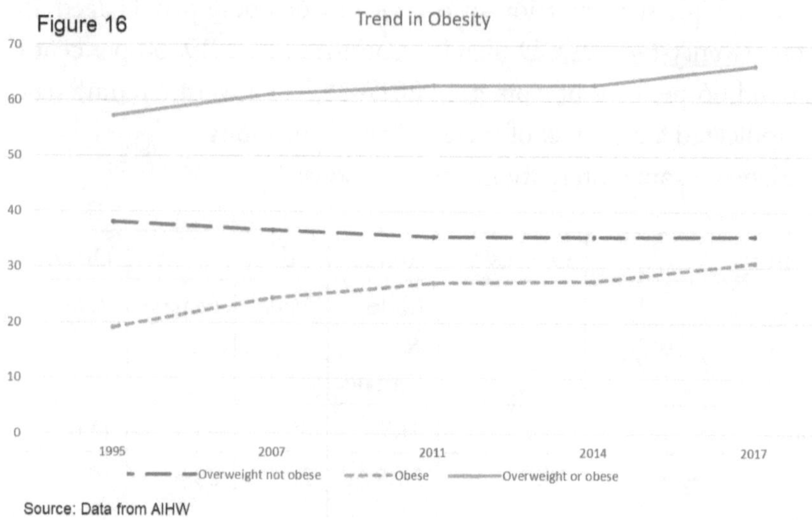


Figure 16: Trend in obesity

## Causes

*Eating Too Much*

Our bodies evolved to be efficient at utilising the food that we eat. Most of the stuff that we eat gets absorbed in the small intestine. There are some exceptions. For example, we cannot break down cellulose, the complex carbohydrate found in many plants, including grass. Cows evolved by creating extra stomachs which contain bacteria which assist in digesting cellulose. We have learned that there is no point in eating grass, but we do have to eat other fibre, which we cannot digest, because it keeps our gut healthy.

Earlier, I said that every day the average man eats food containing about 3,000 calories (12,500 kJ), but his body only requires about 2,400 calories (10,000 kJ), assuming that he is reasonably active. So what happens to the extra calories? They get stored as fat. The other storage compound that the body uses is glycogen. This is a complex carbohydrate found mainly in the liver. As it is a carbohydrate, it easily converts into and from glucose. Sportspeople use this process. Before they exercise, they eat complex carbohydrates, which are absorbed as



CHRIS GILFORD

glucose and get stored as glycogen. During the second hour of their race or match, they convert it back to glucose, so it can be used by their muscles. Fat is an efficient substance for long-term storage. Gram for gram, it can store twice as much energy as carbohydrates.

So if you eat too much, you store what you don't need as fat. This is simple science – there is nowhere else for it to go. Your body does this because we evolved from hunter-gatherers. Their food supply was variable. The tribe might get lucky and kill a large animal which would feed all of them for a few days, but it might be a week before they get another good meal. They need a mechanism to supply nutrients to supplement their subsistence diet of seeds and berries.

Men tend to store their excess fat around the belly, often called middle-aged spread or a beer gut. Women tend to put it on around their buttocks and thighs. However, when they go through menopause, it tends to shift to the belly. Fat around the belly is a particularly bad predictor of heart disease.

There has been debate in the medical literature for half a century about whether fats or carbohydrates are more to blame in causing weight gain and poor health. British researchers tended to favour carbohydrates, especially refined sugar, as being more important, whereas American researchers favoured fats. The Americans were influenced by the big sugar corporations who heavily funded research to show how bad fats were. However, in recent years, the pendulum has swung the other way, and now sugar is generally considered to be the greater evil. This difference in opinion is, like the situation with BMI versus waist-hip ratio, is counterproductive. It gives the message that if experts cannot decide which is bad, maybe neither is.

The truth is that both fats and carbohydrates are bad for you in excess. Eating too much is the major cause of obesity, so what are the others? The commonest are lack of physical exercise, genetics, and medical reasons.

*Lack of Physical Exercise*

Exercise is really good for your overall health, but it rarely reduces weight on its own. You have to do an enormous amount of exercise to counteract the calories from overeating. In fact, if you suddenly start exercising seriously, you may find that you actually put on weight since muscle weighs more than fat. This was discussed in the previous chapter.

*Genetics*

Genetics research has really taken off in the last twenty years, thanks to the human genome project, and scientists are discovering that genes play an enormous role in our health. An article in the *Lancet* reported that they had identified over 200 genes which had an effect on the way our bodies process food. This does help explain why some people can eat huge amounts and not put weight on, whereas others cannot, but whether it may help create effective treatments is debatable. I suspect that it will be decades before any are available, and they are likely to be very expensive.

*Medical Reasons*

Medical conditions are often blamed for weight gain, and hypothyroidism is the one most likely mentioned. Yes, the thyroid hormone does regulate the body's metabolism, and a deficiency of thyroid hormone dose lead to weight gain. However, once the condition is treated, your metabolism should return to normal levels.

Cushing's syndrome is caused by excess of a hormone (ACTH) secreted by the pituitary gland, causing excessive secretion of cortisone by the adrenal glands. Again, this leads to weight gain, but this should be reversed when the underlying condition has been treated.

Steroids like prednisone are used to treat a variety of conditions including asthma and some forms of arthritis. They also cause weight gain, particularly if the dose is high. It is important for the patient to adjust their diet to avoid weight gain since this will exacerbate the asthma or arthritis.

Prader-Willi syndrome is a rare genetic disorder, affecting about 1 in 20,000 at birth. There are a number of symptoms and signs, but the important one here is uncontrollable hunger, to the extent that parents have to use locks on all food storage places including refrigerators. If they eat as much as they want to, obesity and diabetes are inevitable.

*Psychological Reasons*

This is an emerging area in people who are morbidly obese as there is a chicken-and-egg problem. Does obesity cause psychological problems, or is it the other way round?

**What Problems Does Obesity Cause?**

People who are overweight or obese, compared with those with healthy weight, are at increased risk for many serious diseases and health conditions. These include:

- all causes of death (mortality);
- high blood pressure (hypertension);
- high LDL cholesterol, low HDL cholesterol, or high levels of triglycerides (dyslipidemia);
- type 2 diabetes;
- coronary heart disease;
- stroke;
- gall bladder disease;
- osteoarthritis (a breakdown of cartilage and bone within a joint);
- sleep apnoea and breathing problems;
- many types of cancer;
- low quality of life;
- mental illness such as clinical depression, anxiety, and other mental disorders;
- body pain and difficulty with physical functioning.

A new one that has been added is cognitive function, which is similar to intelligence. A 2022 paper in the *Journal of the American Medical Association* found that higher body fat percentage and visceral adipose tissue were associated with more cardiovascular risk factors, vascular brain injuries, and lower cognitive scores.

## Treatment of Being Overweight or Obese

To put it most simply, there are absolutely no effective treatments available. There is no magic pill or operation that will allow you to eat whatever you like and lose weight or not put it on in the first place. The only way of losing weight is to reduce your food intake. It is simple science. If you eat more than your body needs, the excess food will be converted into fat and get stored somewhere on your body. There is nowhere else for it to go. Your body was programmed tens of thousands of years ago to store fat for a rainy day or more likely for the period near the end of the dry season when all the waterholes have dried up and the animals that you normally hunt have disappeared.

One of the problems with eating and people's weight is that there can be a wide variation in people's metabolism, in particular the BMR, the basal metabolic rate, the amount of food they need just to stay alive without even moving. This is like the amount of fuel a car needs when it is idling at a red traffic light.

Many people believe that exercise helps you lose weight or rather that the only reason that they cannot lose weight is that they are unable to exercise due to lack of time or painful knees etc. The truth, however, is somewhat different. There is no doubt that your health will improve if you exercise. This applies to everybody, not just those who are overweight. If you start exercising, you may actually put a little bit of weight on because your muscle mass will increase, and muscle weighs more than fat. You have to do an awful lot of exercise to actually lose weight as a result of the exercise alone. You only lose weight by eating less, but you do need to do some exercise to improve your health. Most people who exercise actually eat a little more as a reward for the exercise.

The only 'treatments' (note the inverted commas) that are used are just gimmicks that try and fool you into eating less than you otherwise would. Various medications have been on the market for the last fifty years, but none do exactly what people want.

Phentermine was developed by the pharmaceutical industry to raise the basal metabolic rate. It is a derivative of amphetamine, otherwise known as speed. It works by reducing hunger so you don't eat as much. It does help people lose weight. Unfortunately, it has some side effects. It has a tendency to keep you awake, so to avoid insomnia, it is taken in the morning. A more serious problem is that when you take it, you tend to lose muscle rather than fat. It is, however, a popular treatment, but there is a myth about its effectiveness. Many people use it and then come back wanting a repeat prescription. They often say that it was very effective and that they lost 10 kg while they were on it. However, I have noticed that when I check their record, the actual weight loss is far less and may even be zero. They have convinced themselves that it worked, presumably to justify its high cost.

There is an assumption that the pharmaceutical companies will be able to make a drug that enables someone to eat as much as they like and not put on weight. As noted in chapter 5, there is a new drug, semaglutide, which was developed to treat diabetes but was found to have the side effect of producing weight loss. There was a trial to assess this, reported in 2021, but there was a catch in its design.

Each participant had to make lifestyle changes. Participants received individual counselling sessions every four weeks to help them adhere to a reduced-calorie diet (500 kcal deficit per day) and increased physical activity (with 150 minutes per week of physical activity, such as walking, encouraged). Both diet and activity were recorded daily in a diary or by use of a smartphone application. The results were initially encouraging. For the first twenty weeks, they lost on average 2 per cent of their starting weight every four weeks. However, after that, the weight loss slowed down and plateaued after sixty weeks at a 16 per cent weight loss. They also found that weight started to climb after the drug was ceased at the end of the trial. There is no data on whether it works in people who do not go on a diet or exercise. I suspect that it doesn't. The drug worked by reducing appetite. In other words, the participants decreased their food intake.

News of the drug spread on social media, and it became very sought after, and many people have been trying to use it for weight loss, to the extent that there is now a worldwide shortage of it. In Australia, it is not indicated for treatment of obesity and so will cost about $130 a month. (For someone with diabetes, it costs a maximum of about $30 a month, but there are strict regulations about who can get the subsidy.)

How useful is this drug? Probably not very. The people who would benefit most are those with a BMI of, say, 35. After a year, they will still be obese and will have to continue taking it, and the long-term benefits and side effects are not known.

Another drug was launched with a different mode of action back in 2006. Orlistat stops you from absorbing fat. If you do eat fat while taking it, the fat stays in your intestines and gets passed out in your faeces. This is actually quite unpleasant since you pass large quantities of very smelly diarrhoea with a lot of wind, and it floats and is difficult to flush away. It will not be much fun in a public toilet. The drug therefore encourages you to greatly reduce the amount of fat you eat, so no more burgers and chips or fried chicken, but this is not what you want, is it?

Various operations have been devised to assist with weight loss. A common one is the laparoscopic adjustable gastric band, commonly called a lap band. It is an inflatable silicone device placed around the top portion of the stomach. It works by slowing the consumption of food and thus reducing the amount of food consumed. Although most patients who have the procedure lose weight, the average weight loss is only half the loss required to get down to the ideal weight. For example, a person who is 180 cm tall, who therefore should get down to 80 kg, and starts at 120 kg only loses on average 20 kg. This is enough to alleviate some of the problems of obesity, but it will not bring their life expectancy up to what it should be. The advantage of the lap band is that no cutting is carried out, and the band can be removed if required.

Gastric sleeve surgery is a more complex procedure in which most (about 85%) of the stomach is removed, leaving only a narrow tube. It does appear to be more effective than the lap band, but the risks are higher, and it is irreversible. The success rate is a little better than lap band, with patients losing about 61 per cent of their excess weight after the procedure. One study noted that 34 per cent of patients who had

had it performed still had a BMI of over 35 five years later, i.e. they were still morbidly obese.

So why does the surgery fail to live up to expectations? Because people continue to eat what they want. For a few weeks after the surgery, they will feel bloated; but gradually, the stomach will adjust, and so they will be able to go back to eating what they always have.

People who take part in eating competitions 'exercise' their stomach so it increases in size, sometimes up to five times normal. This enables them to eat huge quantities of food such as sixty or more hotdogs. This is just what happens when people have bariatric surgery and don't keep to a very strict diet.

So neither medication nor surgery seems to have a good success rate. There are some people who have successfully lost a lot of weight and kept it off. They said that they had a eureka moment when they realised that the only person who could do it was themselves. The only solution that was going to work was for them to modify what they eat and put up with feeling hungry from time to time. Some people use the excuse 'my blood sugar is low' and so have a snack. Far better to get a glucometer (they are not that expensive) and find out what your blood sugar really is. Nine times out of ten, it will be normal.

Those who successfully lost weight found that formal diets do work, but it was easier to just follow sensible rules. The rules that some found easy and effective are listed in appendix 1.

**Normalisation of Obesity**

Statistics show that over half the population of the Western world are now either overweight or obese, and the rate is higher in Australia. This makes people who are within the ideal weight range feel that they are underweight. This is not helped by the way that many writers describe their heroes. They are always tall and usually overweight, with the excuse that it is all muscle.

We can now easily check out the height and weight of celebrities. For example, the actor Tom Hanks is 1.83 m tall, and for his role in the 2000 movie *Castaway*, he slimmed down from 102 kg to 77 kg, so his BMI went down from 30 to 23. The general feeling is now that his weight of over 100 kg is 'normal' and 'healthy', but the science says that it should reduce his life expectancy. However, in the last chapter, I said that the life expectancy of Oscar winners was increased by four years, and he has won two Oscars but not for *Castaway*.

## Dealing with Obesity

Governments around the world are trying to tackle the problem by throwing money at it. Every few months, we hear of a new initiative to tackle the obesity epidemic; and still, it gets worse. The issue is that those who have it do not consider it a problem and resist attempts to discuss it. In some cultures, being overweight is seen as a sign of affluence. Many older Chinese people remember the great famine of the 1960s caused by Mao Zedong when millions died of starvation. They now believe in seeing that their descendants are overweight to give them some help in case a famine ever recurs.

Karumba is a small town in the Gulf of Carpentaria in Far North Queensland. It has a permanent population of about 600, but this swells to over 2,000 every year from Easter to October. Hordes of grey nomads make their annual migration from NSW, Victoria, and South Australia to escape the winter in the South. There are similar scenes all across northern Australia in this period.

They travel in a large 4WDs with a tinny tied on the roof, towing a caravan. The journey to Karumba from the southern states takes about a week, and then they take up residence in one of the caravan parks, in the spot that they reserved the previous year. They spend their time fishing in the gulf, bringing in barramundi, snapper, and grunter. Most of them are couples aged in their sixties and seventies, and a large proportion seem to have a chronic disease, and they are proud of the fact that they are still going strong. They can often be seen around the bar, many of the men leaving their shirts unbuttoned at the top, displaying the scar from their coronary bypass operation as proudly as a digger displaying his medals on Anzac Day. 'Don't worry about me. I've been fixed up' is the unspoken message.

          CHRIS GILFORD

The nearest hospital and doctor to Karumba is at Normanton, 70 km away so when I was based in Normanton, I would drive twice a week to Karumba to hold a clinic there. One particular afternoon, one of the grey nomads came to see me, complaining of pain in his knees. He wanted some painkillers. I asked him a few more questions, looked at his knees, and then asked him to stand on the scales. He was 115 kg and 175 cm tall so a BMI of 37. I then gently suggested to him that perhaps his knees might improve a little if he lost some weight. He then looked me straight in the eye and said, 'I am entitled to be this weight. It is a privilege I have earned.' I should have said that it would be his privilege to put up with excruciating pain while he waited for a knee replacement, but I took the easy way out and gave him some painkillers.

Afterwards, I thought about what he said, which is why I remember it so clearly. It was obviously a line he had used many times before. Equally, obviously, it clearly demonstrated that he thought that his weight was normal, and he had absolutely no idea that it was jeopardising his health.

A 2015 study published in the *Lancet* showed that obesity and extreme obesity can reduce life expectancy by up to eight years and deprive people of as many as nineteen years of healthy living. If the life expectancy is now about 80, this means that, on average, people with obesity can expect to have poor health from the age of 53 before dying at 73. In other words, they won't be able to 'enjoy' their retirement.

More opposition to the idea that obesity is harmful comes from the opposite problem. Anorexia nervosa is a mental illness in which sufferers have a distorted image of their body. They imagine that they are overweight and strive to lose weight by starving themselves. It is estimated to affect 2.9 million people and resulted in about 600 deaths worldwide in 2013. One group at risk of anorexia are fashion models. So some countries – including Italy, Spain, Israel, and France – have enacted legislation on underweight models.

So let us put this into perspective. Those who die from anorexia usually do so at a young age, and so on average, they lose about fifty years of their expected life. So the total loss of years of life due to anorexia is around 30,000 years. So what about obesity? There are estimated to be about 600 million people with obesity, each of which may lose five to ten years of life. So the total loss of years of life due to obesity is more than 3 billion years.

| Problem | Years lost | Preventive legislation |
|---|---|---|
| Anorexia | 30,000 | Yes |
| Obesity | 3,000,000,000 | No |

Table 20: Anorexia and obesity

One major problem with obesity is that people deny that they eat an excessive amount. This has been demonstrated conclusively on the British TV programme *Secret Eaters*, shown on Channel 4 and also seen on Australian TV. In each episode, an overweight couple or family are filmed at home and, wherever they go, recording everything they eat. They are then confronted with the footage showing how much they have eaten and told how many calories they have consumed. They are always amazed at the amount of food consumed. They had obviously given prior consent to being filmed and had no idea beforehand how much they normally eat. It is as though the extra snacks they were taking were done so automatically and did not reach their level of consciousness. I am quite sure that this is a widespread problem.

Most of my obese patients say something similar to 'I only have half a lettuce leaf for lunch, so how can I eat less than that?' While I was in Karumba, I happened to observe one such couple who had described their normal lunch in similar terms. They were in the pub late one afternoon, having a snack which consisted of a large plate of chips smothered in mayonnaise. I saw them a couple of days later and asked if they ever had afternoon snacks at the pub, and they said, 'Never.'

Portion sizes have increased gradually. The George Institute for Global Health revealed that, between 1995 and 2012, Australians consumed increasingly large portions of unhealthy food. Over this period, slices of cake and pizza have increased in size and content, resulting in a 66 per cent increase in the number of kilojoules of energy.



CHRIS GILFORD

Although these foods were the worst offenders, size increases were also seen in cereal bars, ice creams, and processed meats.

Many foods have started out as being healthy but have gradually morphed into something unhealthy. A Caesar salad sometimes now looks more like bacon and eggs smothered in mayonnaise and garnished with a piece of lettuce.

US television has also been glamorising the concept of enormous meals. *Ginormous Food* was a series broadcast on Food Network, an American cable and satellite television channel, and shown here on SBS. In this series, a presenter travels around the USA, trying to find the biggest and tastiest foods in America. The programme shows people eating things such as a 'five-pound, nine-inch-high burger overflowing with chilli cheese fries, bacon, and chipotle cream sauce'. In some cases, anyone who eats a complete meal of this size is presented with a certificate for doing so or inducted into the Hall of Fame.

There was another TV programme a few years ago called *The Obesity Myth*. It looked at a clinic in Melbourne in which the doctor was at pains to tell patients that it was not their fault that they were obese; it was the fault of their genes. However, the ancestors of these Obese patients would have had the same genes, but they were not obese, so the environment has to play a big part. Also, the doctor was confronted by patients who had been told on the previous visit that they had to follow a strict diet, and a urine test would show if they had. Lo and behold, the urine test showed that they had not been following the diet, so whose fault was that?

The ranges of weight that are deemed to be healthy are derived from analysis of life expectancy. In 2016, the *British Medical Journal* conducted a meta-analysis of 230 studies with 3.74 million deaths among 30.3 million participants. They found a relationship between the relative risk of dying and a person's BMI. The risk was lowest for people with a BMI between 20 and 25 but was about 70 per cent higher with a BMI of 35 and 4 times higher with a BMI of 45.

There were similar results in an article in the *Lancet* in 2018, and they demonstrated this in two charts. The hazard ratio is a tool used by epidemiologists and in this case roughly means the chance of someone

with a particular BMI dying compared with the chance of someone
with a BMI at the bottom of the curve. For example, a male with a BMI
of 40 has almost double the risk of dying compared with someone with
a BMI of about 24.

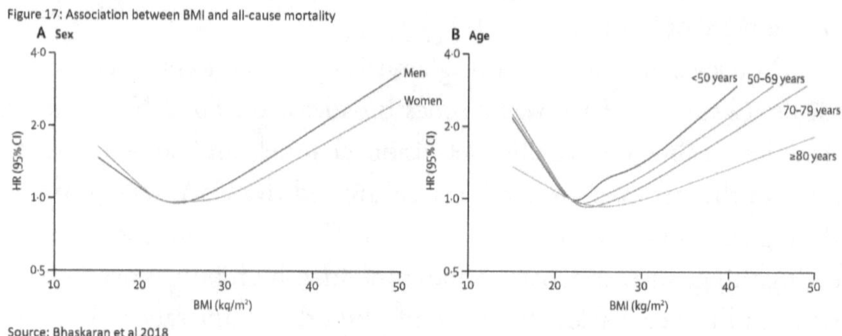


Figure 17: BMI and mortality

They said:

We observed a J-shaped association between BMI
and all-cause mortality, with lowest mortality at 25
kg/m². BMI was associated with mortality risk from
every main category of cause except for transport-
related accidents. For cancer, cardiovascular, respiratory,
blood and endocrine [includes diabetes], digestive,
musculoskeletal, and urogenital causes of death, the
lowest mortality was at 21–25 kg/m².

One interesting point is that it shows how important it is for people
below the age of 50 to have a BMI of about 22–23.

**Healthy Weight Range**

If you don't believe that being obese is bad for your health, have
a look round the waiting room at your local medical centre. You will
notice that the majority of people waiting there are overweight or obese.
All the obese people think that obesity is normal; they never think that

    CHRIS GILFORD

the reason that the waiting room is full of obese people is that those of normal weight don't need to see a doctor so often.

The problem is now worse because there is such opposition to the notion that obesity is bad. Obese people complain about 'fat shaming', but this only happens when they refuse to accept that their obesity is a problem and that the health professional has tried every other tactic to explain the issue. They also talk about 'fat stigma' and say that they are discriminated against because they are fat and complain that this discrimination is legal. (It is legal in Australia, unless the obesity becomes a disability.) There is an enormous resistance by many obese people to acknowledge that their weight is a problem. GPs are encouraged to talk about a patient's weight but may well be hesitant about doing so as it is likely to alienate the patient who may decide to change doctors. The issue, then, becomes the elephant in the room.

One incentive that I did see work was pain reduction. I had an overweight patient who developed gallstones. One of the symptoms that these can give you is pain after a fatty meal. The standard treatment for gallstones is to remove the gall bladder. The patient I had weighed 110 kg. She saw the surgeon and was put on the waiting list for surgery. She was told that by eating a low-fat diet, she could avoid episodes of pain. She was six months on the waiting list and lost 20 kg. She had the surgery but went back to her usual diet and regained all the weight in less than three months. I was tempted to write to the surgeon and tell him that the operation was successful but had actually decreased her life expectancy.

Unfortunately, fat shaming and fat stigma are harmful. It has been shown that experiencing weight stigma reinforces lifestyle behaviours that contribute to obesity. Trends in 'blame, shame, and stigma' have contributed to fat positivity. Obese people do not fear 'fat' but prejudice, discrimination, and exclusion.

I looked at the BMIs of the patients in Normanton and plotted their distribution on a graph. This is seen in the following figure.

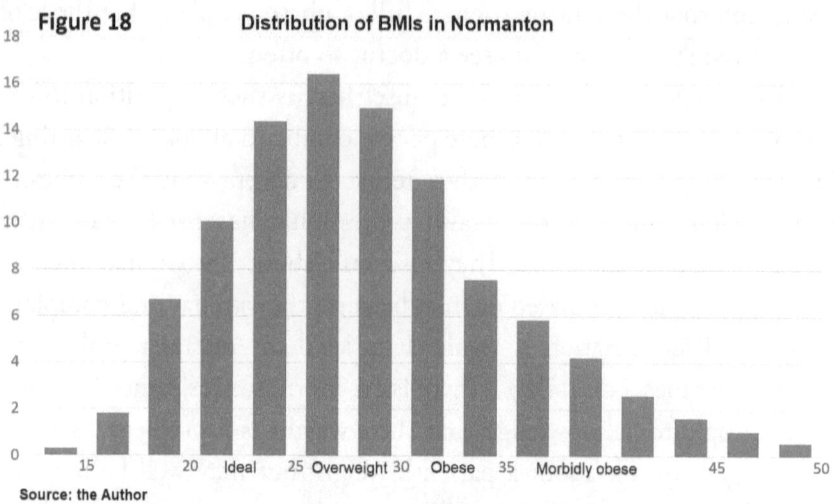


Figure 18: Distribution of BMIs in Normanton

Only 33 per cent had a BMI of less than 25 so were not overweight or obese. Fifty-one per cent were overweight or obese; 16 per cent were morbidly obese.

I think that most of the people who claim discrimination and say they experience fat shaming and fat stigma are morbidly obese. They are clearly people in whom any form of treatment has not worked and also who do not think that obesity is harmful, the fat deniers. They are like the anti-vaxxers, the people who refused Covid vaccinations. That is fine if it is only their own health that is suffering. Unfortunately, they are starting to influence those with a BMI between 25 and 35, who are obese or overweight. Their weight has slowly increased over several years but is not causing them any problems at present. If given the correct information, they should be able to get the self-control to reduce their weight and so increase their quality of life and their life expectancy.

The fat deniers claim discrimination, but as I see it, the actual discrimination is in the opposite direction. Consider these examples.

*Air Travel*

On a recent flight, I had about 10 kg of excess baggage, so I had to

     CHRIS GILFORD

pay extra at $7.70 per kilo. However, the man behind me at check-in had no excess baggage, but he was very obese, weighing probably about 130 kg. He did not have to pay anything extra, even though the total weight of him, plus his baggage, was much greater for him than for me.

When you fly in an aeroplane, weight is critical. Pilots calculate the total weight of the aircraft, crew, passengers, baggage, and fuel. This must be less than the MTOW (maximum take-off weight) for that aircraft. If the total weight is higher than the MTOW, then the aircraft may not be able to take off; or worse, it may be able to take off but then be uncontrollable and crash. This has really happened and killed everyone on board. It was shown on an episode of *Air Crash Investigations*. If you fly in an aircraft with less than about ten seats, you are asked for your weight; but for larger aircraft, and this means virtually all commercial flights, the airlines use a standard figure for passengers' weights. This standard weight is about 81–86 kg for men and 66–71 kg for women. The lower figure is used for the largest aircraft, the higher for medium-sized aircraft.

Therefore, those who weigh less than the standard weight are subsidising those who weigh more. In other words, the airlines discriminate against people who are thin.

*Clothing*

When you go to a clothes shop, you see racks of the same garment but of differing sizes, but the price is the same regardless of size. I bought five T-shirts, identical apart from size, and measured them. The same principle would apply to any other garment, but T-shirts were the easiest – and cheapest. 'Seams' means the total length of all the seams.

| Size | Weight (g) | Seams (cm) |
| --- | --- | --- |
| Small | 126 | 320 |
| Medium | 142 | 332 |
| Large | 153 | 350 |
| X Large | 160 | 356 |

| XX Large | 183 | 368 |

Table 21: Size of T-shirts

Small garments need small amounts of cloth, and the time (and therefore cost) taken to stitch a seam depends on its length and therefore the size of the garment. It seems obvious to me that it costs less to make a small garment than a large one. Fat people and thin people are paying the same price for clothes even though the manufacturing cost is different. In other words, clothing suppliers discriminate against people who are thin.

*Health Insurance*

Health insurance premiums are adjusted for your age but not for any other risk factor such as obesity. Thin people do not need bariatric surgery, so why should they pay the premium for cover that includes bariatric surgery? When I was in Normanton, several patients had knee replacements. All but one were obese; the remaining one was overweight. Orthopaedic surgeons confirm that these figures are typical. So thin people are very unlikely to need a knee replacement. So why should they pay the same premium as a person who is obese and therefore much more likely to need a knee replacement? Again, health funds discriminate against people who are thin.

*Restaurants and Cafes*

People who like to keep their weight under control often find that a standard restaurant meal is too large but have difficulty getting a small meal. Asking for two entrées instead of an entrée and a main course often attracts a disdainful look from the waiter. A restaurant may produce an entrée-sized main course, but they don't seem keen at reducing the price. More discrimination.

I could give more examples of how society discriminates against people who are thin. This discrimination must cease, meaning that

          CHRIS GILFORD

prices must be tailored to the size of the person. Getting overweight and obese people to pay more for services such as these would be one way of helping convince them that they are costing society more.

## So What Can the Government Do?

Governments should be very careful about whom they listen to. Many of the experts whom they talk to have a vested interest in not solving the problem. A surgeon who has decided to specialise in bariatric surgery is hardly likely to advise the government that the procedure should never be subsidised either by the government or the health funds.

Until now, the federal government has resisted attempts to get funding for medications and surgery for obesity. Overeating can be considered an addiction, and the government has been quite successful in dealing with another addiction, namely, smoking. This has already been considered, but one of the strategies has been to push the price of cigarettes ever higher and higher. It has been known for decades that smoking is bad for your health, but the widespread dissemination of this fact made little difference to smoking rates. Similarly, the fact that obese people have a shorter lifespan does not seem to be a sufficient incentive for people to lose weight.

At present, governments give tacit approval for people to put on weight. We now have bariatric versions of hospital equipment, ambulances, and wheelchairs. Retrieval aircraft suitable for conveying morbidly obese patients are now available. Every year or two, governments announce a new initiative for dealing with obesity and commit further millions of dollars to its solution. Unfortunately, the message that many people receive is 'It doesn't matter if you get fat – the government will look after you.' So they should stop spending money on the problem. Governments should institute policies that will educate everybody about the cost to both the individual and the whole country of obesity.

Medicare produces data showing the number of services per capita by sex and age. It looks like this:

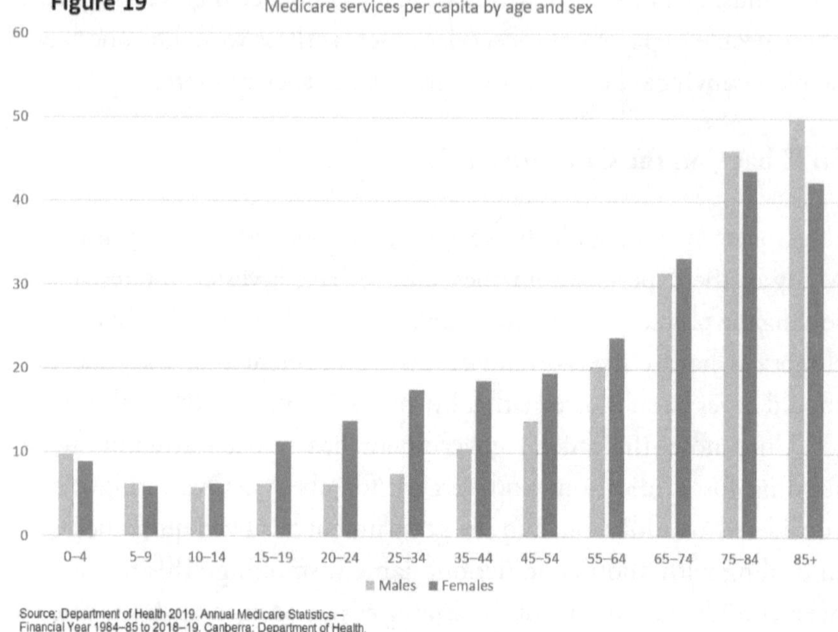


Figure 19: Medicare services by age

Women use more services than men during their childbearing years, but men finally overtake them in their seventies.

The federal government gathers an enormous amount of data about us from Medicare and the Pharmaceutical Benefits Scheme (PBS). Every time you see a doctor or collect medication from a pharmacy, the government knows about it, almost in real time. They know or can easily infer what chronic health problems you have. What they do not know at present is your weight and height. It will only require a small software patch to the medical software that GPs use for them to get this information. There is hardly a privacy issue here in that they already know so much about your health. With that information, it will be easy to produce a graph, similar to the one above, of the average Medicare benefits plotted against BMI. I think it might look like this:



CHRIS GILFORD

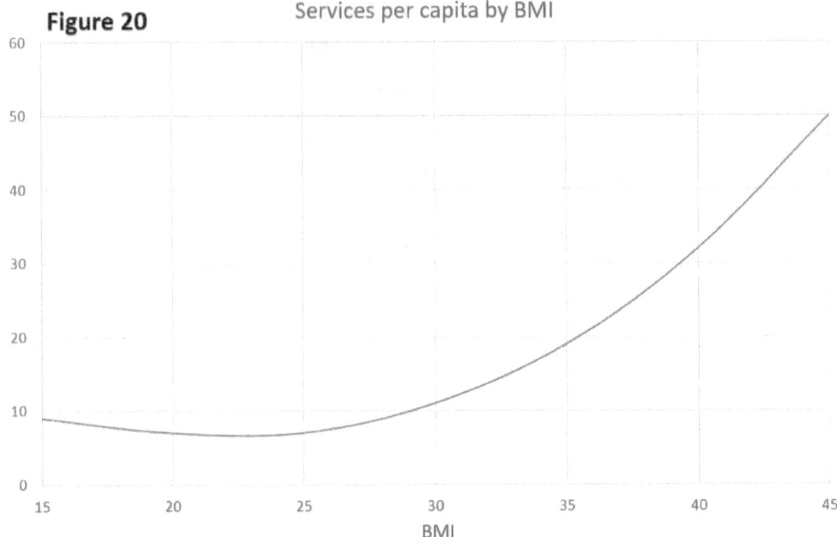


Figure 20: Hypothetical Medicare services by BMI

Also, they should make it more expensive for people who are overweight. These extra costs should start to have a graduated effect on people who are only slightly overweight, so they realise that if they continue to gain weight, life will become much more expensive. A recent prime minister has stated, 'If you want people to stop doing something, you tax them.'

It is really important for younger people, that is, those under 30, to shed excess weight. The professor of medicine at McGill University said in a recent study:

> The more an individual weighs and the younger their age, the greater the effect on their health, as they have many years ahead of them during which the increased health risks associated with obesity can negatively impact their lives.

I suspect that governments are concerned about fat stigma and fat shaming, so they have been trying 'soft options' to deal with obesity. By that I mean having cosy chats with all the various parties to try and gently suggest that people need to try to lose weight. This has achieved absolutely nothing. The proportion of people who are overweight has increased virtually in a straight line for the last twenty years. It is time for governments to take real action. They need to legislate; after all, that is their job. They may almost certainly upset those with a vested interest in selling high-fat, high-sugar food, but most of the major players are headquartered overseas and pay little tax here. We are almost at full employment at present, so job losses will not be a problem.

The Health and Wellbeing Queensland report on obesity has just (November 2022) been released and is primarily concerned with obesity in children. They point out that

> It is the environmental factors that are making unreasonable demands on parents, and like antismoking legislation which made it easier to quit and to not take up smoking, we need to regulate the environment so that it is easier for parents to maintain a child's healthy weight.

Appendix 2 contains a list of my suggestions for educating people about the consequences of being fat and regulating the environment. Hopefully, they will not provoke responses of fat shaming or fat stigma. A couple need some further explanation.

The government should stop subsidising medication for people who are obese. This could initially start with a BMI of 40 and then reduce by 1 each year down to 30. If this sounds unethical or radical, consider the restrictions on prescribing statins used to lower cholesterol. They state that a patient must be on a low-fat diet while they are taking it. Now if you are on such a diet, you will lose weight. Therefore, everybody who has been on a statin for more than ten years should now be in the normal weight range. Therefore, stopping the subsidy for medication for people who are obese is merely a logical extension to existing regulations.

Stop subsiding elective surgery for obese people if their symptoms will improve with weight loss. The classic example here is knee replacement surgery. Studies now show that weight loss is as effective



CHRIS GILFORD

as knee replacement in relieving the pain in knees from osteoarthritis. I am not trying to suggest that losing weight cures osteoarthritis, but it will certainly delay and possibly eliminate the need for surgery. It is also easier and safer for the surgeons to operate on patients who are not overweight, and there will be fewer complications. All patients with painful knees say that the reason that they are overweight is that they cannot exercise, but when they have had the surgery, none of them lose weight. Recent studies have also shown that for couples who cannot conceive, weight loss (if the woman is obese) is as effective as IVF.

Change the building codes so that the normal way of moving from one floor to another is by the stairs rather than by a lift or escalator. All commercial buildings are required to have a staircase to be used instead of the lift in case of fire, but it is usually hidden behind doors, and there is the fear that if you use it, you might never get back inside, or you might set all the alarms off. If our federal MPs go and shop in Canberra Centre, they will find a building in which it is almost impossible to find a staircase to get from one floor to another. This has two effects – it deprives people of exercise and increases greenhouse gases from the generation of electricity needed to propel the escalators and lifts.

## Conclusion

Obesity is one of the biggest threats to human existence, on a par with climate change, and we need to tackle it urgently.

Finally, what if obesity continues to get worse? The AIHW report in 2020 said that obesity will bankrupt the nation. The Health and Wellbeing Queensland Report 2022 confirmed the seriousness of it. What will happen when there is no money to pay for healthcare or enough staff to care for all the obese people? The answer is grim because what happens if you have a sick animal that you love, but you cannot afford the vet bills?

We need to plan now about what to do if the situation does not improve. Perhaps the next step should be to start waging war against the giants of the food industry, the fast-food chains that sell unhealthy food. We could threaten them with more extreme measures.

The war in Ukraine has taught us that food security is much more uncertain than we had been led to believe. I don't think that many people, myself included, realised what an important food producer Ukraine was.

The world's population is now (at the end of 2022) about 8 billion, and it is set to increase to about 12 billion by the middle of the century. This estimate had been reduced about ten years ago as the general increase in civilisation that has been apparent until now tends to reduce the birth rate as more women become educated and enter the workforce. However, the current uncertainty might cause an increase in birth rate and a higher maximum population.

These factors, uncertain food security and rising population, make it far more likely that the world will run out of food in the foreseeable future.

During the Second World War, Britain, which relied heavily on imported food and other products, found that its supply was being severely reduced by the German U-boats which were sinking thousands of tons of cargo every month, mainly in the Atlantic. Germany's food supply was also in jeopardy; this was one of the reasons that Hitler implemented the Holocaust – there would be fewer mouths to feed. Britain's solution was rationing and started preparing for it in 1939 even before the onset of hostilities. It continued until the middle of 1954.

Introducing rationing might help solve both obesity and food security. I can see how it might be implemented. In WWII, it was done with ration books and stamps, but now we would use smartphones. Everyone would get a monthly allowance of so many calories, grams of fat, and grams of sugar. Whenever you go to the supermarket, the checkout computer totals the amount of calories, fat, and sugar and deducts this amount from your allowance. If you run out, you can't buy any more food. This would have to apply to restaurants and cafes as well. There would be lots of details to be worked out, but a draconian measure like this might be required.

# CHAPTER 8

# Injury, Violence, Crime, and Punishment

A T FIRST SIGHT, this might appear to be a strange topic in a book dealing with health problems. The reality, though, is that all these factors have a substantial effect on people's health as they can cause chronic health problems and disability and shorten people's lives.

Looking first at mortality, the ABS publishes the number of deaths at each five-year age group as in this graph for 2021.

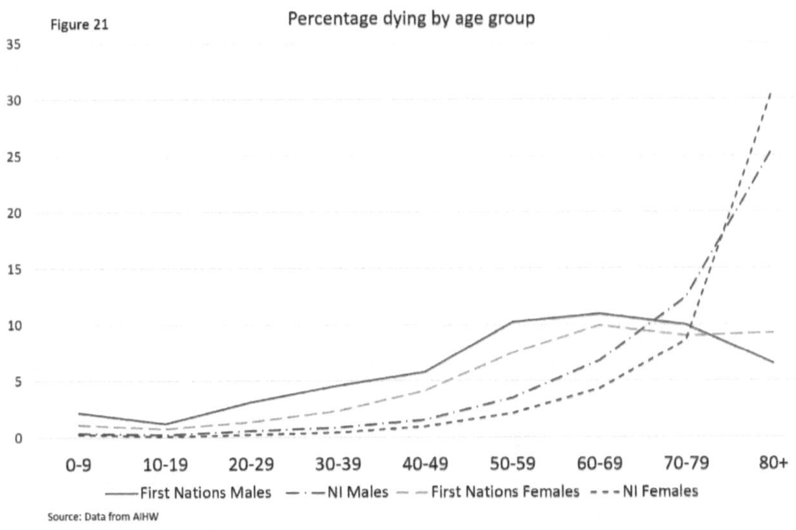


Figure 21: People dying by age group

We can add up the percentages for those under 35, and we find the following for the proportion of each group (by sex and Indigenous status) that died below the age of 35 as follows:

|                                          | Male | Female | Ratio: M/F |
| ---------------------------------------- | ---- | ------ | ---------- |
| First Nations                            | 8.83 | 4.19   | 2.11       |
| Non-Indigenous                           | 1.59 | 0.81   | 1.96       |
| Ratio: First Nations/non-Indigenous      | 5.55 | 5.17   |            |

Table 22: Percentage of deaths below 35

So over five times as many First Nations compared with non-Indigenous people die before the age of 35, and this is almost the same for both sexes. Also, the rate for males is double that of females, even though females probably have a greater mortality from medical problems during their childbearing age.

Why age 35? I could have used 20, 30, 40, or 50, but age 35 gives us the greatest ratio of First Nations to non-Indigenous – 5.43 – and also the greatest ratio of males to females – 2.10.

Why are all these young First Nations men dying? Most of them are from injuries due to accidents, assaults, and homicides. About 20 per cent are due to suicide, which, of course, is a tragedy and something that governments have been trying to fix. However, the other 80 per cent are probably also preventable.

Homicide refers to when one human being kills another and includes murder, manslaughter, and situations of insanity and self-defence. In Mornington Island, five people were killed between 1995 and 2015 so an average of one person every four years. Their average age was 23. The young age of these victims is sufficient to lower the median age at death over this period by almost one year, so it is one of the causes of 'the gap'. During my eleven years in Normanton, there were two homicides, which is a similar rate to Mornington Island, the only difference being that both of the victims were over the age of 35. Assaults and accidents also cause death and significant disability and consequently a reduced life expectancy in victims.

The Australian Institute of Criminology (AIC) publishes biannual reports on homicides in Australia. The latest one, published in June 2022, covers the period 1 July 2019 – 30 June 2020. The rate was 1.02

per 100,000, which was a little higher than previous years, but the general trend is a gradual reduction.

To put the Australian rate into perspective, I have taken data from selected countries from the UN Office on Drugs and Crime:

| South Africa | 33.5 | New Zealand | 2.6 | Australia | 1.0 |
| Mexico | 28.4 | Canada | 2.0 | China | 0.5 |
| United States | 6.3 | France | 1.2 | Indonesia | 0.4 |
| India | 3.0 | United Kingdom | 1.2 | Japan | 0.3 |

Table 23: Homicide rates in selected countries

Homicides are broadly classified as domestic, acquaintance, and stranger. Fortunately, over the last thirty years, both domestic and acquaintance homicides have decreased from about 0.7 per 100,000 to 0.3 per 100,000, according to the AIC. However, stranger homicide has hardly changed at about 0.2 per 100,000.

Domestic homicides can be further classified by the relationship between perpetrator and victim. Intimate partner homicides comprised 56 per cent of domestic homicides and 17 per cent of all homicides. In 80 per cent of the intimate partner homicides, the victim was female; but for all homicides, 65 per cent of victims were male. As regards the offenders, 87 per cent were male.

The AIC report also looks at ethnic background.

| Offender<br>Victim | First Nations | Non-Indigenous |
| --- | --- | --- |
| First Nations | 25 | 11 |
| Non-Indigenous | 4 | 131 |

Table 24: Ethnic background of victims and offenders

In over 90 per cent of cases, the offender and victim had the same ethnic background. For the 25 cases where victim and offender were both First Nations, the population was 820,000, so the homicide rate was 3.16; but where both were non-Indigenous, the relevant population was 24.63 million, so the homicide rate was 0.53. In other words, the First Nations homicide rate was six times higher than the non-Indigenous rate. In both Mornington Island and Normanton, the homicide rate was about one person every four years in a population of 1,200 so a rate of 21 per 100,000. This is seven times the rate for First Nations people in the rest of the country, and nearly forty times the rate for non-Indigenous.

One of the elders on Mornington Island told me about an incident that occurred when she was much younger. A group of five or six men had travelled by boat to one of the other neighbouring islands to settle some dispute. They were never seen again. People on the other island denied all knowledge of the matter but were subsequently seen wearing clothes that had belonged to the supposed victims. Everyone presumed that they had been killed.

Homicide is the ultimate crime of violence towards another person. But there are lesser crimes of violence between people which end up with one of them being seriously injured. These are assaults, according to the criminal codes in Australia, and generally form two groups.

The serious one is 'assault causing grievous bodily harm', abbreviated to GBH. Grievous bodily harm means (a) the loss of a distinct part or an organ of the body, (b) serious disfigurement, or (c) any bodily injury of such a nature that, if left untreated, would endanger or be likely to endanger life or cause or be likely to cause permanent injury to health, whether or not treatment is or could have been available.

The less serious one is assault occasioning bodily harm, which is defined as any bodily injury which interferes with health or comfort. This can be as little as someone exhaling smoke into your face or spitting at you. However, the common injuries include the result of being punched or lacerations, bruises, sprains, and strains.

I have analysed my data from Normanton to give an idea about how many people suffered from injuries that were at least moderately severe. By this I mean a fracture, dislocation, or wound that caused internal damage. Therefore, I excluded superficial lacerations, bruises, sprains, and strains. I have the records of 612 First Nations adults with meaningful data. A quarter, 156, had suffered injuries, the majority of which were due to an act of violence. In most cases, the injuries occurred in someone who drank alcohol to excess. All my figures are likely to be underestimates due to the method of data collection.

Many of these are found in the context of domestic violence, which is acknowledged by First Nations leaders as they have publicised the problem: 'domestic violence – not part of our culture'.

The commonest injury is the broken jaw from being punched in the face. The victim has pain and difficulty talking and eating and has to be flown to a major city for treatment. These days, a plate is screwed into the bone to hold the pieces together; but in the past, the treatment was to wire the jaw so that the fracture would heal on its own. This meant that the victim had to consume liquidised food through a straw for six weeks while the fracture healed.

In Normanton, there were thirty-three people who had had a broken jaw, twenty-two male and eleven female. Of the total, seven had had their jaw broken twice.

The *Australasian Medical Journal* published an analysis of jaw fractures in WA from 1999 to 2009. They found that jaw fractures were ten times as common among First Nations people compared with non-Indigenous and that the number of fractures was stable over that period. They looked at the number of admissions to hospital for jaw fractures and found 1,752 cases in the First Nations WA population, which was 58,700 in the 2006 census. This would equate to thirty-six cases in the ten-year period in a town the size of Normanton.

The perpetrator may also suffer, often sustaining a fracture to one of the bones of the hand, most commonly the fourth metacarpal, the one that the ring finger is attached to. There were twelve of these, but this figure may well be a lot less than the true figure as many would not report it. If the perpetrator gets a cut on their knuckle from the victim's teeth, it may become infected, sometimes called a tooth-knuckle injury. Human teeth have more bacteria than dog teeth do. One person in Normanton had a hand which got infected in this way, and since he delayed getting treatment, the finger had to be amputated. When he got back to Normanton after treatment, he blamed his partner for the fact that he lost his finger, not himself. His main regret was that he could not use his right hand any more to punish her.

Sometimes a person who is angry and thought about punching someone hits the wall instead. Builders told me that they were often called on to repair fist-sized holes in the plasterboard of First Nations houses. Sometimes it is not a wall that gets punched but a plate-glass window. This can be incredibly dangerous if it shatters. The resultant fragments are very sharp and typically cause a deep laceration of the inside of the upper arm of the perpetrator. This is where a large artery and many nerves run. If the artery is severed, the person can bleed to death in a matter of minutes before an ambulance arrives. If they survive, the rest of the arm may be deprived of its blood and nerve supply and have to be amputated.

Three people in Normanton had injuries from punching a plate-glass window. Two of them had to have the arm amputated after attempts to reattach the blood vessels had failed. The third had injured the nerves supplying the arm, and so the arm was partially paralysed.

There were ten injuries from a firearm being discharged, at least three of which were self-inflicted. After questioning them about this, often years later, the usual response was, 'I did some silly things back then when I was on the drink.' One told me that he did it to try and impress a girl whom he was interested in, but it did not work. He also said that the pain was far worse than what he imagined it would be.

Eye injuries from punches that resulted in blindness were common, with nine people being blind in one eye and one in both eyes.

Severe head injuries in which the person is punched on the head or hit with a weapon were also common. The weapon in this case may be any object that is handy. Examples include rocks, bricks, baseball bats, chairs, or even expensive items like video recorders. The victim may also be kicked, and when the victim wakes up, they always claim that the perpetrator was wearing steel-capped boots even though very few were found in Normanton. Unfortunately, some do not wake up and remain permanently semi-conscious; others are profoundly brain damaged.

     CHRIS GILFORD

Stab wounds were very common. The vast majority, too numerous to mention, were only superficial, needing only a few sutures. However, there were at least twelve where the knife had done serious internal damage, and the patient had to be flown out by RFDS. One had penetrated the heart, two the lungs, and three the abdominal cavity. In one case, the knife had penetrated the liver, causing massive internal bleeding. We found out what happened later, when his partner came into the hospital. She said that they were both drunk and had been arguing. She waited until he fell asleep and then knifed him. Her explanation was that 'some people won't take a telling'. Some stab wounds were self-inflicted, usually to the left arm, where the nerves were damaged.

'Do you still throw spears at each other?' asked the late Prince Philip in 2002. He was speaking to the First Nations leader and successful businessman William Brin at the First Nations Cultural Park in Queensland. Fortunately, this was taken to be typical of many of the inappropriate comments he made. The question may be politically incorrect, but it is also extremely valid, for had it been asked on Mornington Island, the answer to the question would have to be a definite 'yes'. The logo of the Mornington Island Shire shows three men holding spears. It can be seen at https://www.mornington.qld.gov.au/.

Many people have been treated at Mornington Island Hospital having had spears thrown at them. In many cases, the spear has penetrated their chest and caused a punctured lung. This allows air to move out of the lung into the surrounding pleural space, known as a pneumothorax. Often, there is substantial bleeding to the extent that a fluid level can be seen on an X-ray of the chest. A pneumothorax can be a life-threatening emergency but one which can be treated easily by inserting a tube into the chest cavity to let the air and/or blood escape. In a ten-year period, there were 13 cases of traumatic pneumothorax from spears, which would have been 13 more homicides without medical intervention. I came across a referral letter for a patient who was being flown out by the RFDS and was described as being 'the third and most stable of our stabbings this evening', which sums up the situation quite well.

There are, of course, other reasons why people get injured, and most of these are called accidents. Motor vehicle accidents tend to cause the more serious ones due to the speed that is involved. In chapter 6, I mentioned those where an unrestrained child has died in this way. Many years ago, I attended a conference where a speaker who worked in a community in the north of WA noticed the high rate of injury that was sustained by people, mainly children, being ejected from a ute as they had been riding unrestrained in the back of them. I have had to deal with the consequence of this practice on two occasions. In one, a young girl had sustained a punctured lung. In the other, I was called into Mornington Island Hospital at 3 a.m. to see four teenagers who had been in the back of a ute. They were cruising round town when the driver suddenly turned a corner, and they were all thrown out. Fortunately, they were only travelling slowly. Two of them had fractures and had to be evacuated by RFDS.

Kowanyama is a dry First Nations community, about four and a half hours' drive on a gravel road north of Normanton. Every couple of months, a group of people from Kowanyama would get a thirst for some grog and make the return trip, loading up their 4WD with as much as it would carry. On one occasion, they started sampling the grog on the way back and came to grief with some fatalities.

Stupidity behind the wheel is not confined to First Nations people. Two brothers in Karumba had an argument at the pub where they had been drinking and, while intoxicated, drove their utes at each other, writing them both off. I wonder how they explained this to their insurance companies. The combination of alcohol, adrenaline, and testosterone is a toxic cocktail and probably explains most of the increased number of male deaths below the age of 35.

Quad bikes are notoriously dangerous, and steps have been taken in the last twenty years to try and make them safer. There have been a number of fatalities of jackaroos working in cattle stations. One First Nations father in Normanton acquired one and took his four children on a ride across a paddock on it. Unfortunately, they hit a termite mound and rolled over. All the children had limb fractures and had to be evacuated, requiring two RFDS aircraft. The father was lucky that there were no fatalities. However, no one should rely on luck to avoid tragedy.

The number of assaults in Normanton and on Mornington Island keeps the police busy, and there is a complement of ten to twelve in each community for populations of around 1,200, or 1 per 100 residents. In contrast, Queensland has about 12,000 officers for a population of 5.2 million or about 1 officer for 430 residents. This in itself is an indicator of the increased level of crime in these communities.

Another indicator is found in the court system. The magistrates' court in Mornington Island sits about two or three days a month. The local justice group Junkuri Laka published a regular newsletter with a list of forthcoming events in the community, including the court days, with a list of those who needed to attend. The newsletters for April 2016 listed a total of 140 residents who were due to attend the two court days that month. So that was about a fifth of the adult population. Most charges were about alcohol possession, but there were a few public nuisances and being drunk in a public place. The newsletter gave advice, saying it was important to turn up: 'DO NOT just stay away as the Magistrates will issue a warrant and you'll end up in the watch house.' The court also dealt with more serious charges such as assaults, and every month I would have to write out statements describing the injuries that the victim had received and how it might affect their lives.

For less serious offences, the perpetrator might be fined. I am sure some readers might have been issued with a speeding ticket, and most will pay it in a lump sum. In Mornington Island, hardly anybody pays a fine as a lump sum. The fines are handled by the State Penalties Enforcement Registry (SPER), which is a division of Queensland Revenue Office. The perpetrator, through their solicitor, pleads poverty, and a repayment regime of five to ten dollars per fortnight is arranged. One of the police officers told me that residents of Mornington Island collectively owed SPER several million dollars and that the community had the highest per capita debt in Queensland.

If someone is convicted of a crime and sentenced to a period in prison, they are flown to Townsville. One of the police officers told me that there were then twenty-nine Mornington residents in prison, and this was not unusual. He also said that about 40 per cent of the males and 6 per cent of the females had been to prison at some stage of their life.

This high rate of incarceration may have tragic sequelae. There was a royal commission into deaths in custody about twenty years ago, but a 2003 report found that juvenile offenders (median age about 18 years) with a history of past imprisonment in Victoria had death rates that were nine times as high for the young male offenders as those of other young males of the same age and forty-one times as high for young female offenders as those of other young females. This has been confirmed by other studies since then.

Obviously, there are few alternatives to imprisonment for serious crimes like homicide or grievous bodily harm. However, many of those in prison have not done anything violent, but their crime is that of disobedience. They have repeatedly ignored court orders or otherwise failed to show respect for the court, and the whole situation has escalated. This could be a breach of a domestic violence order or just repeatedly failing to turn up at court to answer charges. It is therefore an absolute tragedy when such a person's life comes to an end in prison or later, but it is completely avoidable.

It was my impression that the number of assaults carried out by females was steadily increasing, and this has been borne out by a 2012 report by the AIC, looking at assaults in 1996–7 and 2009–10. Over this thirteen-year period, the number of assaults by males increased by 18 per cent, but the increase was 49 per cent for females.

As regards the victims, a report by the AIHW on the hospitalisation rate for young people due to assault showed the opposite – a 29 per cent increase for males and 19 per cent for females between 1996–7 and 2005–6. Their report also noted:

> Both fatal and non-fatal assaults involving young people contribute greatly to the global burden of premature death, injury and disability. Violence among young people harms not only its victims, but also their families, friends and communities and adds greatly

to the costs of health and welfare services, reduces productivity, decreases the value of property and disrupts a range of essential services.

They counted the number who were hospitalised for injuries, and the rate is expressed per 100,000 population. Overall, the rate was 162 in 1996–7 and increased to 205 in 2005–6. They looked at the rates in different population groups in 2005–6 and found the following:

| | Rate | | Rate | Ratio |
|---|---|---|---|---|
| Young First Nations females | 1,078 | Other young females | 46 | 23.4 |
| Young First Nations males | 1,000 | Other young males | 295 | 3.4 |
| Very remote areas | 1,820 | Major cities | 213 | 8.5 |
| Disadvantaged areas | 333 | Prosperous areas | 164 | 2.0 |

Table 25: Characteristics of assault victims

This increase of injuries due to violence is worrying. It does seem to be the consequence of a general increase in the level of anger which leads to aggression that now seems to be widespread everywhere in society. Reality TV shows such as the cooking or renovation competitions are manipulated to raise the level of aggression between the participants to provoke verbal abuse because it makes good television, that is, higher ratings and therefore higher advertising revenue.

Road rage and air rage have emerged as problems for travellers. Children's sports are being disrupted by parents attacking each other or threatening the referee. It is hardly surprising that this then increases and triggers physical assaults. The availability of mobile phones has enabled instant broadcasting of altercations. Some of the fights that take place in First Nations communities can be viewed on YouTube.

## Prison

Some First Nations people appear to benefit from a period in prison. When they get back to their community, we can see an improvement in their health probably because they have had no access to alcohol, although they might have found some marijuana. They often eat a better diet than they had at home, they have been getting their medication regularly, and many of them go to the gym to work out. They can have video conferences with their family, and the equipment at the hospital is used for this, so the hospital staff get glimpses of how well they look.

In Normanton, there were more crimes of burglary probably because there was a much larger non-Indigenous population. This could be because First Nations people did not want to steal from their own people or because the takings from a non-Indigenous house would probably be larger.

My own house was broken into half a dozen times, on one occasion breaking down the back door with a large rock. Once, I had recently returned from a holiday in Vietnam and had some Vietnamese currency left over – notes of 1 million dong. The burglars must have been delighted with their haul but dismayed when they discovered how little they were worth. On another occasion, some teenagers took some $100 bills which I had taken overseas as emergency cash. They spent them in the town but didn't realise that the shopkeepers would know straight away that the money was stolen. On another occasion, a girl took a camera, and the police found her. The police asked me to have a meeting with her and her mother to help resolve the matter. I asked her where the camera was, and she said she had thrown it away. I asked her why she did it, and she just shrugged and said, 'Because'. I presumed that it was just boredom and that it kept her entertained for an hour or two. She had left school but not tried to get a job. Her mother was horrified, but I don't think the girl cared less.

In conclusion, injury, violence, and crime are all much commoner in First Nations communities, and so it is hardly surprising that the rate of incarceration of First Nations people is higher than in the general population. This argument does not seem to have been considered by those who complain of the high incarceration rate. The best way of trying to deal with this is to support families and see that children are raised with high moral standards. The WHO (2007) has stated:

> Effective interventions identified to reduce violence among young people include life skills training programs; preschool enrichment to strengthen bonds to school, raise achievement and improve self-esteem; family therapy for children and adolescents at high risk; and educational incentives for at-risk high school students.

Laying a better groundwork, especially education, will see that young adults get jobs, and then wealth, status, and good health will follow.

# CHAPTER 9

# Health Programmes

WHEN I WAS a student in Sri Lanka, on my days off I travelled around the country by bus and train and got to talk with the local population. One of them asked where I had come from, so I told him England. He then grasped my hand and shook it vigorously. 'Thank you. Thank you. Thank you,' he said. 'You built everything in this country – the schools, hospitals, roads – so every time I meet someone from England, I thank them.'

The 1979 Monty Python film *Life of Brian* contains a scene where Reg, an activist played by John Cleese, is trying to whip up support for an uprising against the Roman imperialist aggressors. He has to concede some consequences of the Roman occupation: 'All right . . . all right . . . but apart from better sanitation and medicine and education and irrigation and public health and roads and a freshwater system and baths and public order . . . what have the Romans done for us?' If you change 'Romans' to 'white fellas', this becomes the attitude of many First Nations people.

These are two contrasting views of colonialism at opposite ends of the spectrum. The constitution divides responsibility for health between the federal and state governments. The state governments run the hospitals and community clinics, whereas the federal government funds medical services outside hospitals through the Medicare programme, pharmacy services through the Pharmaceutical Benefits Scheme, and aged care.

**State Governments**

State governments are responsible for public hospitals and community clinics. Since there are few private medical practices or pharmacies in remote areas, they have traditionally been responsible for the vast majority of health services to remote communities. They already had infrastructure in place, such as hospitals and schools. Therefore, they have been able to increase services within the existing operating framework.

For health, there are some differences between the way the services are delivered between the states and territory. For example, for communities of around 1,000 residents, Queensland prefers to have a hospital with a resident doctor where patients can be admitted, whereas in the Northern Territory all patients who require admission are evacuated to larger centres (mainly Darwin and Alice Springs).

The worst figures for life expectancy and childhood mortality occur in remote areas, so it is important to understand the services that are provided in remote areas. I am using Mornington Island as an example as I worked there for a few years. It is run by the North West Hospital and Health Service, the local division of Queensland Health, based in Mount Isa. The hospital has a twenty-four-hour emergency department, inpatient beds, outpatient services, and community health. Community health work mainly out in the community, visiting people in their homes, doing basic checks, and helping ensure that people attend clinics. The doctor runs a daily GP clinic as well as seeing patients in the ED. There are visiting specialists and allied health professionals most weeks using the rooms in community health, which is in one wing of the hospital. Patients with serious illnesses who need specialist care or surgery are flown out by RFDS either to Mount Isa or Townsville. There is an X-ray machine but no radiographer, so some of the nurses are trained to do basic X-rays. Pregnant women have their antenatal care on the island but leave four weeks before their delivery date to stay in the town where they will birth. The ambulance service is located at the hospital but managed separately.

Any patient who is admitted to the hospital may have a relative or friend stay with them in the hospital to help with their social needs. When patients are attending specialist or allied health appointments in Mount Isa or Townsville, their travel and accommodation costs are paid by the health service, and if they are admitted to hospital, they can take a relative or friend with them, with their costs paid.

**Federal Health Programmes**

Medicare and the Pharmaceutical Benefits Scheme are the federal government's methods of funding medical and pharmacy services. These include all services outside hospitals and state-run community clinics and so include all GPs and specialists in private practice and retail pharmacists.

An AIHW report in 2005 on expenditure on health services for First Nations people in 2001–2 found that the federal government spending per capita was about $900 on First Nations people and $1,000 on non-Indigenous, but for state/territory governments, it was $3,600 and $2,200 respectively.

The federal government realised that state governments were funding most of the medical services in remote areas due to the absence of private clinics and so set up an agreement with the states. Under this scheme, Medicare funds many of the services provided by GPs in remote areas, even though the doctor is an employee of the state health service. The patients are all bulk-billed and the Medicare benefits are paid directly to the state health service. According to the original agreement in the early 2000s, the money was supposed to be used in the community where it was generated, with a local committee formed to decide how it should be spent; however, this did not happen in Normanton. Since the mid-2000s, they have also been funding allied health services including dentistry, physiotherapy, and psychology.

Medicare benefits for GPs have undergone a gradual change over the last twenty years. Until then, the benefits were only paid to doctors for specific medical items such as consultations or surgeries.

The Enhanced Primary Care package was introduced in 1999 and initially consisted in new items for medical practitioner involvement in multidisciplinary case conferencing and care planning for people with chronic and complex needs, and items for annual health assessments for

First Nations people aged 55 and over and for non-Indigenous people 75 years of age and over (the older person's health assessment).

In 2004, the Strengthening Medicare package was introduced, and this included new bulk-billing incentive payments, items for allied health services provided to patients with chronic disease management plans, health assessment items for residents of aged care facilities, First Nations people aged between 15 and 55, First Nations adult health check, and an item for GPs undertaking a medication management review of a resident of an aged care facility in collaboration with a pharmacy.

In 2005, GP Medicare rebates were increased from 85 per cent to 100 per cent of the schedule fee. In addition, the Round-the-Clock Medicare initiative was introduced, with new item numbers for non-urgent services provided in evenings and weekends. These essentially reinstated the item numbers that had been removed in about 1987. In addition, the Enhanced Primary Care items were replaced by the chronic disease management items for patients with a chronic or terminal medical condition, declaring the term 'Enhanced Primary Care' obsolete.

In 2006, there was a mental health initiative, Better Access to Psychiatrists and Psychologists, requiring GPs to create mental health care plans and a child health check for First Nations children.

Similar changes were made almost annually since then, with doctors getting a greater proportion of their income not from consultations but from case conferences and preparing management plans. As a secondary goal, this meant that the government was able to collect more and more data on what diseases people have and how their doctors are treating them. For example, there are specific items for patients with diabetes, asthma, or any mental illness. The government already had knowledge of what surgical treatment anyone had had.

All this was being done before there was any proof that there was any health benefit for patients.

## Pharmaceuticals

As regards pharmaceuticals, there are three ways in which the federal government provides extra subsidies to First Nations people or those in remote areas.

Firstly, there is the section 100 scheme. Section 100 gives the minister the power to subsidise medication outside the normal Pharmaceutical Benefits Scheme. There are two main circumstances in which this applies. One is the provision of highly specialised medication, such as anti-cancer drugs. The other is the provision of medication to remote First Nations communities, in which the medication is supplied free of charge to all members of that community, including non-Indigenous.

Secondly, there are a number of medications on the Pharmaceutical Benefits Scheme which are only benefits if the patient is First Nations.

Thirdly, there is the process called simply 'Closing the Gap' in which the medication is free (if the patient is a pensioner) or at the pension rate (for non-pensioners). This scheme is for First Nations people, but there are restrictions – the GP must be in an accredited practice participating in the Indigenous Health Programme, the patient must be a registered patient of that practice, the medication must be for prevention or treatment of a chronic disease, and the doctor must believe that the patient will not take it unless it is free or heavily subsidised. The prescribing software that doctors use checks these details and prints a code on the prescription. However, most patients do not understand the restrictions – they believe that 'Closing the Gap' means automatic free medication – and pressure the doctor to manually override these checks.

## Other Federally Funded Programmes

These are the programmes that generally come under the umbrella term 'Closing the Gap'. The federal government's publicity department has done a good job at promoting the programme through its agencies including Oxfam, holding sausage sizzles, and manufacturing thousands of T-shirts, posters, bumper stickers, and all the other paraphernalia used to bring a government programme to people's attention.

The federal government is restricted in the way it can provide funding. Under the constitution, it cannot interfere in areas that are the states' responsibilities, but it can channel funding through independent corporations. The federal government has had little infrastructure in the communities and so has put the provision of services out to private tender. In some cases, an established organisation has obtained the contract to supply services; but in others, a new organisation has been created specifically for this purpose. Billions of dollars have been spent to try and address the inequalities.

## Visiting Health Services

There are also visiting medical services funded by the federal government. The Royal Flying Doctors Service and other aeromedical services are funded by both federal and state governments but also receive significant donations from industry and voluntary donations. The RFDS is well known as providing aeromedical retrieval services and inter-hospital transport throughout most of Australia. However, they also provide medical, nursing, and allied health services to areas that do not have an existing service. The RFDS send child health nurses every week or two to Mornington Island to check the health of children and carry out their routine vaccinations.

The federal government has also created and funded programmes using resources provided by state health departments. The federally funded specialists who visit Mornington Island include the following:

ICOP, the Indigenous Cardiac Outreach Programme, comes three to four times a year. As well as a cardiologist, there is a cardiac ultra-sonographer who does echocardiograms, and a liaison officer.

IROC, the Indigenous Respiratory Outreach Clinic, has two teams for adults and children, each of which comes twice a year. As well as respiratory physicians, they have respiratory technicians who do respiratory function tests.

The Deadly Ears Programme comes twice a year for a week. There is a team of ENT consultants, anaesthetists, theatre technicians, and nurses. They conduct clinics and then set up an operating theatre and carry out several operations such as inserting grommets or removing adenoids.

## Alcohol Rehab Centres

State governments have addressed the issues of substance abuse for a long time. In Queensland, the department is known as ATODS (Alcohol, Tobacco, and Other Drugs Service), and there is usually a nurse in each community to provide this service.

The federal government started establishing a number of residential rehab centres about ten years ago. One was built at Normanton and opened in 2014 and is known as the Normanton Recovery and Community Well-Being Service and has a twenty-bed residential facility. It was planned for residents of the lower gulf – Normanton, Doomadgee, and Mornington Island. Initially, it was proposed to site it about five kilometres from the town, a distance that would discourage most people from walking into town to access alcohol, but the cost of providing services such as power and water were prohibitive, so a site was selected adjacent to the hospital, even though it is only just over a kilometre from three pubs. It is currently run jointly by the Salvation Army, who has a long history of providing rehab services, and Gidgee Healing, the Aboriginal-controlled health service based in Mount Isa.

## Aboriginal Medical Services

The federal government has assisted in setting up over 150 health corporations which run over 300 medical services throughout Australia which are aimed specifically at First Nations people. Many of them are members of National Aboriginal Community Controlled Health Organisation (NACCHO), and according to their website, naccho.org.au:

> The National Aboriginal Community Controlled Health Organisation (NACCHO) is the national leadership body for Aboriginal and Torres Strait

      CHRIS GILFORD

Islander health in Australia. NACCHO provides advice and guidance to the Australian Government on policy and budget matters and advocates for community-developed solutions that contribute to the quality of life and improved health outcomes for Aboriginal and Torres Strait Islander people.

As well as doctors and nurses, they employ Aboriginal health workers who assist in providing more culturally appropriate services. They often have vehicles which are used to bring their patients to the service. They work hard to ensure that all possible services are supplied to their patients since much of their funding is conditional on them meeting targets, such as the number of health checks that have been performed. Some of them employ administration staff whose sole job is to check that all these are carried out.

On Mornington Island, the established agencies include North West Remote Health, Mission Australia, Save the Children, and the PCYC. However, according to the CEO of the shire, in 2017, there were 46 service providers running 105 programmes.

## North West Remote Health

North West Remote Health started life as the Townsville and Rural Division of General Practice. In 1992, the federal government started funding the divisions of general practice. They were set up to form associations of GPs within a geographical area to enable GPs to access better services for their patients. The Townsville and Rural Division of General Practice changed its name in about 2003 to North and West Primary Health Care and, at about that time, won a tender to provide allied health services (including physiotherapy, occupational therapy, speech therapy, and dietetics) to the gulf communities (mainly Normanton, Doomadgee, and Mornington Island). In 2010, they also started supplying GPs to work in these areas.

The Rudd government looked at the role of the divisions of general practice and set out to replace them with Medicare Locals. Many of the divisions, including North and West Primary Health Care, just transitioned into the new entities, so in July 2011, it became the Central and North West Queensland Medicare Local.

The Abbott government changed the structure of these organisations again, and in July 2015, it changed its name to North West Remote Health (NWRH) and became a subsidiary of Western Queensland Primary Care Collaborative Limited (WQPCC), which was established as a non-profit company by the Western Queensland Primary Health Network.

NWRH was providing allied health services and visiting GPs and was running the aged persons hostel. It had taken over the aged persons hostel in 2016 from another organisation which ran other hostels in First Nations communities. However, in July 2017, the provision of allied health services and visiting GPs was taken over by Gidgee Healing – see below.

## Oxfam

According to their website, they helped launch the Close the Gap campaign more than a decade ago to raise awareness around the gap in health outcomes. I could not find any specific programmes, but they perform an administrative role to strengthen Indigenous community organisations and promote and advance the representation of First Nations people. They help raise the profile of Indigenous communities to decision-makers and assist in procuring grants for them. They are responsible for much of the publicity material for Closing the Gap.

## Mission Australia

According to their website,
Mission Australia is a non-denominational Christian charity that has been helping vulnerable Australians move towards independence for more than 155 years. Every day we support people nationwide by combating homelessness, assisting disadvantaged

families and children, addressing mental health issues, fighting substance dependencies, and much more. We're generously supported by our funders, partners and tens of thousands of everyday Australians, who make the work of our tireless volunteers and staff possible. Together, we stand with Australians in need until they can stand for themselves.

The majority of Mission Australia's services receive government funding, and in some cases from a combination of local, state and federal bodies. We engage in rigorous and competitive tender processes to run programs on behalf of government and benefit communities. The services are run like small businesses, with profit and loss statements submitted to the funding body. However, government funds do not cover all of our services, nor the back-office roles that support our community workers and enable us to plan ahead and stand up for vulnerable Australians. This is why we value the strong and continuing support provided by generous members of the community and corporate sector.

Mission Australia runs three programmes in Mornington Island: Safe House, Women's Shelter, and Safe Haven.

The Safe House provides accommodation for young people who are unable to stay at home for a variety of reasons. The women's shelter is a safe place for women to go if they are feeling unsafe at home or need some time out. Children in their care can come as well. It was established in 1980. Safe Haven operates the night patrol that helps people under 18 years get home safely at night. Staff work between 8 p.m. and 1 a.m. seven nights a week and drive around the community finding young people who might need transport.

## Save the Children

According to their website,

Save the Children is one of Australia's largest aid and development agencies dedicated to helping children. We work hard to protect children from harm and help them access quality education and health services. With more than 90 years working with children, we are at the forefront of saving children's lives when disasters strike and create lasting change for children and their families through our long-term development programs. We have programs in 31 countries, including Australia, where we work in every state and the Northern Territory. Save the Children started helping children in Australia in the 1950's. Our first Australian programs focused on early education for Aboriginal and Torres Strait Islander children. With significant growth since then, we now run education and child protection programs for disadvantaged communities in urban, regional and remote locations right around Australia.

About two-thirds of their funding comes from government grants, the rest from donations, private and corporate.

Save the Children operates a children and family centre, the building was completed in about 2013. It is a thirty-nine-place day care centre tailored to the needs of Mornington Island children and families. The centre maintains a welcoming learning environment that celebrates and reflects its community, enables safe exploration, and provides high-quality educational programmes that extend children's knowledge and skills.

## PCYC Queensland

Police-Citizens Youth Clubs (PCYC) Queensland is a trusted and respected charitable not-for-profit that delivers a broad range of youth-focused activities and programs, school age care, gym and fitness, and more for everyone. Together we're building safer, healthier communities through youth development. Since 1948, our staff and volunteers have been working in partnership with the Queensland Police Service to meet local community and youth needs. Today, PCYC supports more than 73,000 members across our 54 branches from the tip of Cape York to the Gold Coast hinterland. There are 38 branches in First Nations communities.

Importantly, PCYCs are a vital and key point of engagement for young people who are at risk, disadvantaged or disengaged. Our clubs and programs provide opportunities for young people to have positive experiences, get involved in a wide range of activities, and learn from great mentors and community leaders including our serving Police officers. Almost 90% of our work is funded through your kind donations and our services for the community. The remaining is from government funding and significant in-kind support from our founding partners. Any surplus revenue goes straight back into our programs and facilities, as well as the communities we serve — ensuring we deliver on our vision, now and in the future.

There are also agencies which have been specially created to provide services, and these include Gidgee Healing and a legal service, Junkuri Laka.

## Gidgee Healing

Gidgee Healing is an Aboriginal community-controlled health service dedicated to making a long-term positive impact on the health and well-being of Aboriginal and Torres Strait Islander families.

Based in Mt Isa, they provide a broad range of high-quality primary healthcare services across the Mt Isa, north-west, and lower gulf regions of Queensland. It has been the agency for several government-funded initiatives.

For example, in 2016, Gidgee Healing expanded its Mums and Bubs programme into the gulf communities of Mornington Island, Doomadgee, and Burketown. Local health workers based in Doomadgee and Mornington Island ensure parents and families have ongoing support within their community. Based in Mount Isa and travelling fortnightly to each of these communities, there will also be a team of midwives and child development specialists.

**Junkuri Laka**

Junkuri Laka is an organisation owned by the people of the Wellesley Islands, the group of islands which includes Mornington Island.

> Our work is in the areas of law, justice and governance, where we are involved in many activities. Our work goes from standing up for our people in court to organising community service projects; from assisting native title corporations to mediating conflicts in the community; from talking with the government about alcohol regulations to publishing a newsletter. All our work is aimed at making things right. Whether that is between people, between our people and the government or between individuals and the criminal justice system, or even about making things better for our people by making our community stronger and more independent.

In 2007, the Mornington Island Restorative Justice (MIRJ) project was initiated after the dispute resolution branch (DRB) received requests from visiting magistrates, police, and community justice groups for assistance to provide mediation services to remote communities experiencing high levels of conflict. The DRB within the Queensland Department of Justice and Attorney General (DJAG) manages the MIRJ project. In the same period, the Commonwealth Attorney General's Department (AGD) offered to partner with DRB in a project on Mornington Island which had been identified as a project location in the Restorative Justice Action Plan with funding sourced through the national petrol sniffing strategy. Because of its fragility and remoteness, Mornington Island was also identified in the commonwealth remote service delivery strategy. The mediation service started in October 2011.

## Other Agencies and Services

Mirndiyan Gununa is an Aboriginal arts and culture organisation based on Mornington Island, Queensland, Australia. It has a First Nations–majority staff who deliver locally relevant community programmes that produce internationally significantly artwork. Some of the local artists have had their work displayed in the Ian Potter Centre, part of the National Gallery of Victoria.

There are many other agencies supplying services to Mornington Island, but I do not know who they are. I apologise if any of the information in this chapter is incomplete or incorrect.

# CHAPTER 10

# First Nations Culture in an International Context

CULTURE REFERS TO the way that people live their life and how their ideas, history, values, and beliefs affect the way they behave. It has an impact on what people eat, how they dress, how they celebrate events, how they respond to challenges, and how they enjoy themselves. Cultural practices vary widely around the world and gradually evolve, but the fundamental principle is the same everywhere – we all want to see that our children grow up and have a better existence than we have had but also that they know and understand their ancestors' origins and way of life. The five key elements of First Nations peoples' culture are land, family, law, ceremony, and language.

First Nations people make a number of claims about their culture, claiming that they are in some way different from everyone else. It is worth looking at some of these in detail.

## Attachment to the Land

First Nations people emphasise that they have a strong attachment to their land. They say they have a strong spiritual relationship with it, as well as relying on it for the necessities of life, including food and shelter. However, I question the implication that their attachment is unique and far deeper than that found in other cultures.

From 1788 to 1823, the colony of New South Wales was a penal colony made up of convicts, soldiers and their wives, and a few free settlers. A total of over 160,000 convicts were sent to Australia until transportation ceased in 1868, 20 per cent of them women. Obviously, the convicts had no choice in the decision to migrate to Australia, and probably many of the soldiers did not either. Free settlers had started to arrive in larger numbers in 1793, but in 1815, there was a policy to promote migration, and about two-thirds of those who arrived between then and 1850 had their fares paid by the colonial government. Living and working conditions in New South Wales and the other colonies were better than in Europe, thus the attraction of moving to a new country. It is estimated that, by 1850, about 187,000 free settlers had arrived, bringing the total non-Indigenous population to over 400,000.

In 1851, gold was discovered in Australia, and this attracted many migrants from Europe and also from China. As a result, the non-Indigenous population of Australia trebled between 1848 and 1858. It reached about 3.8 million by federation in 1901.

In contrast, the population of the UK, where the majority of settlers came from, was 27 million in 1851 and 38 million in 1901. Therefore, less than 1% per cent of the people living in the UK chose to travel to Australia. So the vast majority of people living there chose to ignore the prosperity of Australia, the assisted passages, and the chance of making their fortune on the goldfields. They were too attached to the land that their family had lived on for generations.

First Nations people were correct when they contrasted their attachment to the land with the attitude of the migrants with whom they came into contact. However, generalising this to everyone else in the world is an error.

All round the world, there are people who have been displaced from their traditional lands for many reasons, and this has been going on for centuries. In the Old Testament, several chapters are devoted to the Jews' invasion of lands that had been promised to them by God; and since then, they have put an enormous amount of effort into hanging on to it, despite others having claims over it.

The desire to explore the world and ignore one's roots may well come from an inherited gene as this desire does seem to run in families. It is likely to be a recessive gene, meaning that descendants of those who have it will tend to lose it, and so their behaviour will revert to the norm of staying in one place. Most Australians now have an attachment to the area where they grew up. They may head overseas for a gap year, but most return. Real estate agents tell us that most people stay in the same suburb when they move house, unless there is a pressing need, such as a job, to move elsewhere. The 1997 film *The Castle* shows the attachment a family had to their home when it was threatened by redevelopment.

Recently after floods and bush fires, we have seen how most people whose houses have been destroyed by natural disasters prefer to rebuild in the same place rather than moving to somewhere else where the risk of destruction is less.

I am not denying that the First Nations people of Australia have an attachment to their land. I am just saying that most Australians have a similar attachment, and therefore, we all understand it.

## Family

First Nations people stress the importance of their family. Again, this is a universal characteristic of human beings and several other species of animals and birds. The misconception probably arose for the same reason as the attachment to the land. Many of the people whom First Nations people first came into contact with had left their families behind, particularly the soldiers and convicts, but those who stayed in Europe did so because of their strong attachments to their family. First Nations people do, however, use terms for their relatives differently from non-Indigenous people. They use words for various relatives such as 'sister', 'brother', and 'cousin' differently from non-Indigenous people. This may represent a problem with the way these words have been translated from the original language into English, rather than a conceptual difference. In any case, the vast majority of non-Indigenous people are interested in finding out who their family are and enjoy tracking down 'long-lost' relatives or finding out whether they are descended from someone famous. Adoptees are now able to find out more easily who their ancestors were. Many people take pleasure in researching their family tree, and there are television programmes about people who have done this.

 CHRIS GILFORD

## Ceremony

Ceremonies play an important part in First Nations people's culture. They are still performed in many parts of Australia but mainly in Arnhem Land and Central Australia. The most well-known is the Garma Festival, which is held each year near Nhulunbuy in north-eastern Arnhem Land. They are often performed at important parts of a person's life, such as coming of age or marriage or death. Attendance at the initiation or coming-of-age ceremonies was generally confined to persons of the same gender. Often, the ceremonies were and are held to try and ensure a good supply of plant and animal foods.

Elsewhere in the world, there are ceremonies to mark important events in people's lives. Marriage and death are two, but the equivalent of coming-of-age ceremonies and rituals are ones that take place under the auspices of churches or other religious bodies and include confirmation, baptism, circumcision, and bar mitzvah. Churches often have Harvest Festivals in which the congregations gives thanks for the food that has been grown. Every time we watch the NZ All Blacks play rugby, we are reminded of one of the important Maori rituals – the haka.

## Cultural Heritage

First Nations people claim that they have a 'rich cultural heritage' and are justly proud of it. UNESCO, the United Nations Educational Scientific and Cultural Organisation, maintains the World Heritage list of places around the world which represent our legacy from the past, what we live with today, and what we pass on to future generations. Our cultural and natural heritage are both irreplaceable sources of life and inspiration. In 2022, there are now 897 cultural sites, 218 natural sites, and 39 mixed sites.

There are now twenty sites in Australia on the World Heritage list, twelve of which are classified as natural, four as cultural, and four as mixed natural and cultural. Three of the four purely cultural sites are the Royal Exhibition Building and Carlton Gardens in Melbourne, the

Sydney Opera House, and the Australian Convict Sites (in WA, NSW, Tasmania, and Norfolk Island). The fourth is

- The Budj Bim Cultural Landscape, located in the traditional country of the Gunditjmara people in south-eastern Australia, consists of three serial components containing one of the world's most extensive and oldest aquaculture systems. [It is about 250 km west of Melbourne and was used as an eel farm.]

The four mixed sites are as follows:

- Kakadu National Park is noted for the cave paintings, rock carvings, and archaeological sites which record the skills and way of life of the region's inhabitants, from the hunter-gatherers of prehistoric times to the First Nations people still living there.
- The Willandra Lakes Region, which includes Lake Mungo, contains some of the earliest evidence of *Homo sapiens sapiens* outside Africa. It includes a cremation site dating to around 40,000 years ago, the oldest in the world. *(However, it is not the oldest ritual burial in the world.)*
- The Tasmanian Wilderness constitutes one of the last expanses of temperate rainforest in the world. Remains found in limestone caves attest to the human occupation of the area for more than 20,000 years.
- Uluru-Kata Tjuta National Park features spectacular geological formations that dominate the vast red sandy plain of Central Australia. Uluru, an immense monolith, and Kata Tjuta, the rock domes located west of Uluru, form part of the traditional belief system of First Nations people.

How does this compare with the rest of the world?

There are numerous sites of rock art dating from prehistoric times throughout the world. There are rock paintings found in Spain and Sulawesi (Indonesia) dating from about 40,000 years ago. There are rock engravings about 60,000 to 70,000 years old in France and South



CHRIS GILFORD

Africa. The oldest traces of rock art in South America have been dated to 26,000–22,000 BCE. In the Pyrenees between France and Spain, there are remains of human settlement – stone circles, caves, and a dolmen – dating from 40,000 to 10,000 BCE. SG̱ang Gwaay in Canada is a site where Haida communities lived 14,000 years ago.

If you look up 'rich cultural heritage' in an internet search engine, you will find over 40 million entries, with contributions from nearly every country in the world.

## Storytelling

First Nations people stress their history of storytelling – tales that have been handed down over the generations. They were told with differing levels of details depending on who the audience was. They covered subjects such as history, cultural practice, values, laws, and responsibilities.

The same is true in the rest of the world. For thousands of years, storytelling was the only method of passing information down through the generations. Gradually, as each culture developed a written language and the materials needed for writing down the language, the stories were recorded in a medium that lasted for long periods.

The *Epic of Gilgamesh* is generally considered the earliest 'book' written. Gilgamesh probably lived in Mesopotamia between 2800 and 2500 BCE, but the earliest clay tablets on which it was inscribed date from 2100 to 1800 BCE, so the story can only have been passed down the generations initially by storytelling.

There are many other examples of stories that have been handed down in this way and subsequently written down. They include the following: the Old Testament in the Bible, *The Arabian Nights*, Icelandic sagas, Greek and Roman myths, Norse/Scandinavian mythology, *Beowulf*, and Indian poems such as *Ramayana*. Our children grow up with fairy tales and nursery rhymes. Many can be traced back to a time before written records, and it was left to authors like the Grimm brothers and Hans Christian Andersen to write them down.

There is now the World Oral Literature Project, based in Cambridge

(UK) and Yale (USA) Universities, which aims to document and make accessible endangered oral literatures before they disappear without record. To quote from their website (www.oralliterature.org):

> For many communities around the world, the transmission of oral literature from one generation to the next lies at the heart of cultural practice. Performances of creative works of verbal art – which include ritual texts, curative chants, epic poems, musical genres, folk tales, creation tales, songs, myths, legends, word games, life histories or historical narratives – are increasingly endangered. Globalisation and rapid socio-economic change exert complex pressures on smaller communities, often eroding expressive diversity and transforming culture through assimilation to more dominant ways of life. As vehicles for the transmission of unique cultural knowledge, local languages encode oral traditions that become threatened when elders die and livelihoods are disrupted.

Music and dance have been found in many ancient cultures. There are depictions of dance in cave drawings in India that are 9,000 years old. We also know that music and dance were important in ancient Egypt. Traditional folk songs, often with narrative verse, are found in many cultures. The dancers from Mornington Island took part in the opening ceremony of the Sydney Opera House in 1973.

Recently, a song man from Kowanyama, a First Nations community on the eastern side of the Gulf of Carpentaria, complained that there was no one who wanted to take over his role. Singing in the *corroboree* is an ancient tradition passed down through generations. He is now recording the songs which are in the local dialect, which itself is dying out.

Elsewhere in the world, many folk songs have been preserved in various ways. A number of classical composers have journeyed through their countries, listening to the folk songs, writing them down, and then arranging them, often for full orchestra. In particular, Percy Grainger



CHRIS GILFORD

was born in Australia but left here at the age of 12 and became passionate about British folk music. Other composers who used European folk music include Brahms, Grieg, and Dvorak. So why don't the current generation of First Nations singer-songwriters go round First Nations communities collecting and preserving the old songs?

## Traditional Hunting

First Nations people are permitted to continue many of their traditional practices, even though they would be in breach of the law for non-Indigenous people. Some of the traditional rules are followed, for example, in parts of Cape York, dugongs could be approached, killed, and eaten only by older initiated men. However, in many cases, hunting and fishing practices have incorporated new materials. Metal was unknown until the Chinese and Malay people arrive within the last millennium, spears are now made of aluminium instead of timber, crowbars and car springs replace digging sticks and adzes, fishing nets are made of nylon instead of bush fibre, guns may be used on large prey, and aluminium dinghies replace dugout canoes.

Elsewhere in the world, Indigenous people can have dispensation regarding hunting regulations. For example, the Inuit in Alaska hunt whales in breach of the International Whaling Commission, but unlike the Japanese whaling industry, this is rarely reported.

## Effect of White Settlers

In an earlier chapter, I described the two major harmful periods in recent history, the near extermination of First Nations people and the stolen generation. It is interesting to compare the two since they both lasted about sixty years:

|  | Frontier Wars | Stolen Generation |
| --- | --- | --- |
| Period | 1860–1920 | 1910–1970 |
| Numbers involved | 200,000–500,000 | 20,000–100,000 |

| Reason | Extermination | For their benefit |
|---|---|---|
| Subject of the 'Sorry' speech | Not specifically | Yes |
| Subject of a parliamentary report | No | Yes |

Table 26: Impact of colonialists on First Nations people

Warfare has been a feature of life throughout the world for millennia, and memories of past conflicts remain within our collective memory as can be seen by the war memorials in every town and city. Many Australians have made their pilgrimage to Gallipoli to remember those killed in the First World War. I have not been to Gallipoli, but I did visit the Normandy beaches a few years ago, I found the experience very moving. It gave me a glimpse of the feelings that Stan Grant describes when he visits the sites of the massacre of his ancestors nearly 200 years ago. We therefore understand the need for First Nations people to remember those who were killed in the Frontier Wars.

*Stolen Generation Comparison*

The practice of forcibly taking members of a culture away from their families, transporting them huge distances, and then trying to get them absorbed into a different culture has been occurring for thousands of years all round the world. The most common reason for doing this is slavery.

The earliest records of slavery date from the first cities in the Middle East about 5,000 years ago. The Romans were known to have slaves, generally getting them from lands that they had conquered. It spread from there to almost every other culture. Sir Thomas More was lord high chancellor in England in the early sixteenth century. He was a devout Roman Catholic and was in conflict with King Henry VIII. In 1516, he wrote a book, *Utopia*, a work of fiction about an ideal island state in which slavery is a feature of utopian life, and every household had two slaves. The slaves are either from other countries (prisoners of war, people condemned to die, or poor people) or criminals. The



CHRIS GILFORD

Catholic Church endorsed the book, including the slavery, and More was canonised in 1935.

The colonisation of the Americas from the sixteenth to the nineteenth century created the slave trade as large numbers of workers were required to work in the cotton and sugar plantations. The slaves were largely supplied by West African colonies and were transported to the USA, Caribbean islands, and Brazil. The anti-slavery movement started at the end of the eighteenth century, and most of the slave trade across the Atlantic ceased by the middle of the nineteenth century. By then, over ten million Africans had been transported.

Most people therefore believe that the slave trade ceased in the nineteenth century, but sadly, it did not. Slavery was used by a number of regimes throughout the twentieth century, mainly by dictators. Hitler made vicious use of slave labour to help the war effort. Apart from prisoners of war, nearly six million foreign workers from countries to the East were registered to work in agriculture and munitions. Hitler was, of course, particularly brutal towards the Jews. Stalin sent millions of dissidents to work in Siberia. Japan used large-scale forced labour, mainly from Korea, China, Indonesia, and Burma. Mao Zedong made the entire population subservient to the party, moving many out of cities to work as agricultural labourers. There was a similar policy in Cambodia under Pol Pot.

Even in the twenty-first century, slavery continues. It is currently estimated that there are now about twenty to thirty million slaves throughout the world. Many African countries still traffic slaves across borders. Mauritania is the country with the most, where they are considered to be inheritable property, but the biggest slave markets are in Nigeria. A 2005 report by the US State Department estimated that 600,000–800,000 people were trafficked across international borders annually, of whom 80 per cent were women and children. Most of these are sex slaves, whereby they are controlled by confiscation of their passports and debt bondage.

The current obsession with being 'woke' has seen campaigns to remove statues of people involved in the slave trade. I would have thought that it would be far more useful to have a campaign to really abolish modern slavery throughout the world. However, no one seems to be doing this probably because it is dangerous and will require travel to unpleasant parts of the world. Perhaps knocking down statues is more fun.

Another process of forcibly taking people away from their families was the punishment handed out by courts in England and Scotland from the seventeenth to the nineteenth century. Transport to the colonies, as outlined in a previous chapter, was common. About 50,000 were sent to North America and 160,000 to Australia. The convicts were supposedly allowed to return home after completion of their sentence, but few chose to.

## Indigenous People in Other Countries

According to Amnesty International, there are 476 million Indigenous people around the world and spread across more than 90 countries. They belong to more than 5,000 different Indigenous peoples and speak more than 4,000 languages. Indigenous people represent about 5 per cent of the world's population.

The UN Department of Economic and Social Affairs is aware of the problem and currently lists the gaps in life expectancy as follows: Guatemala, 13; Panama, 10; Mexico, 6; Nepal, 20; Australia, 20; Canada, 17; New Zealand, 11. They note in particular the alarming levels of diabetes, stating that worldwide over 50 per cent of Indigenous adults over age 35 have type 2 diabetes, and these numbers are predicted to rise, putting the very existence of some Indigenous communities at risk. The poor levels of health are especially felt by Indigenous women, with disproportionately high levels of maternal and infant mortality.

The United Nations has made the Declaration on the Rights of Indigenous Peoples. The basic ones are the right to self-determination; the right to cultural identity; the right to free, prior, and informed consent; and the right to be free from discrimination.

Australia, Canada, the USA, and New Zealand all have significant populations of Indigenous communities, and they have been compared many times. A review by the AIHW in 2011 compared sixteen papers published since 1990 on this subject. The only other Indigenous people who live in westernised nations are the Sámi in Scandinavia. It is interesting also to see that terms like 'native' and the concept of someone being 'mixed blood' are acceptable in other countries.

*USA*

When I was growing up in the UK, one of the common games played in schoolyards was cowboys and Indians. The group would be divided into two teams which would take on some of the characteristics of the original combatants. These games were probably prompted by the popular TV programmes shown in the 1950s and '60s, the 'westerns'. They were as common then as the crime/detective/forensic dramas are today, with IMDB listing 618 titles. They included *The Lone Ranger*, *Rawhide*, *Laramie*, *Wells Fargo*, *Bonanza*, and *Cheyenne*, all of which were based on the events in the USA in the middle of the nineteenth century, when white settlers were heading west against the 'Red Indians' who were trying to hold on to their land.

These days, they are usually known as Native Americans, though the term 'American Indian' is still used, except in Alaska, so a common classification is American Indian and Alaska Native (AIAN). They make a distinction between those who are full blood and those who are mixed blood. Those who are full blood make up about 1.3 per cent of the population of the USA and mixed blood about 3 per cent. The states with the highest proportion of Native Americans are Alaska, Arizona, Montana, New Mexico, North and South Dakota, and Oklahoma, all of which are in the western half of the USA. There are many tribes, the biggest being the Navajo and Cherokee. Seventy per cent now live in cities, Los Angeles having the highest number, and 22 per cent in reservations. They were granted US citizenship in 1924.

There is debate about when the first Native Americans arrived in North America. It is generally thought to be about 15,000 years ago, but the range is from 30,000 to 10,000 years ago. Sea levels were much lower during the last ice age, resulting in a land bridge between Siberia and Alaska. Researchers have proposed the existence of an ice-free corridor across what is now North-West Canada which would have facilitated travel through that region.

In June 2022, the *Lancet* published a major study of the change in life expectancy of different races in the USA between 2000 and 2019. They looked at blacks, Asian/Pacific Islanders, Latinos, whites, and American Indian and Alaska Native. The statisticians in the USA group Asians, mainly Japanese, and Pacific Islanders together, abbreviated to API, even though they differ greatly in their health status, the Asians' health being much better.

| Race | LE in 2000 | LE in 2019 | Improvement |
| --- | --- | --- | --- |
| Black | 71.4 | 75.3 | 3.9 |
| API | 82.8 | 85.7 | 2.9 |
| Latino | 79.5 | 82.2 | 2.7 |
| White | 77.2 | 78.9 | 1.7 |
| AIAN | 73.1 | 73.1 | 0.0 |

Table 27: Life expectancy of different races in the USA

The study confirmed 2018 findings by the CDC that showed most gains in life expectancies for all racial-ethnic groups occurred between 2000 and 2010 but then largely stagnated, in part due to higher rates of overdose deaths and suicide.

It is interesting that the blacks have done so much better than the Native Americans. One possible explanation is a consequence of legalisation of abortion in the USA after the *Roe v. Wade* decision in 1973. There was a significant drop in the number of mainly black babies who were not wanted by their mothers and so grew up in a life of crime and had early deaths.

The blacks are mostly descended from slaves, the Native Americans from people dispossessed of their land. I am not going to try and draw any conclusion from this.

Oxfam's Australian website says, 'We've played a lead role in transforming the Close the Gap campaign for Indigenous Health



CHRIS GILFORD

Equality from a popular movement into a force that has shaped government policy and continues to do so by elevating the role of Aboriginal and Torres Strait Islander organisations.'

Recently, they produced a poster which said, 'The United States, Canada and New Zealand have substantially and rapidly reduced the mortality rates for their indigenous peoples. With the political will Australia could do the same.' The table above shows that this certainly is not the case for the USA as the gap there has widened.

*Canada*

In Canada, there are three separate groups of Indigenous people: First Nations people, Inuit, and Metis. Canadians now consider the terms 'Indians' and 'Eskimos' to be pejorative. The First Nations people came across the land bridge from Siberia about 15,000 years ago and settled mainly in western Canada, with smaller numbers in the East. They now form the largest ethnic group in Northwest Territories, Saskatchewan, Manitoba, and the northern parts of Ontario and Quebec and form about 5 per cent of the Canadian population.

The Inuit are descendants of a group that moved eastwards from western Alaska about 3,000 years ago. They now live mainly in the province of Nunavut, northern Quebec, and north-west Greenland and comprise about 0.2 per cent of the Canadian population.

The Metis are descendants of mixed-race unions between First Nations people and European settlers, usually First Nations women and Frenchmen who were working in the fur trade industry. Their highest numbers are now in the provinces of Manitoba, Saskatchewan, and Northwest Territories, and they form about 1.5 per cent of the whole Canadian population.

The life expectancy was reported in a 2019 study as follows:

|  | Male | Female |
|---|---|---|
| First Nations | 72.5 | 77.7 |
| Metis | 76.9 | 82.3 |

| Inuit | 70.0 | 76.1 |
| White | 81.4 | 87.3 |
| Gap between white and First Nations | 8.9 | 9.6 |
| Gap between white and Metis | 4.5 | 5.0 |
| Gap between white and Inuit | 11.4 | 10.2 |

Table 28: Life expectancy of different races in Canada

*New Zealand*

New Zealand was first settled by the Maori in the middle of the fourteenth century, having travelled by canoe from the Society Islands (French Polynesia). Their ancestors had, in turn, travelled from Taiwan hundreds of years earlier.

Cook visited in 1769, claiming it for Britain, and European settlement began soon after the establishment of the colony of New South Wales. There was conflict with the resident Maori people, partly resolved with the Treaty of Waitangi in 1840. Hostilities broke out a few years later, and the fighting continued for nearly thirty years with nearly 3,000 killed, three-quarters of them Maori. Maori people now comprise 16.5 per cent of the NZ population.

After the Second World War, there was widespread migration by some of the Polynesians and Melanesians living on Pacific Islands, mainly Samoa, Tonga, the Cook Islands, and Niue. They came for job opportunities and were an important source of cheap labour for New Zealand's fledgling economy. They are known as Pasifika. Their numbers have grown over the last seventy-five years, and they now form 8 per cent of the NZ population, and there are now more Pasifika living in New Zealand than in their original countries.

Life expectancy is as follows, from the Stats NZ data published in 2021:

| | Male | Female |
| --- | --- | --- |
| Maori | 73.4 | 77.1 |

| Pasifika | 75.4 | 79.0 |
| White | 80.0 | 83.5 |
| Gap: Maori – white | 7.6 | 7.4 |
| Gap: Pasifika – white | 5.6 | 5.5 |

Table 29: Life expectancy of different races in New Zealand

*Scandinavia*

The Sami inhabit northern areas of Norway, Sweden, and Finland, and a few are found in the north-west of Russia. Their ancestors migrated from what is now SW Russia in about 2000 BCE. There are now approximately 100,000 in total. They are particularly known for their reindeer herding. There have been few studies comparing their health with that of a control group, but one in 2012 showed that

> life expectancy and mortality patterns of the Sami are similar to those of the majority population [non-Sami people in northern Norway]. Furthermore, Sami lifestyle seems to contain elements that reduce the risk of developing cancer and cardiovascular diseases, e.g. physical activity, diet rich in antioxidants and unsaturated fatty acids, and a strong cultural identity.

The 2011 AIHW report compared the life expectancy of First Nations people of Australia, NZ, Canada, and the USA with their white populations, but the data is from 2000. I have added data for the Sami people.

| | % Indigenous | Indigenous Life Expectancy | White Life Expectancy | Gap in Life Expectancy |
| --- | --- | --- | --- | --- |
| Australia | 3.2 | 60 | 79 | 19 |
| New Zealand | 24.0 | 70 | 78 | 8 |

| | | | | |
|---|---|---|---|---|
| Canada | 6.7 | 73 | 79 | 6 |
| USA | 4.3 | 72 | 77 | 5 |
| Scandinavia | 0.5 | 78 | 76 | NS |

Table 30: Life expectancy differences in five countries

The life expectancy of the Indigenous Sami people appears to be two years longer than the reference population of others living in the same area, but the result is not statistically significant. Nevertheless, they do seem to be doing much better than other First Nations people. Perhaps they have a lot to teach us.

# CHAPTER 11

# Analysis of Closing the Gap

I N CHAPTER 1, I quoted from the 2020 Closing the Gap report that was prepared for the prime minister. The ABS publishes reports of life expectancy every five years and is yet to publish them for the 2021 census, so the report states:

> In 2015–2017, life expectancy at birth was 71.6 years for First Nations males and 75.6 years for First Nations females. In comparison, the non-indigenous life expectancy at birth was 80.2 years for males and 83.4 years for females. This is a gap of 8.6 years for males and 7.8 years for females.

Combining these figures with the ones in previous reports yields the following table.

| Life Expectancy Gap | Males | Females |
| --- | --- | --- |
| 2005–7 | 11.4 | 9.6 |
| 2010–12 | 10.6 | 9.5 |
| 2015–17 | 8.6 | 7.8 |

Table 31: Life expectancy gaps over ten years

There appears to be a slight improvement, and contradicts the figures of mortality rates that were in the 2020 Closing the Gap report. However, these figures do not show the full picture. According to the ABS censuses in 2006 and 2021, the total population of First Nations people increased from 455,016 to 812,728 people, or by over 78 per cent. This is an enormous increase.

Although some of this was due to an excess of births over deaths, more analysis is needed. The ABS tables show the breakdown by age, so we know the number of First Nations people over the age of 5 every five years. However, we should expect that some of the people who were alive at the time of one census died before the next census. Assuming life expectancy is about 60-70, about 1.5 per cent of people die each year, or about 7.5 per cent over the five-year period. This means that there were about 60,000 extra First Nations people recorded in the 2011 census that were not in the 2006 census and similarly for the next two censuses. I hope you can follow what I have done in the following table as I have tried to find out how many there are:

| | A<br>(from ABS) | B<br>(from ABS) | C = A - B | D = A ×<br>92.5%<br>From 5 yrs.<br>before | E = C - D |
|---|---|---|---|---|---|
| | Total First Nations | Total children <5 years old | Total >5 years old | Total from previous row, less 7.5% who died | Increase in 5 years |
| 2006 | 455,016 | | | | |
| 2011 | 548,370 | 67,416 | 480,954 | 420,890 | 60,064 |
| 2016 | 649,168 | 73,265 | 575,903 | 507,242 | 68,661 |
| 2021 | 812,728 | 85,941 | 726,787 | 600,480 | 126,307 |

Table 32: Increase in number of First Nations people

These increases add up to 255,032. So where did the extra people, or 30 per cent of the current First Nations population, come from? It is possible that a few were overseas previously, but that number will be fairly small. The extra people must be those who chose to identify themselves as First Nations in 2021 but did not in previous censuses.

 CHRIS GILFORD

Over the last decade or two, there has been a government policy to encourage people of First Nations background to identify themselves as such.

Neville Bonner was a senator for Queensland from 1971 to 1983. He is credited with being the first person with First Nations ancestry to be elected to Parliament. However, there is another contender. David Kennedy was elected to the House of Representatives in a by-election for the seat of Bendigo in 1969 but was defeated at the general election three years later. Although he has First Nations ancestry, he did not identify as such until some years later. He would therefore be the sort of person who would be counted in early censuses as non-Indigenous but in later ones as First Nations.

My hypothesis is that the 250,000 who were counted as First Nations in 2021 but not in earlier censuses would be people who could walk in both worlds and so would probably have a life expectancy somewhere between that of First Nations and non-Indigenous people. If we make this assumption, we will probably find that the corrected life expectancy may not have decreased as much as the report says. However, we will have to wait until the ABS releases the 2021 life expectancy figures to get a definite answer as the extra 126,000 people in the 2021 census will have a more noticeable effect.

I looked further at these figures and realised they still did not make any sense to me. They certainly did not fit with my experience in Normanton and Mornington Island. On Mornington Island, I looked at the age at which people were dying – the median ages of death were 47.5 for males and 54 for females, and it was similar for First Nations people in Normanton. The 2020 Closing the Gap report did talk about remoteness contributing to reduced life expectancy, giving the figures of 6.2 (male) and 6.9 (female) between major cities and remote or very remote area.

These adjusted figures are still about ten to fifteen years less than the life expectancy figures quoted for First Nations people in remote areas. A recent report into the NSW town of Wilcannia stated that most First Nations men there were dying in their forties.

The WHO publishes a list of the ranking of countries by their life expectancy. Australia has just moved up from fourth to third highest in the world. If there was a country called 'First Nations Australia' with a life expectancy of 62.5 (average for men and women), it would come in at 150$^{th}$, ahead mainly of those sub-Saharan African countries that have been ravaged by HIV. Mornington Island would come in at 175$^{th}$ out of 183 countries.

What do all these figures show? 'There are lies, damned lies and statistics' is a quote attributed usually to Mark Twain or British prime minister Benjamin Disraeli. It probably only means that life expectancy is not a good measure of the success or failure of Closing the Gap. Another is needed.

## Why Has Closing the Gap Failed to Deliver?

The organisations and people responsible for First Nations health can be divided into three main groups. Firstly, there are governments – federal, state, and to a lesser extent local government – who legislate and provide the funding. Secondly, there are the agencies and health providers who provide the services. Thirdly, the consumers – the First Nations people themselves – who receive the health services.

## Governments' Role

The federal and state governments appear to be working hard to deal with the problem as shown by the number of programmes that have been initiated as outlined in an earlier chapter. The government's publicity departments have done a good job at promoting the programmes, holding sausage sizzles, and manufacturing thousands of T-shirts, posters, bumper stickers, and all the other paraphernalia used to bring a government programme to people's attention.

One of the most visible programmes is that of bringing down the cost of medication. Prescriptions have 'CTG' printed on them by the medical software that doctors use. Whenever a prescription is written for a First Nations person, they assume that it will be covered by the

            CHRIS GILFORD

Closing the Gap programme and are very disappointed when told that it isn't. For example, it only covers chronic conditions, not acute illnesses.

One of the other criteria for CTG prescriptions is that the doctor must decide that the patient is 'unlikely to adhere to their medicines regimen without assistance through the measure'. Does a doctor have enough information to make this decision? The usual reason that someone now on benefits cannot afford the $6.80 for a prescription is that they do not have the money because the cost of food has gone up.

SBS had a TV series, *First Contact*, in which various non-Indigenous people visited First Nations people and, in some cases, stayed in their houses. On one occasion, one of the visitors assumed that their host received extra Centrelink benefits as they were First Nations and was surprised when they were told 'no'. However, what their host failed to mention was the extra services that they did receive, like CTG, that otherwise they would have to pay for.

Governments seem to like spending lots of taxpayers money and think that it solves problems. How often do we hear an interchange in *Question Time* like this: 'What is the government doing about this problem?' The answer is usually something like this. 'In the last budget, we spent hundreds of millions of dollars on it, which is far more than the opposition did when they were last in office.' They think that spending the money solves the problem and don't look to see whether it actually made any difference.

Dambisa Moyo is a Zambian woman who overcame many disadvantages to get an education at Oxford and Harvard Universities and became a consultant to the World Bank. She wrote *Dead Aid*, in which she argued that the billions of dollars sent from wealthy countries to developing African nations has done more harm than good and that there are better ways of helping address the desperate poverty that plague millions.

## Agencies That Provide Services

Apparently, there are forty-six service providers in Mornington Island, but no one seems to know who many of them are. There must be quite a few who have therefore made little impact on the community. The shire CEO says that he has asked them about this, but in many cases, they either do not reply or say they cannot reveal any information due to privacy concerns, or it is 'commercial in confidence'. Where we do have some information, we find that they have to conform to strict guidelines – they are funded for one particular purpose and cannot use their funding for anything else.

Many of the agencies are not well managed. Two of them in Mornington Island were in administration. There have been many instances of fraud in First Nations communities. There has been an investigation into the Northern Territory government's Employment Provisional Sum policy. This was a scheme which assists companies that employ First Nations workers. It is thought that the level of fraud is in the millions, and six companies were referred to the NT Police for investigation.

There are gaps in services that cannot be filled although the resources are present. For example, at the hospital, there is a common problem with trying to get intoxicated patients home in the evening. They may be well enough to go home and just sleep it off but too intoxicated to walk home unaided. We were often unable to locate relatives who could collect them in a car or walk home with them. There is no taxi service. There is, however, a night patrol bus, which is funded to drive round the streets at night to look for any children who should be at home in bed and take them there. The women's shelter has accommodation for women who are at risk of being a victim of assault, and they have transport. However, neither will transport or accept any woman who is intoxicated. Occasionally, it is possible to use a brief window at 10:45 p.m. when the nurses change shifts (with an overlap), and one can quickly drive someone home. Sometimes there is no alternative to admitting them to the hospital, so they have a sleep and go home in the morning.

There is also duplication of services. Gidgee Healing has been funding a chronic diseases GP, a child and maternal health GP, a visiting midwife, a visiting paediatrician, and nurses to carry out child vaccinations. The expressions 'chronic diseases GP' and 'child and maternal health GP' are, of course, oxymorons – GPs, by definition, do not specialise; they deal with all problems for both sexes and all ages. The clue is in the name – general practitioner. There are already visiting midwives and paediatricians from Queensland Health, so why are more needed? Again, the RFDS provide child vaccinations very efficiently – the take-up of vaccinations in Mornington Island is one of the highest in the country. If nothing is broken, why try and fix it? I am seriously concerned that more patients will slip through the net. I can foresee the case of a pregnant girl who will tell each provider that she is seeing the other but is, in fact, not seeing anyone. She will eventually appear at the hospital in labour, having had no antenatal care at all.

This fragmentation of services can lead to problems. If a patient is referred by Gidgee to a specialist in Mount Isa, the specialist's letter will go back to Gidgee. If when the patient arrives home they get into trouble and go to the hospital in the evening, the hospital may not know about the referral. A lot of patients think that if you use a computer, it has all the information needed and that it is unnecessary to explain about seeing the specialist.

## Service Providers Continually Changing

In chapter 1, I described the way in which one organisation had evolved from a division of general practice, then a Medicare Local, and then North West Remote Health, a subsidiary of Western Queensland Primary Care Collaborative Limited. There are consequent changes in organisational structure, management style, personnel, and other aspects such as logos, uniforms, and stationery.

Government programmes usually run on a three-year cycle. The first year is spent assessing the situation, finding premises, and recruiting staff. Real work is done in the second year. In the third year, there is uncertainty about whether the programme will continue. Little work with clients is done since either the staff are busy writing reports or they leave since they don't like the uncertainty about whether they will continue to have a job. Those who stay often only know a couple of weeks before the end of the financial year whether their jobs will continue.

**Wrong Targets**

As well as being given strict guidelines about how government money should be spent, the service providers also are given targets to monitor their performance, and they are required to meet these to continue their funding. Although these targets may appear useful to the accountants, often, they do not give an indication of whether the community is benefiting.

The latest Closing the Gap report (July 2022) gives the data for the number of health checks that are carried out, as well as the life expectancy, broken by jurisdiction but only for NSW, Qld, WA, and the NT. There is little, if any, correlation between the two variables. There is no measurement of whether the patient made any change to their lifestyle or risk factors as a result of the health check.

The number of referrals that are made to another health provider is a target for some agencies. So a patient who is a diabetic may get referred to a dietician, diabetic educator, podiatrist, and eye specialist. Four referrals made – wonderful. However, no one follows up to find out whether the appointments were made and whether the patient actually attended the appointments.

Another one is the number of management plans that were created out. They started as part of the Enhanced Primary Care policy about eighteen years ago. The name was changed in 2005 to chronic disease management. There are several components, and they also include team care arrangements. Since there is a Medicare item number for these, it is easy for the government to keep track of the numbers.

There are similar changes throughout the world, with governments trying to change health delivery and the way chronic disease is managed. But is this making any difference to health outcomes? There has been little research in the effectiveness of chronic disease management plans (DMPs) in Australia, but there have been many studies carried

     CHRIS GILFORD

out overseas. Here is a selection. In 2003, the WHO concluded the following:

- Most of the evaluated DMPs for chronic conditions have been shown to improve the management and control of the disease. There is a wide body of evidence on this for diabetes, depression, chronic heart failure, and cardiovascular diseases.
- There is evidence that DMPs improve providers' adherence to evidence-based standards of care.
- There is no evidence about which components of a DMP are most important for improving quality of care.
- There is no evidence of a direct link between DMPs and significant reductions in mortality or of improvements in quality of life.
- There is no evidence on DMPs' cost effectiveness.

By 'management and control' they meant the mechanics of the patient's journey through the health system.

A report in the *New England Journal of Medicine* in 2011 concluded that 'disease-management programs did not reduce hospital admissions or emergency room visits, as compared with usual care' and further that there were no cost savings.

A review in the *British Medical Journal* in 2016 evaluated the effectiveness of chronic care models for type 2 diabetes. They found the following:

- One year of multifaceted care slightly improved HbA1c and cholesterol levels in patients with newly diagnosed diabetes but not in patients with established diabetes, compared with usual diabetes care.
- Compared with usual care, multifaceted care did not significantly change quality of life of the diabetes patient.
- Finally, measured for screen-detected diabetes only, the risk of macrovascular and microvascular complications at follow-up

was not significantly different between intervention and control patients.

There have been many more reports looking at the effectiveness of chronic disease management plans. There are a very few studies which have shown small improvements in outcomes, but the vast majority shows no improvement in health, and none was cost effective.

There are studies which show that chronic disease management plans do improve control, but almost invariably, they rely on subjective data. Asking, 'Do you think you are managing your disease better on the CDM plan compared with beforehand?' almost always gets a positive response, even though objective tests might show otherwise.

Doctors are expected to carry out 'evidence-based medicine', in other words making sure that any treatment prescribed will definitely help the patient. This should also apply to administrative aspects.

## Service Overlap

With the large number of agencies providing services, there are some overlaps in services sponsored by the various providers. I was at a meeting of representatives of various agencies in Normanton. I think that over twenty organisations were involved. Three of them were supplying youth mental health support, and so they divided up the workload by the ages of the clients, which meant that some families had different members seeing different practitioners. It did not work well.

I have already mentioned the duplication of ante-natal care and vaccinations in Mornington Island.

## Continuity of Care

Several studies have shown that everyone's health is better if they have a regular GP. General practice has evolved over the years from solo and small practices into large medical centres with large numbers of doctors, nurses, and allied health practitioners. You may not get to see the doctor of your choice on each occasion, but since all practices

　　　CHRIS GILFORD

are now computerised, the doctor you see will have all your history on display.

In Mornington Island, the hospital has been the centre for medical care for decades. Gidgee Healing now has their own doctors. However, they are using a completely different medical software. Although it is claimed that each system's data may be read by the other provider, this is a potentially dangerous situation. Medical software is very complex as the software checks the data that is typed in and shows warning messages if something conflicts with an event in the past. It will not be possible to integrate sequential data such as blood pressure readings. It is helpful to be able to show patients a graph of their blood pressure and how it changes when medication doses have been altered, but this will not be possible. It will be time-consuming to write a good referral letter as each system will only have half the data.

Many of the agencies providing services seem obsessed by privacy. They are very reluctant to divulge information to other providers in the community. They disallow even informal chats between staff of the agency and the hospital staff, unless the patient has given written consent to the exchange of information. I agree that there may be isolated cases where some information is very sensitive and does need to be kept completely secret, but the consequences of not being easily able to transfer information could be catastrophic.

**Programmes Abandoned**

Over twenty years ago, a First Nations organisation in Normanton obtained government funding to construct a cultural centre. I believe that this was meant to be a multifunctional building that would serve as a meeting place and somewhere for the local painters to display their artwork and probably some other roles as well. The funding was first obtained in the mid-1990s, but there were delays getting it built, and the cost of construction increased significantly, and no further funding became available. In 2005, the organisation finally got round to building it but chose not to reduce its size but to build as much of it as they could with the several hundred thousand dollars they had been given. This turned out to be just the floor and the roof, and there it has remained for over fifteen years. There was an attempt a couple of years later to put in a toilet block, but this was only partially completed and subsequently vandalised. The large 'carport' can be seen on Google Earth 750 metres north-east of Normanton Hospital. It measures about twenty-two by seventeen metres. This is typical of buildings that have been constructed with government funds and then abandoned.

## Consumers

Consumers – the First Nations peoples – are the third group involved in the provision of healthcare. It may be surprising to think that First Nations people may not be using the services provided, but as the proverb says, 'You can take a horse to water, but you cannot make it drink.'

I have observed another almost fatalistic reason. When I started in Normanton, the federal government, as part of its plan to move control of First Nations health to First Nations people, was funding an organisation called the Karboyick Larkinjar Aboriginal Corporation for Health. It was run by Jerry Callope, whom I knew quite well. One of the things he did was to organise a health summit in Normanton to include the nearby communities of Doomadgee and Mornington Island. I was invited to attend as an observer, but I was not permitted to ask questions. I went to the opening session in which Jerry gave the opening address. He said, 'I am an Aboriginal person, and so I am going to die twenty years earlier than if I had been born to white parents.' I would have liked to have been able to point out to him that this was unlikely, given that he did not smoke or drink alcohol and lived in a clean house which was not overcrowded, but I was prevented from doing so.

I read recently of a study carried out which shows a similar self-defeating attitude in another culture. A researcher tested boys from the Indian subcontinent for their skill in computer games. They were asked their names and age, and then their scores were ranked. The test was repeated, identical in every way except they were also asked their caste, their position in society. The researcher found that in the second



CHRIS GILFORD

test boys from a lower caste did worse than boys from a higher caste, whereas in the first test their scores were equal. In other words, when the boys had to think about their low caste, they did worse.

Another aspect that I witnessed in First Nations communities was the general attitude to deaths, and most of these occurred in hospital. If it was a traditional elder or anyone else in the community who was over about 70, it was viewed as an absolute tragedy that was totally unexpected even if they were known to have a chronic illness. Huge numbers of the community would file in to pay their last respects even in the middle of the night. It actually became a rather spiritual event, even for members of the hospital staff. On the other hand, if a younger person died, it seemed to be taken as a matter of course, with no one questioning why they had died decades earlier than they should, and no one connected their death with the avoidable illness that they had due to the lifestyle they led.

So it appears that many First Nations people believe that their health is bad just because they are First Nations and that there is nothing they themselves can do which will improve matters. So why give up things that you enjoy such as drinking and smoking as it will not do any good?

The various programmes that have been set up provide assistance for people to manage almost all their lives. More and more of the community feel that they do not have to make any effort to help themselves or members of their family. Some of the service providers appear to agree with this.

The local justice group Junkuri Laka appears to reinforce this. In a recent newsletter, where they comment on the amount of youth crime, they write:

> It is therefore vitally important that the problem is stopped now, and that will only be possible if the services dealing with children focus all of their attention and resources at keeping the kids from hanging round the streets at night and getting into mischief. (JL newsletter, May 2016 No.2)

The services referred to are the PCYC, Save the Children, and Mission Australia's Safe Haven. What about the children's parents? Isn't it their responsibility? In the rest of the country, parents supervise their children. They control the amount of time they can spend away from home in the evening and how much time they can spend on their phones and tablets and regulate bedtimes. If a child breaks the rules, they are grounded. There is no government funding for parents who supervise their children appropriately and make sure they get to school.

The most likely reason that children are roaming the streets at night is that their parents are drinking. The way to get the children off the streets is by controlling the alcohol, and governments have shown themselves to be unaware or incapable of solving this problem. If children are roaming the streets at night, they will be too tired to go to school the next day, and so their education will suffer.

**Consumer Attitudes**

On 13 February 2008, PM Kevin Rudd apologised to the First Nations people of Australia. His speech in Parliament opened with this sentence:

> Today we honour the Indigenous peoples of this
> land, the oldest continuing cultures in human history.

The phrase 'oldest continuing culture' has become a mantra, and it has been repeated countless times with pride by First Nations peoples. In 2008, it was thought that ancestors of Australia's First Nations peoples arrived less than 50,000 years ago; but in 2011, researchers analysed DNA and found that they were part of an early wave of human expansion out of Africa, between 62,000 and 75,000 years ago.

Research into this subject is evolving, and it is probable that an older culture will be found in Africa. Some research papers now insert a qualifier such as 'among the oldest cultures on earth'. Given that the scientific data was lacking, why did Kevin Rudd say it? I suspect that he said it to try and empower the First Nations peoples of this country. He probably thought that it would increase their status, and from Michael Marmot's theory, this would lead to lower mortality. Sadly, this has not happened.

I think that some First Nations peoples may have taken this phrase further than empowerment, and it has given them a sense of entitlement, the belief that they are inherently deserving of privileges or special treatment. Entitlement is a personality trait which affects how people see the world and what they expect from other people. Unfortunately, it can lead to disappointment and depression when their aspirations are not realised.

A sense of entitlement is found across all ages and cultures but does seem to be more common among millennials, whereas the philosophy among baby boomers and Generation X was 'Life's a bitch, and then you die', an expression first used in the *Washington Post* in 1982.

An additional reason for this may come from some of the Closing the Gap advertising material which the federal government and many agencies produced in large quantities in the early years of the programme. They included bumper stickers, posters, and T-shirts. Some of them feature a secondary slogan: 'Demand Indigenous health equality'. It makes health equality sound like a commodity similar to an item on the supermarket shelves as it uses the same sort of language. This is a photo of part of a poster that I found in Mornington Island:

Photo by the Author

Figure 22: Close the Gap Poster

It implies that all someone has to do is go to a health facility where someone will wave a magic wand, and somehow, better health will be conferred on them because the government is supplying the money. There is no suggestion that the person has to do something for themselves.

I think that the word 'demand' is also an issue. It gives some legitimacy to people demanding more services which may be inappropriate or unnecessary. It shifts responsibility away from personal lifestyle choices and preventive measures. There are other examples of these. When Prozac was first available in Australia as a treatment for depression, I got several requests from patients who were not depressed but just felt that it could give them a 'high'. Many people request unnecessary surgical procedures, and cosmetic surgeons get their share of these.

In First Nations communities, it tends to be more for ancillary services. If a patient is travelling to another city for surgery, then they can have an escort (relative or friend) to accompany them if it is medically necessary; the escort's travel is paid by the state government. It



CHRIS GILFORD

is obviously reasonable for someone to have an escort for major surgery such as heart surgery. However, the bar for what is medically necessary is being continually lowered so that an escort will now be sanctioned for virtually any surgery, however minor, and for investigations and consultations. This is actually rather selfish, particularly in Mornington Island. The aircraft that are used for practically all journeys into and out of the community are almost always full, and they are often booked up two weeks ahead. Therefore, if someone is taking an unnecessary escort, someone else might miss out on their appointment or surgery.

Another issue with travel is that although the flight and accommodation are paid for, the patient does have to pay for transport from the airport to the city. This can be an issue and has been addressed in one of the Closing the Gap programmes. However, it is interesting to compare the amount of paperwork needed to access this, and it gives an insight into how governments operate. If a patient is seriously ill and needs to be evacuated to a tertiary hospital by the Royal Flying Doctor Service (or another aero-medical retrieval service), then all I had to do was make a phone call even though this service costs in excess of $10,000. To get a commercial flight costing, say, $500 to the city for an outpatient appointment, I had to fill in a two-page form, a lot of it just ticking boxes. However, if the patient wanted a $50 taxi voucher from the airport to the city, then I had to see if the patient had had a GP management plan prepared within the last year and, if not, create one and also fill out an application form explaining in detail why the service is required and how it will benefit them. There is a Medicare item number for preparation of a GP management plan – no. 721 – with a fee of $121, so it costs the government this amount to provide a $50 benefit.

## Compliance

In a health context, compliance means the extent to which the patient complies with taking medication, turning up to outpatient appointments, and following the advice of health professionals. Compliance with taking medication is, at best, fair. Studies have shown that among the total population of Australia, only about 60 per cent of people take their medication as directed, regardless of cultural background. Of the rest, half may take their medication only some of the time. For lifestyle factors, the figures are far worse. Very few people actually follow advice as to diet, exercise, smoking cessation, and alcohol moderation.

Unfortunately, compliance with medication is worse in First Nations people. Most First Nations people get their medication completely free, or at the concession rate, so the cost of medication is not an issue. In Mornington Island and Normanton, most people on chronic medication get it dispensed in blister packs which is known to aid compliance. However, even with these, many people do not take their medication correctly.

Compliance can also include the extent to which people attend appointments or remain in hospital when advised to do so. Many people in Mornington Island do not attend appointments at the hospital even if community health staff go round to their house to give them a lift. They can be too busy playing cards or drinking alcohol. Many do not get to the airport in time for their flight. They often cancel the flight with a variety of excuses, often too late for someone else to use the seat. A common excuse is not having any money for incidentals at the destination, even though they usually have a couple of weeks' notice of the flight. Many people who are admitted to hospital discharge themselves against medical advice. A significant number of them run into problems after they have gone home and have to call the ambulance to get taken back to hospital to complete their treatment.

A number of people have been trained as Aboriginal Health Workers, which is a job title that does not exist among non-Indigenous people. They have basic training in health and take basic observations such as blood pressure and blood sugar and pass on health messages to the rest of the community. However, most of their time is spent finding community members, delivering their medication, and checking that they turn up for appointments or flights. This is in itself an acknowledgement that First Nations people are less compliant than non-Indigenous people.

Patient with kidney disease who are on dialysis often do not dialyse as often as they should. It is possible to get away with missing dialysis

 CHRIS GILFORD

for a couple of days, but it becomes critical if four or five days are missed. They become overloaded with fluid which puts a strain on their heart, which may already be in poor shape. This becomes an emergency. Several of these dialysis patients have had to be flown out of Mornington Island under these circumstances.

This is particularly common around the time of a funeral. Funerals are important for First Nations people. Family members travel large distances to attend a funeral of a loved one. The funeral may be delayed to give everyone the opportunity to attend. Some of those who attend may be on dialysis and cannot dialyse when they are away from their home. If they arrive on time and the funeral is delayed, they become overloaded with fluid and have to be flown out, often missing the funeral as a result.

Many people do not regard appointments with health professionals as important. This often occurs when little seems to happen during the consultation. Going to an appointment may be an inconvenience, and if the consultation is short and just consists of the specialist saying, 'Everything is fine. We will see you again in three months,' there does not seem to be much value. Patients gain the impression that they are there to boost the ego of the specialist – 'aren't I a clever surgeon?' – and not for their own health.

Another issue is that many First Nations people seem reluctant to tell health professionals the full story of how they became ill. They believe that investigations will precisely diagnose their problem. Unfortunately, this is totally wrong. About 80 per cent of the patient's problems are diagnosed by the account given by the patient or someone with them. I know of cases where someone has come into a remote hospital with vague complaints, but neither they nor the person with them has told the hospital about an accident they had in the previous day or two. In one case, they had fallen down a flight of stairs; in the other, they had been hit hard on the head. One died, and the other has been left with severe disability, but if the trauma had been reported earlier, the outcomes would have been very different.

So why are First Nations people reluctant to talk to health professionals? I think one reason is the mistrust of 'white fellas' and the fear that they will be criticised or even punished. First Nations people seem to acquire this perception at an early age, and it sticks with them. It probably refers back to the time of the stolen generation or the missionaries, when First Nations children were scared of being taken away by the authorities or brutally punished, even though these practices disappeared decades ago. Health professionals learned many years ago not to be judgemental, to treat every patient on their merits. Many First Nations people complain that they are told that they need to 'get over' and 'move forward' regarding the issues like the stolen generation. On the contrary, no one is trying to nullify the sins of the past, but there must be a realisation that attitudes towards First Nations people have changed radically. So it is even more surprising that some First Nations children are reluctant to talk to health professionals since they would not have had any personal experience of negative responses. They must have been taught about these experiences, and this begs the question why and by whom? Similarly, I used to hear parents or grandparents tell their children, 'Behave, or Doctor will give you a needle,' which, of course, just makes the child cry, and this makes it impossible for the doctor to hear anything when they try to listen to the child's chest.

If you live in northern Australia, west of the Great Dividing Range, and turn on the television, you will find a television channel that is not found in the South and East. This is Imparja, a television station based in Alice Springs, targeted at the First Nations people living in the North. It is First Nations owned and began broadcasting in 1988. Most of the programmes it broadcasts will be familiar as many of them are Channel 9 programmes, but there are a few locally produced programmes. What may not be familiar are the advertisements. Many of them are of businesses in Alice Springs, but a significant number are health messages. These cover a range of topics such as 'Wash your hands after going to the toilet,' 'Remember to take your kids to school,' 'Wear light clothing when you go out at night,' 'Wash your hands before eating,' and 'Don't lie down in the road at night.'

These would appear to be simple rules for everyday living. It is a tacit acknowledgement by the First Nations owners of the station that many First Nations people either do not understand their importance or choose to ignore them. Furthermore, it means that if anyone comments that some First Nations people do not understand principles or basic hygiene, it is not a racist comment.

This highlights a paradox in First Nations society. First Nations people claim, rightly, that there is no overall difference between their mental capacity and that of non-Indigenous people, using parameters such as intelligence, memory, leadership qualities, motivation, perception, or analytical reasoning. And this is borne out by the fact that there are now many First Nations people who are high achievers with bachelor's and doctor's degrees. There are many working as judges, professors, members of Parliament, doctors, journalists, lawyers, accountants, actors, artists, and musicians. There are also high achievers on the sporting arena, winning gold medals at the Olympics and excelling in boxing, football, tennis, and many other sports. Many of them have become household names.

On the other hand, First Nations people also say that they need extra assistance with their health and education and many other aspects of daily living. Normally, if a person needs extra help in doing something, it is because they have a disability, learning difficulties, or something else that can be defined. If you ask why they need extra help, they just say it is because they are First Nations and therefore disadvantaged, implying that no further discussion is needed.

Many First Nations people say that they understand that if they sustain an injury, it may have serious consequences, and they can understand them because the injury is visible. However, they also say they have difficulty with the idea that they can have a serious chronic disease without having any symptoms. This seems to me to lack logic. I suspect that it is an argument that has been put forward in the past to account for First Nations behaviour, but if a First Nations person can understand the argument, then they must understand the concept of a disease without symptoms.

To summarise, there are problems at all three levels — the governments, the agencies, and the consumers — and so solutions are needed at all levels.

# CHAPTER 12

# A New Approach

THE TWO HEALTH targets currently are as follows:

| Outcome | Target |
| --- | --- |
| People enjoy long and healthy lives. | Close the Gap in life expectancy within a generation by 2031. |
| Children are born healthy and strong. | By 2031, increase the proportion of First Nations babies with a healthy birthweight to 91 per cent. |

Table 33: The health targets

For the gap in life expectancy, unfortunately, it is going to take decades before it might begin to be closed. Our health slowly deteriorates from the age of around 20 (remember the cholesterol plaques in the American servicemen) and accelerates in middle age. However, the quality of health of First Nations people deteriorates before this. Assuming that the best programmes are put in place, the increase in life expectancy of First Nations people is likely to be very slow, perhaps just two or three months a year.

Secondly, the ABS only publishes life expectancy figures every five years, so it is difficult to monitor progress.

Thirdly, the life expectancy of non-Indigenous people is also slowly increasing, so the target for First Nations people is getting farther away. However, the rate of increase in non-Indigenous life expectancy may decline. About five to ten years ago, there was discussion about the effect of obesity on life expectancy for the whole population. There were arguments that the life expectancy would soon plateau and that people who are middle aged now would be the first to have a lifespan less than their parents. Therefore, I believe that it should be abandoned as a key indicator of any Closing the Gap plan.

Life expectancy, though, is a very convenient indicator of the overall health of a community as it is a single figure. It will be nice if we could find another single figure that gives an indication of the overall health of a community.

In chapter 9, I showed the figures for the percentage of people who died under the age of 35 in 2021, compared with the deaths at all ages. Here it is again.

|  | Male | Female | Ratio: M/F |
|---|---|---|---|
| First Nations | 8.83 | 4.19 | 2.11 |
| Non-Indigenous | 1.59 | 0.81 | 1.96 |
| Ratio: First Nations/non-Indigenous | 5.55 | 5.17 |  |

Figure 22: Percentage of deaths below 35

So five times as many First Nations people compared with non-Indigenous people die before the age of 35. To put it another way 98% of non-indigenous men live past 35, but only 91% of First Nations men. This is a huge gap. I found the data on the ABS website for the three previous years, and the figures were similar with no clear trend. I couldn't find any earlier figures. I think, though, that this difference clearly represents a gap which could form a key indicator. In addition the numbers are published every year, and could show improvement much more quickly than life expectancy.

I also think it is important that there are three additional targets to ensure that there is a reduction in the rates of the important risk factors at the age of 30. This should also be used to reinforce the idea that preventive medicine is really important. These are:

- the rate of smoking,

- the rate of harmful alcohol drinking, and
- the rate of those who are overweight or obese.

Initially, the last of these should be defined as at present by a BMI of over 25; but ideally, the figure should be reduced below that.

Another indicator that might be considered for comparing the health of First Nations people with non-Indigenous people is the disability-adjusted life year. It not only includes the potential years of life lost due to premature death but also includes equivalent years of 'healthy' life lost by being in states of poor health or disability. In so doing, mortality and morbidity are combined into a single, common measurement. This is a relatively new indicator and is used by the UN and WHO. However, it is still being refined, and it may not be appropriate to use it yet.

The new indicator for child health is certainly useful, but childhood mortality is critical. It also has the advantage that it gives an indication of the health of young children up to the age of 5. It should be reinstated but changed so that it can be compared with the rates for children in other countries. This means changing the denominator from the population (per 100,000) to births (per 1,000).

## How Can the Gaps Be Closed?

I get very irritated listening to people who continually claim that the government is not doing enough for a particular section of the community that they care about without either making any suggestions that might make an improvement or acknowledging that there are limitations in terms of budget and other factors about what the government can do and that it is treading a fine line.

So I feel that there would be little point in me writing this book and you reading it if I did not attempt to offer some suggestions for the solution to the problems of Closing the Gap. On the other hand, it would be very presumptuous of me to even make suggestions about what I think First Nations people could do without extensive consultation. They have obviously been the prime movers in making the changes two years ago. This chapter is therefore aimed at governments and those in power. I will leave it to them to negotiate with First Nations people. All the initiatives that have been undertaken in the last twenty years have certainly advanced their numbers and prominence, and perhaps the status, of First Nations people, but they have done virtually nothing to close any of the gaps.

**Bureaucracy**

I think that much of the federal bureaucracy needs to be dismantled. The federal government funds numerous programmes through third-party agencies. They need to stop this and channel the funds through the relevant state departments of health. I know that there is a certain amount of mistrust between them, but this could be alleviated by the federal government using compliance officers to ensure that funds allocated for a particular purpose are used only for that. Each state department district or region needs to set up First Nations control of the federal funds that have been allocated to it.

Having a single provider will allow for a better exchange of medical data between clinicians, apart from the rare occasions when very sensitive data needs to have restricted access. It will also prevent overlap of services. I realise that this will restrict people from having a choice of provider, but this is a small price to pay for the greater efficiency and better use of public money and avoiding catastrophes that probably occur through poor communication between providers.

Since Closing the Gap is going to take decades, it is pointless having the three-year cycle of programmes and grants. Eliminating this will also improve service delivery and job security.

The government should simplify the pharmaceutical benefits for First Nations people and just let all those on a pension or healthcare card to get them for nothing and all others at the pension rate. Similarly, the requirements for management plans to get taxi vouchers etc. should be eliminated. In fact, all the management plans should be eliminated from the Medicare benefits schedule unless there is any objective scientific proof that they do improve people's health. This will free up a lot of GPs and so help the impending doctor shortage.

## Reducing the Risk Factors

As I said in the last chapter, for the last fifteen years, the whole philosophy of Closing the Gap has been that good health is something that the governments can provide for First Nations peoples without them having to do anything for themselves, and this is reinforced by the secondary slogan 'Demand Indigenous health equality.' The only way that health improves is by people taking individual responsibility for their health, and it is the government's job to facilitate this and also make it clear that good health is an individual's responsibility.

Health will be improved enormously by following these simple rules: lose weight, stop smoking, do more exercise, and don't drink alcohol in harmful amounts. There is no need for health professionals to be involved in this process. Governments, though, do have a role in making regulations to make it easier for people to follow the rules.

One of the main features of First Nations culture is their attachment to the land. They want to live on the land where they have lived for thousands of years. They want to do this despite the difficulties in doing so and the adverse consequences. The difficulties are those of lack or transport and infrastructure, of which the most important is the shortage of housing. The adverse consequences are the poorer health that is inevitable if they choose to live in very remote areas, even after correcting for other variables.

Governments can therefore link these two concepts. The provision of better housing should be a reward for reducing the rate of risk factors in a community. I realise that this is going to get a lot of criticism, but as everything else has failed, I can see no alternative.

There are, however, some things that governments can do to facilitate lowering the rate of the risk factors. Most of these start in childhood.

*Nutrition*

Obesity is caused by poor nutrition, and chapter 8 showed how obesity begins in childhood. Even in the age group 2–4, 25 per cent of non-Indigenous children and 28 per cent of First Nations children are overweight. The figures for non-Indigenous children stay roughly the same until aged 18, when they double over the next ten years, probably coinciding with the age when they leave school. For First Nations children, they increase by about 50 per cent by the age of 18 and then another 50 per cent over the next ten years. Therefore, any intervention needs to start during childhood. Families need to be educated about diet. Obesity can be prevented by reducing the amount of fat and sugar that is eaten and at the same time increasing the proportion of fruit and vegetables.

Every time that there is a community event, one of the ways of attracting people to it is a 'sausage sizzle'. Politicians describe the humble sausage as a 'democracy sausage' at polling stations on election day. In Mornington Island, it was used to promote Closing the Gap events. However, is this useful? Does it set a good example? Sausages contain a large amount of fat and can hardly be described as healthy. A range of veggies and salads will be better but less likely to attract people.

One of the common concerns is the alleged high cost of fresh fruit and vegetables. This is a myth. As one person in Normanton told me, 'After we've done our usual shopping, there's no money left over for fruit and veg.' She thought that 'good food' was to be eaten as an addition to her normal shopping, not as a replacement. Fruit and veg should be the main component of the evening meal, covering about 50 per cent of the plate. They should be the first thing to go in the shopping trolley, not the last. You will be able to cut down the amount of meat you need to buy, and this is more expensive than vegetables.

Another problem with modern life is the amount of food that we eat that is prepared by an organisation that is driven by profit and usually supplied in a form which does not require cutlery. The prime culprits are fast-food outlets.

It is also much better for the planet if we reduce the amount of meat we eat and increase the amount of vegetables. At present, about two-thirds of the land surface of the planet is used for food production, and about two-thirds of this is used for grazing animals, mainly cattle and sheep but also goats, pigs, chicken, turkey, duck, and others.

Another strange thing is the fact that many people are prepared to pay a lot of money for vitamins and minerals, which are completely unnecessary for over 90 per cent of the population. Protein shakes are another unnecessary expense – they are just made from eggs and milk. Many studies have shown that processed food is bad for us, so we should cut down on anything that comes in a tin or jar. The only exceptions should be for some canned vegetables, where the ingredients only consist of the vegetable itself and water.

*Physical Inactivity*

Physical inactivity is the next problem that needs to be addressed during childhood, and here, schools can help enormously. When I was a child, I used to hate being required to play sport, and we had to do about four hours a week; but in hindsight, I am very glad that I was forced to do so. The worst was having to play rugby. I started wearing spectacles at the age of 8, and these had to be taken off for rugby, so I would spend the hour's game running around, unable to see where the ball was, let alone picking it up and running with it. Nevertheless, the exercise was good for me.

Pleasingly, First Nations children did better than non-Indigenous children. The percentages meeting the guidelines were as follows:

|  | 5–12 years | 12–17 years |
| --- | --- | --- |
| First Nations | 60% | 33% |
| Non-Indigenous | 45% | 19% |

Table 34: Children doing enough exercise

Clearly, there is more work to be done for school-age children. However, it is after they leave school that the amount of exercise that people do drops considerably. Most people then stop virtually any form of exercise apart from walking. However, we can look overseas to see a form of community exercising that is much more inclusive.

Tens of millions of Japanese people, so a significant proportion of the population of 125 million, perform a specific exercise routine at least once a week. It is known as *rajio taiso*, and it is a short routine broadcast daily on national radio and is carried out in parks, schools, offices, and factories every day by all generations of Japanese people. Surprisingly, it did not start in Japan but in the USA in the 1920s. Breakfast TV in Australia has broadcast exercise routines, and people may do them in their homes, but I think that the concept needs to be part of the national psyche. Perhaps First Nations communities could show the way.

Lots of parents stand around and watch their children play team sports. Perhaps they would be better served by jogging round the pitch.

The federal government supports community sports, ensuring that there are sports grounds available for everyone, but the amount allocated from the budget is currently decreasing, from $601 million in 2020–21 to 332 million in 2023–24. Perhaps there should be a monetary incentive for people to participate, aimed at those in the poorest areas who might find it difficult otherwise.

*Alcohol*

Restrictions in First Nations communities have not had much success. Recently, the restrictions on Mornington Island have been lifted so that beer is now available, and the hope was that this would end the local production of home brew. Unfortunately, however, this has made little, if any, difference to the situation there. Every community is different, so it is very difficult to generalise. However, it is really important for children to be educated about the harm that alcohol does, and it is really beneficial if they have good role models to demonstrate this, and their parents are in the best position to do this.

*Tobacco*

The campaign to reduce tobacco consumption has had most success. The main weapons have been to increase the price through taxation and to restrict the places where it is legal to smoke. A recent visit to Europe showed me how Australia is a long way ahead of many other countries in this regard. Surely, the next step should be not to further proscribe where people may not smoke but where they may smoke. This could take the form 'Smoking is illegal everywhere except among consenting adults in private.' If smokers feel that this is too restrictive, it is the same restriction for where people may have sex, and this does not seem to cause any problems.

*Education*

Social status, employment, and wealth have all been shown to contribute to a longer life expectancy, but the fundamental requirement for all of them is a good education. Unfortunately, the aspirations of many children now are not to enter a worthwhile occupation but to be a gamer, a YouTube sensation, or a social media influencer.

The figures in chapter 1 showed how the gap in school attendance starts to decrease in year 7, for which the age range is 12–13. Students who drop out at that age are probably setting themselves up for a lifetime of poverty, low socio-economic status, and probably crime. Students need to stay at school and complete year 12 because this will greatly increase their ability to get a good job. Going to university or TAFE gives a further increase. This means that for anyone living in a remote or very remote area, they will have to leave home and go to a city for a few years. They can still visit their home community at regular intervals.

*Remoteness*

Remoteness is an independent risk factor for health and education, but many First Nations people want to continue living in their traditional lands because they have done so for thousands of years. So the question is, can the risk be mitigated?

All round Australia, small towns need a reason for their existence. This is simple economics. There can never be sufficient money generated within a town to pay for all the things that it needs to purchase from elsewhere. They need to have an external source of funds. Three common sources are the following:

- Mines – The workers extract minerals from the ground, they are sold elsewhere, and the money comes into the town as wages for the workers.
- Farming – The farmers and workers sell the meat, milk, wool, etc. elsewhere, and the money comes back.
- Tourism – People from other areas come into the town/resort and spend their money.

A town does not need many of its population to be bringing in the external income, probably only about 10 per cent, the rest being employed by the services industries, such as a school, hospital, and shops that spring up in response to the demand. Obviously, schools and hospitals are funded by external income from state governments. However, if the industry providing the external income suddenly disappears, and this has happened in many places such as mining towns or towns built around a sawmill or abattoir, then the town will die. People move away to find work, and the population may get down to zero. There are over 200 ghost towns in Australia, mostly former mining towns. One of the most famous is Hill End, 75 km north of Bathurst in NSW. At the height of the gold rush, in the 1870s, it had a population of 8,000, with two newspapers, five banks, eight churches, and twenty-eight pubs, but the population dwindled when the gold ran out. It had a brief respite in the 1940s when the painter Russell Drysdale discovered it, but the population is now below 100.

Another type of town is the dormitory town, usually found in a ring round a major city. Some people who work in the city want the small-town lifestyle, so that is where they live and spend their money, which has been earned in the city. Small towns should be reasonably self-sufficient in terms of the occupational roles that are required. These are approximate figures for some occupations in Australia:

|  | No. in Australia | Number pro rata for a town of 1,000 |
| --- | --- | --- |
| Plumbers | 89,800 | 3.6 |

| Electricians | 168,900 | 6.8 |
| Nurses | 350,000 | 14.0 |
| Doctors | 103,000 | 4.0 |
| Lawyers | 83,000 | 3.3 |
| Teachers | 300,000 | 12.0 |

Table 35: Some occupation numbers in Australia

Cities and large towns need more than their share for some of the professions because it is often a business that needs people in particular occupations, not the human beings who live there. Therefore, the number of professionals needed in a town of 1,000 may be about half the number in the table.

This means that once enough First Nations people have been trained to do these roles, there should not be a need for external workers to come in like fly-in, fly-out mineworkers. First Nations people in a community will have ownership of the workforce.

So what about First Nations communities? Often, the only source of external money is Centrelink. However, the amount that comes in is only enough to allow a subsistence type of existence. Everyone in the town apart from the staff at the school, police, and hospital remains at the bottom of the social hierarchy, and so their health remains very poor.

**A Solution – Part 1**

Firstly, what is apparent when living in a First Nations community is that there are a number of households that are dysfunctional. There is a large consumption of alcohol, often home brew. There is partying with loud music being played every night. Fights often break out, resulting in a punch-up, or people take out their aggression on the house, punching holes in the walls or smashing the furniture. Any children living there have difficulty sleeping, so if they do wake up in the morning, they do not get any breakfast and so set off for school hungry. In some communities, the school provides breakfast for them. They either fall asleep in class or are disruptive, thus preventing the others in the class from getting a good education.

Back at home, the rest of the family sleep in because no one has to work. They may get up and go out to a house where card games are played. They may go out to the shops to get food but more likely go to the local takeaway to get chicken and chips. The children finish school and then go round to friends' houses and then start looking for someone who will give them some cigarettes to smoke until they go home and have the takeaway food. The house deteriorates because no one cleans it.

And so the cycle repeats daily. I think that the only way to break this cycle is to have a new type of social worker as a household adviser or mentor for the family.

There is a shortage of housing in First Nations communities, so this can be used as an incentive. A dysfunctional family is granted a new house, complete with furniture, but in return, they have to be watched closely by this household adviser for a period of a few months, and they have to meet some benchmarks every month. Hopefully, this adviser will live close to the family so they are there 24/7 to offer advice. These advisers are to be First Nations people who have themselves raised children of their own and so have practical experience on these matters and also have few, if any, harmful habits. Given the increasing number of people now identifying as being First Nations, it should be possible to find enough for this.

They can advise the family as follows:

- Making sure everyone gets up at the right time and has breakfast
- Seeing that the children get to school on time with healthy lunch boxes
- Helping the adults with their finances
- Helping the adults get jobs if they don' t have them
- Going shopping with them and advising them on healthy food choices
- Helping keep the house clean and in good repair

- Limiting the amount of junk food and sweetened drinks that the children consume
- Limiting the amount of alcohol that the adults drink
- Setting boundaries for the children such as the time spent on their phones or tablets
- Making sure that the children go to bed at an appropriate time and that the house is quiet
- Banning smoking except for well away from the house
- Preventing overcrowding by ensuring that no one else moves into the house, except for relatives visiting for a short time from another community
- Helping them keep the backyard tidy, creating a nice garden, and perhaps growing some vegetables

Hopefully, after a few months, the family will see the benefit of living in a functional house, and so the adviser will be able to leave them to manage on their own so they can go on to advise the next family.

## A Solution – Part 2: Incentive for the Whole Community

There are two issues in housing – improving the existing stock and building new ones. As I indicated earlier, it is very expensive to build in remote communities, but one way of reducing the cost would be to use local tradesmen.

Tradespeople are in short supply in remote communities, contributing to many of the deficiencies of the houses. Young First Nations people should be encouraged to get apprenticeships so they can return and use their skills in their own community. There is no reason why the entire workforce building a house should not eventually be a First Nations crew. To begin with, half the workforce might be licensed builders and tradespeople, with the remainder being apprentices; but after a few years, the apprentices will qualify, replace all the licensed workers, and take on apprentices themselves.

The government should commission new houses in remote

communities, but one of the requirements should be that a percentage of the young adults go away to TAFE and start apprenticeships and then come back to work in their community. Eventually, it will only be the cost of materials that is spent outside the community.

## A Solution – Part 3: Enable More Employment Opportunities

Steps also need to be taken to deal with the lack of employment opportunities in the community, unless it is lucky to have a mine nearby. There have been attempts to set up new businesses in First Nations communities, but most have not been successful, often bogged down by bureaucracy in all its forms. Mark Moran's book *Serious Whitefella Stuff* describes attempts to build a fruit farm in one community, and it ultimately failed. So as I see it, there are several ways of adapting processes that are successful elsewhere. In each case, the community becomes a dormitory town.

Many mineworkers are employed on a fly-in, fly-out basis. They live in a city and work in a remote location. There is no reason why some workers could not do the reverse – live in a remote community and commute weekly or fortnightly to a city for work. In the future, I could even see a situation where an airline had an aircrew who all lived in a remote community. On Fridays, they would fly the aeroplane with community members who worked in the city home, leave the aeroplane parked there over the weekend, and then fly it with all the workers back to the city on the Monday morning.

When I have worked in small towns with a predominantly non-Indigenous population, almost all the nurses came from the local community. In contrast, in Normanton and Mornington Island, most of the nurses came from overseas, and this is also the case in many other remote First Nations communities. We had nurses from India, South Korea, the Philippines, Zambia, and Zimbabwe and probably many more countries, and they were usually on contracts of about six months. Some had left their children behind in their home country, to be cared for by grandparents. This sounds tough for them, but for at least these days, they are able to keep in touch by video calls.

The fruit industry needs many seasonal workers and, to fill vacancies, employs many people from Polynesia and Melanesia but also young backpackers keen to see the world. Why can't First Nations people do this work?

Governments could also create incentives for more employment possibilities by upgrading transport links.

## More First Nations Professionals Needed

As I write, the ABC is running a story about the very high rate of homicide and disappearance of First Nations women in remote communities. I did allude to this in chapter 9, saying that the homicide rate among First Nations people was six times higher than the rate for the whole nation and that 80 per cent of the victims were female.

Spokeswomen were calling for more funding. However, what they really need are more First Nations police officers, preferably half of them to be female. Some of these could train to become detectives, and they would have a far better chance of finding those responsible for all these excess deaths. They might even be able to go undercover, something that a non-Indigenous detective could never do. They also need more First Nations social workers to help recreate the social fabric of the communities.

Similarly, more First Nations teachers might have more success in inspiring First Nations children to complete all their studies, compared with non-Indigenous teachers. I have also discussed doctors and nurses earlier, but we need more First Nations allied health professionals such as paramedics, psychologists, physiotherapists, occupational therapists, dentists, and many others.

It seems that there is a huge number of First Nations people who have become facilitators or coordinators but themselves not actually doing something directly with the First Nations people in the lower half of the socio-economic scale who would benefit most from Closing the Gap.

None of the measures I have described have anything to do with the provision of health services. They are all about reducing risk factors

 CHRIS GILFORD

and improving the functionality of the community, but they require people to get actively involved in these dysfunctional communities. I am hopeful that this will be better at closing the gap than has been done until now.

# APPENDICES

## Appendix 1 – Simple Rules to Lose Weight

- Don't cheat as this is the usual cause of failure.
- Chips do not count as vegetables and so are not allowed.
- For First Nations people, get as much bush tucker as you like – nuts, berries, fruit, vegetables, wallaby, fish, dugong.
- Stop adding sugar to your tea and coffee, and don't use artificial sweeteners. The tea and coffee will taste bitter to begin with, but you will get used to it in about two weeks, and you will find that you have lost your sweet tooth.
- No soft drinks such as cola or lemonade ever. Even the ones with zero calories are unhelpful since you won't get rid of your sweet tooth.
- If you are thirsty, drink plain tap water.
- The only snacks you are allowed are raw carrot, raw celery, or nuts, so keep a supply handy in case you feel hungry.
- Morning tea or afternoon tea are all right, unsweetened, but no cakes or biscuits.
- Breakfast should be cereal (with skimmed milk) or toast. If you want something cooked, try an egg, tomatoes, or mushrooms on toast.
- Lunch should be a salad sandwich, sushi, or equivalent and then a small piece of fruit.
- Use smaller plates for your meals – 25 cm is big enough.
- Evening meal should be at least half vegetables, a quarter carbs – pasta, rice, boiled potato – and a quarter fish or meat, but this is optional, and you can have extra veggies. Have fresh fruit or cheese and biscuits for dessert.
- Don't cook anything in breadcrumbs or batter.
- Take alcohol if you like but only one standard drink a day.

## Appendix 2 – Things the Governments Could Do for Obesity

- Publish data on the health dollar costs of being obese.
- Require airlines to charge passengers according to their weight.
- Require health funds to charge premiums according to people's BMIs.
- Require clothes retailers to charge according to the size of the garment.
- Require all restaurants and cafes to offer half-size meals at, say, two-thirds cost.
- Introduce a sugar and sweetener tax. A sugar tax has been shown to work overseas, but drinks with artificial sweeteners also need to be taxed (perhaps at a lower rate) so people lose their sweet tooth.
- Require all restaurants and cafes to supply plain water for free. This does happen now in good restaurants but not fast-food outlets.
- Stop subsidising medication for people who are obese.
- Stop subsiding elective surgery for obese people if their symptoms will improve with weight loss.
- Change the building codes so that the normal way of moving from one floor to another is by the stairs rather than by a lift or escalator.
- Make lifts only stop every third floor. This does happen in some residential blocks, but it should be universal. People in wheelchairs should have access to a device that allows lifts to stop on each floor, but this should be incorporated into the wheelchair so it cannot be misused.
- Separate the candy bar from the box office in cinemas. This will dissuade people from eating junk food.
- Make it compulsory for waiters and fast-food outlets to try and persuade customers to downsize their meals. 'Would you like to save a dollar by only having the small fries?'

- Salad, not chips, should be the default extra for turning a burger into a meal. There should be no discount when adding a soft drink.
- Reduce the size of cakes and desserts in cafes. The fact that staff are prepared to offer 'two spoons' implies that they know that the portions are far too big.
- Stop café staff from offering fatty extras as in 'Do you want cream or ice cream with your cake?' because it implies that having neither is not an option. Customers must initiate the choice of whether to have any extras.
- Try and reverse some of the factors that have made eating easier. For example, persuade people to buy smaller refrigerators, but with larger fruit and veg shelves.
- Legislate so that supermarkets are laid out in a way that discourages unhealthy eating. Confectionery and drinks with high sugar content should be farthest from the checkout. Put them in a locked cabinet like paint sprays. Prohibit discounting of these and tax them.
- Ban restaurants that offer 'all you can eat for $20'. If you go into one, you can see how people who are already overweight pile their plates high to get the most bang for their buck.
- Legislate that if an organisation employs someone who is obese, then the employee must pay for the extra-strength chairs and other equipment that they use.
- In shopping centres, food halls should be on a separate level and only accessible by stairs.
- Allow employers to take into account a prospective employee's weight when assessing their suitability for a job.
- Turn off all escalators. Make people take the stairs.

# REFERENCES AND FURTHER READING

**Books**

Basedow, H., *Notes on Some Native Tribes of Central Australia*, 1903, David Welch, 2008.

Bottoms, T., *Conspiracy of Silence – Queensland's Frontier Killing Times*, 2013, Allen & Unwin.

Diamond, J., *Guns, Germs, and Steel: The Fates of Human Societies*, 1997, W. W. Norton & Co, NY.

Gillespie, D., *Big Fat Lies – How the Diet Industry Is Making You Sick, Fat, and Poor*, 2012, Penguin Random House, Australia.

Grant, S., *Talking to My Country*, 2016, Harper-Collins.

Marmot, M., *The Health Gap – The Challenge of an Unequal World*, 2015, Bloomsbury Publishing Plc, London.

———, *Status Syndrome – How Your Place on the Social Gradient Directly Affects Your Health*, 2004, Bloomsbury Publishing Plc, London.

Moran, M., *Serious Whitefella Stuff – When Solutions Become the Problem in Indigenous Affairs*, 2016, Melbourne University Press.

Moyo, D., *Dead Aid – Why Aid Is Not Working and How There Is a Better Way for Africa*, 2009, Allen Lane, Penguin Books.

Peasley, W. J., *The Last of the Nomads*, 1983, Fremantle Press.

Stephen, L., *Eating Ourselves Sick – How Modern Food Is Destroying Our Health*, 2017, Pan Macmillan, Australia.

Winchester, S., *Land – How the Hunger for Ownership Shaped the Modern World*, 2021, Harper-Collins.

**Journal Articles and Reports**

Aggarwal, R., Bibbins-Domingo, K., Yeh, R. W., et al., 'Diabetes Screening by Race and Ethnicity in the United States: Equivalent Body Mass Index and Age Thresholds', 2022, *Annals of Internal Medicine*, https://doi.org/10.7326/M20-8079.

Amnesty International, 'Indigenous Peoples', 2022, https://www.amnesty.org/en/what-we-do/indigenous-peoples/.

Anand, S. S., Friedrich, M. G., Lee, D. S., et al., 'Evaluation of Adiposity and Cognitive Function in Adults', 2022, *JAMA Network Open* 5(2):e2146324. doi:10.1001/jamanetworkopen.2021.46324.

Aroda, N. R., Rosenstock, J., Terauchi, Y., et al., 'Randomized Clinical Trial of the Efficacy and Safety of Oral Semaglutide Monotherapy in Comparison with Placebo in Patients with Type 2 Diabetes', 2019, *Diabetes Care* 42(9):1724–32.

Australian Broadcasting Corporation, 'Pub Licence Conditions Spark Civil Liberties', 2005, ABC, https://www.abc.net.au/news/2005-06-09/pub-licence-conditions-spark-civil-liberties/1589200?utm_campaign=abc_news_web&utm_content=link&utm_medium=content_shared&utm_source=abc_news_web.

Australian Bureau of Statistics, Census Data, 2021, Australian government.

———, Deaths, Australia, 2021, Australian government.

———, Australian Health Survey: Biomedical Results for Chronic Diseases, 2013, Australian government.

——, Life Tables for Aboriginal and Torres Strait Islander Australians, 2015–2017, 2018, Australian government.

Australian Commission on Safety and Quality in Healthcare and National Health Performance Authority, Australian Atlas of Healthcare Variation, 2015, Australian government, Sydney ACSQHC 2015.

Australian Department of Health and Aged Care, Syphilis Notifications in Australia, 2022, Australian government.

——, Guidelines for Physical Activity, 2022, Australian government.

Australian Institute of Criminology, Homicide in Australia – Statistical Report No. 39. Ben Serpell, Tom Sullivan, and Laura Doherty, 2022, Australian government.

——, Male and Female Assault Offending in Australia Research in Practice No. 29, 2012, Australian government, https://www.aic.gov.au/publications/rip/rip29.

——, Assault-Related Injuries among Young Australians. Crime Facts Info No. 177, 2008, Australian government, https://www.aic.gov.au/publications/cfi/cfi177.

Australian Institute of Health and Welfare, Australia's Health, 2018, Australian government.

——, Australia's Health Data Insights, 2022, Australian government.

——, National Drug Strategy Household Survey, 2019, Australian government.

——, Aboriginal and Torres Strait Islander Health Performance Framework. Data Tables: Measure 1.20 Infant and Child Mortality, 2022, Australian government.

——, Overweight and Obesity: An Interactive Insight, 2020, Australian government, Cat. No. PHE 251. Canberra: AIHW, https://www.aihw.gov.au/reports/overweight-obesity/overweight-and-obesity-an-interactive-insight.

——, Injury among Young Australians AIHW Bulletin Series No. 60. Cat. No. AUS 102, 2008, Australian government.

——, Comparing Life Expectancy of Indigenous People in Australia, New Zealand, Canada, and the United States: Conceptual, Methodological, and Data Issues. Cat. No. IHW 47, 2011, Australian government.

——, Australian Burden of Disease Study 2011: Impact and Causes of Illness and Death in Aboriginal and Torres Strait Islander People, 2011, Australian government.

——, Expenditure on Health for Aboriginal and Torres Strait Islander People 2010–11: An Analysis by Remoteness and Disease. Health and Welfare Expenditure Series No. 49. Cat. No. HWE 58. Canberra: AIHW, 2013, Australian government.

——, Expenditure on Health Services for Aboriginal and Torres Strait Islander People 2001–2002, 2005, Australian government.

——, Aboriginal and Torres Strait Islander Stolen Generations and Descendants: Numbers, Demographic Characteristics and Selected Outcomes. Cat. No. IHW 195. Canberra: AIHW, 2018, Australian government.

——, The Health of Australia's Males, 2019, Australian government.

——, Australia's Health, 2008, Australian government.

——, A Picture of Overweight and Obesity in Australia, 2017, Australian government.

——, Housing Circumstances of Indigenous Households: Tenure and Overcrowding. Cat. No. IHW 132. Canberra, 2014, Australian government.

——, Aboriginal and Torres Strait Islander Health Performance Framework 2020 Summary Report. Cat. No. IHPF 2. Canberra, 2020, Australian government.

——, Australia's Children. Cat. No. CWS 69. Canberra: Australia's children, 2020, Australian government.

——, Australian Burden of Disease Study: Impact and Causes of Illness and Death in Aboriginal and Torres Strait Islander People 2018 – Summary Report. No. 27. Cat. No. BOD 33. Canberra, 2022, Australian government.

Bhaskaran, K., dos-Santos-Silva, I., Leon, D. A., et al., 'Association of BMI with Overall and Cause-Specific Mortality: A Population-Based Cohort Study of 3.6 Million Adults in the UK', 2018, *Lancet*, http://dx.doi.org/10.1016/S2213-8587(18)30288-2.

Bongaerts, B. W. C., Müssig, K., Wens, J., et al., 'Effectiveness of Chronic Care Models for the Management of Type 2 Diabetes Mellitus in Europe: A Systematic Review and Meta-Analysis', 2016, *British Medical Journal*.

Bricknell, S., 'Trends in Violent Crime', 2008, Australian Institute of Criminology.

*British Medical Journal*, 'BMI and All Cause Mortality: Systematic Review and Non-Linear Dose-Response Meta-Analysis of 230 Cohort Studies with 3.74 Million Deaths among 30.3 Million Participants', 2016, *BMJ* 353, https://doi.org/10.1136/bmj.i2156.

Caleyachetty, R., Barber, T. M., Nuredin, I. M., et al., 'Ethnicity-Specific BMI Cutoffs for Obesity Based on Type 2 Diabetes Risk in

England: A Population-Based Cohort Study, 2021, *Lancet Diabetes Endocrinology*; 9: 419–26. Published online 11 May 2021, https://doi.org/10.1016/ S2213-8587(21)00088-7.

Centre for Disease Control, 'Suicides, Drug Overdose Deaths Named as Key Contributors to Decline in U.S. Life Expectancy', 2018, CDC director.

Chiang, C. L., 'The Life Table and Its Construction: From Introduction to Stochastic Processes in Biostatistics', 1968, New York: John Wiley & Sons, 1968: 189–214.

Coffey, C., Veit, F., Wolfe, R., et al., 'Mortality in Young Offenders: Retrospective Cohort Study', 2003, *British Medical Journal* 326: 1064–67.

Commonwealth of Australia, Closing the Gap Report, 2020, Department of the Prime Minister and Cabinet.

——, Closing the Gap Prime Minister's Report, 2017, Department of the Prime Minister and Cabinet.

Damasiewicz, M. J., and Polkinghorne, K. R., 'Global Dialysis Perspective: Australia', 2020, *Kidney360* 1 (1): 48–51; American Society of Nephrology, https://doi.org/10.34067/KID.0000112019.

Department of Health (Australia), Annual Medicare Statistics – Financial Year 1984–85 to 2018–19, 2019, Australian government. Data accessed by Australian Institute of Health and Welfare (2019), The Health of Australia's Males, AIHW.

——, National Syphilis Surveillance Quarterly Report Quarter 1: 1 January–31 March 2022, 2022, Australian government.

Franklin, J., 'The Cultural Roots of Aboriginal Violence', 2008,

*Quadrant Online*, https://quadrant.org.au/magazine/2008/11/the-cultural-roots-of-aboriginal-violence/.

Gwartney, D., et al., 'Mortality Rate Higher among Bodybuilders', 2016, American Urological Association's 2016 annual meeting, http://www.renalandurologynews.com/aua-2016-misc-urinary-problems/mortality-rate-higher-among-bodybuilders/article/495038/.

Inzucchi, S. E., et al., 'Efficacy of Treatments for Diabetes', 2005, *Diabetes Care* 28:1282–88.

Kruger, E., and Tennant, M., 'Fractures of the Mandible and Maxilla: A Ten-Year Analysis', 2016, *Australas. Med. J.* 9(1): 17–24. Published online 31 Jan 2016. doi: 10.4066/AMJ.2015.2570, https://www.ncbi.nlm.nih.gov/pmc/articles/PMC4748304/.

Lin, A. L., Nah, G., Tang, J. J., et al. 'Cannabis, Cocaine, Methamphetamine, and Opiates Increase the Risk of Incident Atrial Fibrillation', *European Heart Journal*, Oct 2022, https://doi.org/10.1093/eurheartj/ehac558.

Lowitja Institute, Transforming Power – Voices for Generational Change: The 2022 Report for the Closing the Gap Steering Committee, 2022, Lowitja Institute.

Marijon, E., Mirabel, M., Celermajer, D. S., et al., 'Risk Factors for Rheumatic Fever', 2012, *Lancet* 379(9819): 953–964.

McCall, N., and Cromwell, J., 'Results of the Medicare Health Support Disease-Management Pilot Program', 2011, *N. Engl. J. Med.* 365(18): 1704–12. PMID 22047561, doi:10.1056/NEJMsa1011785.

McFarling, U. L., et al., 'Life Expectancy by County, Race, and Ethnicity in the USA, 2000–19: A Systematic Analysis of Health Disparities', 2022, *Lancet* 400(10345): 25–38, https://doi.org/10.1016/S0140-6736(22)00876-5.

Minority Rights Group International, World Directory of Minorities and Indigenous Peoples, 2022, https://minorityrights.org.

Nathan, D. M., et al., 'Efficacy of Treatments for Diabetes', 2009, *Diabetes Care* 32:193–203.

Norum, J., and Nieder, Carsten, 'Socioeconomic Characteristics and Health Outcomes in Sami Speaking Municipalities and a Control Group in Northern Norway, 2012, *Int. J. Circumpolar Health* 71: 10.3402/ijch.v71i0.19127. Published online 20 Aug 2012. doi: 10.3402/ijch.v71i0.19127.

Productivity Commission, Closing the Gap Annual Data Compilation Report July 2022, Australian government.

Queensland Health, The Health of Australian South Sea Islander People in Queensland – An Analysis of Hospital Separation Data, 2011, Division of the Chief Health Officer.

Scientific American, 'The Plants and Animals That Nourish Man', 1976, *Sci Am* 235(3): 88–97, Sept 1976.

Silburn, K., Reich, H., and Anderson, I. (eds.), 'A Global Snapshot of Indigenous and Tribal Peoples' Health', *Lancet*-Lowitja Institute Collaboration, 2016, *Lancet* 379(9819): 953–64.

Silcocks, P. B., Jenner, D. A., and Reza, R., 'Life Expectancy as a Summary of Mortality in a Population: Statistical Considerations and Suitability for Use by Health Authorities', 2001, *J. Epidemiol. Community Health* 55:38–43.

Statistics Canada, Aboriginal Peoples Survey, an Overview of the Health of the Métis Population, Catalogue No. 89-637-X 2009006, 2006.

Stats NZ Tatauranga Aotearoa, National and Subnational Period Life

Tables, 2020, New Zealand government, https://www.stats.govt.
nz/news/growth-in-life-expectancy-slows/.

The *Economist*, 'Australia Is Flailing in the Face of a Meth Epidemic',
2017, *Economist*, Sydney.

The State of Queensland (Health and Wellbeing Queensland), Report
1 – Impact of Obesity on Life Expectancy in Queensland, 2022,
https://hw.qld.gov.au/wp-content/uploads/2022/10/HWQld_
Impact-of-Obesity-on-Life-Expectancy-in-Queensland_
October-2022.pdf.

The World Bank, Population figures.

The World Factbook (CIA), Population figures.

Tjepkema, M., Bushnik, T., and Bougie, E., 'Life Expectancy
of First Nations, Métis and Inuit Household Populations
in Canada', 2019, *Statistics Canada*, https://www.doi.
org/10.25318/82-003-x201901200001-eng.

United Nations, 'Indigenous Peoples', 2022, https://www.un.org/
development/desa/indigenouspeoples.

United Nations Educational, Scientific and Cultural Organization,
'World Heritage List', 2022, UNESCO, https://whc.unesco.org/
en/list/.

University of Cambridge Museum of Archaeology and Anthropology,
World Oral Literature Project, 2022, University of Cambridge,
https://www.oralliterature.org/.

Velasco-Garrido, M., Busse, R., and Hisashige, A., 'Are Disease
Management Programmes (DMPs) Effective in Improving Quality
of Care for People with Chronic Conditions?', 2003, WHO

Regional Office for Europe (Health Evidence Network report), http://www.euro.who.int/document/e82974.pdf.

Wilding, J. P. H., Batterham, R. L., et al., 'Once-Weekly Semaglutide in Adults with Overweight or Obesity', 2021, *N. Engl. J. Med.* 384: 989–1002.

World Health Organisation, Preventing Injuries and Violence: A Guide for Ministries of Health, 2007, WHO, Geneva.

# INDEX

Queensland 3-4, 11, 47, 55, 183, 189, 194, 198
Queensland Council for Civil Liberties 122
Queensland government 58
Queensland Health 4, 113, 189
Quetelet, Adolphe 147

# R

rajio taiso 247
rates
    attainment 11-13
    drugs and crimes 177
    employment 12-13, 19
    foetus' growth 95-6
    foetus survival 95
    homicide 177-8, 254
    hospitalisation 48, 143, 184-5
rationing 174
Red Indians 213
referendum council 58
refrigerators 146
Reg (Life of Brian character) 188
remoteness ix, 8, 11-13, 141, 221, 248, 264
    impact of 142-4
rent inspection 138
residential rehab centres 194
resin *see* hashish
rheumatic fever 78-9, 89, 267
rheumatic heart disease (RHD) xii, 78-9, 81, 138
risk factors vii, 25, 39, 70-2, 79, 81, 93, 95-6, 98, 107-8, 135, 137, 143, 149, 168, 226, 244, 267
rock arts 206
*Roe* v. *Wade* 214
Romans 32, 36, 210
Round-the-Clock Medicare initiative 191
Royal Flying Doctors Service (RFDS) 48, 125, 144, 182, 193, 225

rubbing alcohol *see* isopropyl alcohol
Rudd, Kevin 58, 232
Rudd government 195
rules, simple health 244
rum 119
rum colony *see* New South Wales (NSW)

# S

*Saccharomyces cerevisiae* 114
safe sex 85
Salvation Army 194
Sámi 213, 217-18
*Sarcoptes scabiei* 88
Saskatchewan 215
Save the Children 195, 198
scabies 88
Scandinavia 217
Scandinavians 33
school attendance gaps 8, 10, 112
school sores 89
screening, of population at risk 85
sealed orders 53
*Secret Eaters* 162
Section 100 scheme 192
semaglutide 77, 157
sepsis 89
septic arthritis 87
*Serious Whitefella Stuff* (Moran) 253
services, ancillary 234
1763 royal proclamation 53
severe head injuries 180
sewerage systems 38
sexually transmitted infections (STIs) 84-5, 88
shire 64
slave trade 210-11, 211-12
slaves 210
small towns 48, 160, 248-9
smallpox 39-40, 44
smartphone 66, 146
smokers 129